THE WAKE

THE
WAKE

The Deadly Legacy of a Newfoundland Tsunami

LINDEN MacINTYRE

HarperCollins*Publishers*Ltd

HarperCollins books may be purchased for educational, business
or sales promotional use through our Special Markets Department.

HarperCollins Publishers Ltd
Bay Adelaide Centre, East Tower
22 Adelaide Street West, 41st Floor
Toronto, Ontario, Canada
M5H 4E3

www.harpercollins.ca

Library and Archives Canada Cataloguing in Publication information
is available upon request.

ISBN 978-1-4434-5202-1

Maps by Mary Rostad

Printed and bound in the United States of America
LSC/H 9 8 7 6 5 4 3 2 1

To
men and women
who work hard
and die
slowly

In Memoriam

Peter Quirke
Alice MacIntyre
Patrick O'Flaherty
Michael "Uncle Mick" Slaney
Roger Slaney
Kevin Pike

*The difficulty is that the need is terrible and so unjust,
and schemes of development take long to mature, and meanwhile
a people are deteriorating and dying by inches.*
—LADY MARY JANE HOPE SIMPSON, JULY 25, 1935

I've met a lot of old friends and there's a lot of them dead and gone.
—DAN RORY MACINTYRE, JANUARY 27, 1961

All sorrows can be borne if you put them in a story . . .
—ISAK DINESEN, NOVEMBER 3, 1957

CONTENTS

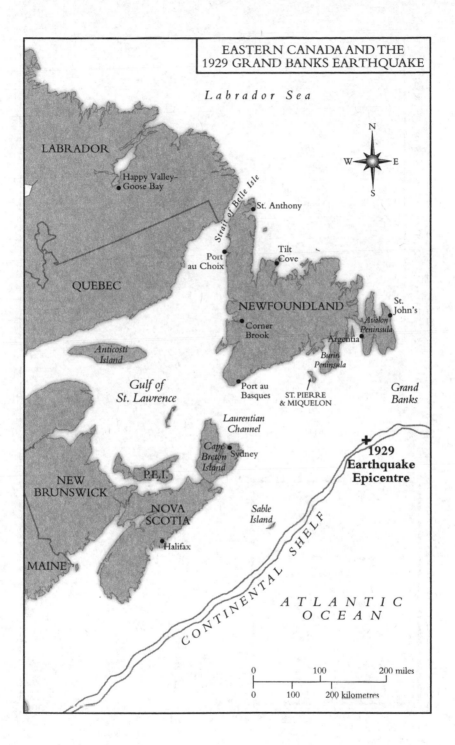

EASTERN CANADA AND THE
1929 GRAND BANKS EARTHQUAKE

Labrador Sea

N
W — E
S

LABRADOR

Happy Valley-
Goose Bay

St. Anthony

Strait of Belle Isle

Port
au Choix

Tilt
Cove

QUEBEC

NEWFOUNDLAND

St.
John's

Corner
Brook

*Avalon
Peninsula*

Argentia

*Burin
Peninsula*

*Anticosti
Island*

Port au
Basques

ST. PIERRE
& MIQUELON

*Grand
Banks*

*Gulf of
St. Lawrence*

*Laurentian
Channel*

*Cape
Breton
Island*

Sydney

+
**1929
Earthquake
Epicentre**

P.E.I.

NEW
BRUNSWICK

NOVA
SCOTIA

*Sable
Island*

CONTINENTAL SHELF

MAINE

Halifax

*ATLANTIC
OCEAN*

CONTINENTAL SHELF

0   100   200 miles

0   100   200 kilometres

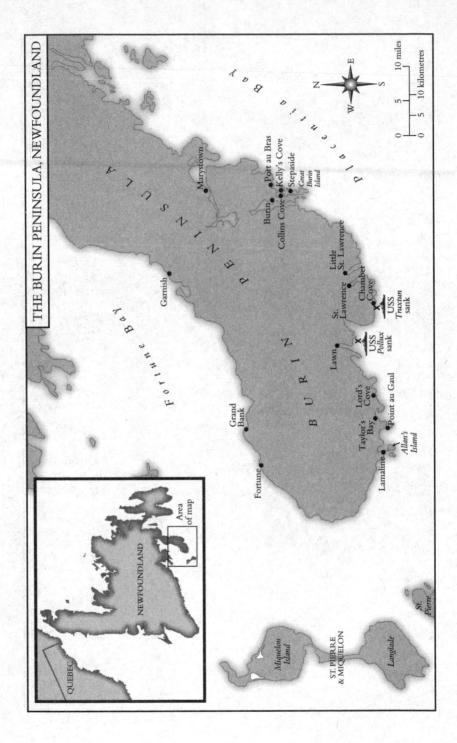

THE BURIN PENINSULA, NEWFOUNDLAND

Placentia Bay

Marystown
Port au Bras
Collins Cove
Kelly's Cove
Burin
Stepaside
Great Burin Island

PENINSULA

Garnish

Little St. Lawrence
St. Lawrence
Chamber Cove
X USS Truxtun sank

Fortune Bay

BURIN

X USS Pollux sank

Lawn

Lord's Cove
Taylor's Bay
Point au Gaul
Allan's Island

Grand Bank

Lamaline

Fortune

10 miles
10 kilometres
5
0   5   0

N
W   E
S

Area of map

NEWFOUNDLAND

QUEBEC

Miquelon Island

ST. PIERRE & MIQUELON

Langlade

St. Pierre

Conversations with the Dead I

i.

Here's the beginning of a story. A conversation. It's late 1968.

We were talking about mining. My father had just given it up. Had a new surface job near home. I was visiting for a weekend. We were in a pub. It had a name that I forget, but it was called Billy Joe's by everybody.

—How's that, the new job?

—Good. I think I'll get a dog.

—A dog.

—I work alone now, and a lot of night shift. A dog would be company.

—Good idea.

He talked a bit more about the dog and the new job, taking care of pumps for a water utility. And about the mining work he'd done since he was around sixteen. He coughed a lot.

—How's the health?

He looked away, frowned.

We shared a room once, in a camp. Northern Quebec. Somewhere between Senneterre and Chibougamau. I'd be awake half the night listening to him cough, breathing heavy when he wasn't coughing.

—Health is great. Had a complete checkup before I left the last job. A hundred percent.

—Really?

—It's what the doctor said.

I wanted to ask more about the physical. Who was the doctor? But another man arrived and sat down at our table. Peter MacKay. The Glendale MacKays. Someone he'd grown up with. Then the conversation was in Gaelic, spoken softly. I listened hard, struggling to follow.

A friend of mine came by the table. A friend from school. Dennis. I joined him for the afternoon. I'd catch up with my father later. No problem. Resume the conversation. More about his health. About that doctor. Whenever.

Next day, my father drove me to the airport.

We didn't speak much on the drive. And the way things turned out, we never spoke again.

He was fifty years old when he died four months later.

ii.
~

Not so long ago, I had a dream.

We seem to be compelled to make sense of dreams by giving them a shape and meaning, even when, probably, they're only fragments of illusions.

But some dreams have structure and their own memorable logic. The one I clearly remember happened to me on the morning of May 22, 2017. It was shortly before dawn. I know that because it woke me and I wasn't able to go back to sleep. I got up and wrote it down.

I was in a small room. And my father was in the room. It was as if he had been waiting for my arrival. He looked exactly as he had the last time I saw him. I saw him in the dream as I had seen him for the last time, alive, that day years ago, after Billy Joe's.

I said,

—I have to ask you something.

He nodded.

—*Do you remember August 1942?*

He smiled.

—*Why does it matter?*

—*There was a fatality in the Iron Springs mine on August 19. I was wondering if you were there.*

—*Yes, he said. A fatality. A man fell down the shaft. There were two who fell.*

—*And one survived . . .*

—*His leg snagged in the timber. That saved him.*

He shook his head and laughed a little.

—*So you were there.*

—*No. I was away. Rennie Slaney told me all about it.*

Then I remembered: he married my mother in August 1942. Maybe that's why he was away.

I said,

—*I understand they laid the dead man out in the lunchroom.*

—*Yes. I heard that too. There was nowhere else.*

—*If you had been there . . .*

—*It would have been my job.*

—*You were underground captain.*

—*I was.*

—*You were only twenty-four years old in August 1942.*

He frowned, shrugged.

—*So?*

—*That was young.*

—*Not so young back then.*

iii.

~

As will happen sometimes, a dream continues. A continuing conversation somewhere in the soul.

—So why the sudden interest?

—You had a lot of stories but never told them. Not to me.

—I doubt if you'd have listened.

—But we never talked much anyway when you were living. You weren't around much. It was after you died, I realized that you were, in many ways, a bit of a mystery.

—A mystery, eh?

—An enigma.

—If you say so. But would it have been any different if I were around more?

—We'll never know. You were, for long periods of time, an absence, an empty place at the end of the kitchen table.

—Well, the table wasn't empty, right? Nobody went hungry. I was away because I was working. But didn't we room together later? In Newfoundland and Northern Quebec? Didn't we talk then?

—You were a shift boss. I was the lowest of the low. Underground labour. We were more like co-workers. We never talked about what really matters: who we are, what we think, what we need.

—Some things are hard to talk about.

—We joked, gossiped, laughed, played cribbage, drank beer, smoked cigarettes. But never really talked.

—Fair enough. So talk.

—I want to tell a story about why so many in your generation of miners died too young.

The memorable shrug. His signature.

—I want to talk about why you and so many like you put your lives and health at risk in places that were essentially unregulated; why, even when there was regulation, especially in the remote places, the safety of the workplace was usually at the discretion of mine owners.

—It was called earning a living.

—Risking life and health?

—Life and health are always a matter of common sense, no matter who or where we are, or what we do.

4

—But sometimes common sense collapses under the pressure of earning a living, especially when you're young.

—Which was why I got out when I did.

—But still you died when you were relatively young.

—There's that. But fifty wasn't so young for my crowd. It was pretty old, actually.

—Because of how you worked?

—Everything. How we lived in general.

—So how does common sense stack up beside the realities of livelihood? Profit-making? Masculine bravado?

He just shrugs. Again.

—Has anything changed?

—I doubt it.

iv.

~~~~

But what I really need to know is how he will react to the story I am about to tell; how approximately fifteen hundred sensible miners working in a small, remote community risked their lives because they were unaware of the perils that surrounded them.

How normal instincts of self-preservation were blunted by desperation. How entire communities were left impoverished and numb by an earthquake that was followed by a tsunami, and by the collapse of the fishery that had provided a livelihood for centuries.

And how they became hard-rock miners, seduced by promises of shared prosperity from a mine promoter from New York.

Things he knew but never spoke about when he was living: how more than three hundred of these unsuspecting men were doomed to die slowly, badly, because of conditions in their workplace; how hundreds of the others would live out their lives struggling to breathe, their mobility severely compromised.

Many of these men worked with or for him in a little mining town called St. Lawrence, on the south coast of Newfoundland.

And I want to know if he'd agree that what happened there is a story that has relevance today for vulnerable workers in many other places, in Asia and Africa and Latin America. That the story of what happened in St. Lawrence, Newfoundland, is kind of universal, a continuing saga of abuse and exploitation by an industry that thrives in conditions of political disorder and economic desperation.

Perhaps another conversation, for another dream, or a nightmare.

So here's the story. It's about a place and people, and men who became hard-rock miners because of a barely imaginable convergence of events. It's also about him.

It started with an earthquake.

It ended with a plague.

Prologue

To circumnavigate an island in the North Atlantic is to achieve a unique perspective on some of the most striking scenery in North America—the plunging hillsides, the cliffs darkened by a sea that seems to pound them violently even when the winds are lazy—the sudden sense of solidarity and shared curiosity with adventurers who passed this way centuries ago. And yet, in the larger sweep of time, it was not so long ago at all, but a blink in the lifespan of a world that has been shaping this topography for more than two million years.

As the earth's temperature fell during what we now know as the last ice age (ten to eighty thousand years ago), water froze into glaciers that covered the top of the planet, including all of what is now called Canada. Oceans, created by a great continental rift that began more than one hundred million years before the glaciers, dropped fifty fathoms, exposing what we now see, looming and unapproachable, before our eyes. It occurs to the anxious modern mind that the process that required tens of thousands of years to freeze the top of the planet is now working in reverse, accelerated to the point where a thaw is discernible in the span of a single human lifetime.

We are now warned that the seas are rising again. But twenty-five thousand years ago, the seas withdrew. Humans learned to fashion tools and weapons from metal instead of stone, to refine minerals for making heat and energy, food and light—a marriage of human creativity and the bounty of the elements. Timeless geophysical events would set the stage for apocalyptic destruction, but also shape the opportunities for our deliverance. The nutritious soil sprang green with vegetation. People evolved, thrived and spread, adapted, reproduced and struggled to repurpose rock and soil and trees and other species for food and shelter. In time, humanity was intimate with the surface of the planet, or most of it. At home on top of nearly all the oceans.

But what lay deep beneath the surfaces of land and sea would, until modern times, remain mysterious, and even now, except where wealth was an incentive, a matter of indifference to all but those with arcane interests—the scientists and the dreamers.

And yet, it is easy to imagine the land we see, travel, live upon, stripped of its familiar vegetation and reproduced beneath the oceans. The highlands and lowlands, the cliffs and valleys, the mountains and fjords and canyons and vast plains that account for more than 70 percent of the earth's surface—a world that remains mostly inaccessible to mortals. But we are able to know it and see it in our mind's eye because it is merely a bald continuation of what we see around us.

FOR North Americans, the nearest and most familiar and accessible part of that hidden world is the Atlantic continental shelf, a submerged landmass that projects outwards from the shoreline, relatively shallow, until it begins to slope down through the continental rise, yielding to the vast Sohm Abyssal Plain, a hilly expanse, in places several miles below the surface of the ocean.

As the slope descends, it is split and criss-crossed by steep trenches and canyons, which both deliver and collect sediment from the land and from the ocean bottom, where the sea is shallower. One such trench, the Laurentian Channel, extends from the confluence of the St. Lawrence and Saguenay Rivers, delivering sediment from erosion and glaciation to the underwater edge of where the continent once ended.

During the height of the ice age, the east coast of what is now called North America extended more than a hundred miles farther than at present. A larger, wilder Hudson River carved an immense channel, not unlike the Colorado River did the Grand Canyon, across the continental slope before the waters rose again.

The submerged valleys and the canyons there became collection systems for detritus—silt, stone, sand—accumulated over a span of time that can only be approximated. Time that is inconceivable to ordinary mortals except as abstract ages, epochs, eras. Time measured in the millions of years, never mind millennia.

And then, in the vastness of nature, as in human experience, there comes a moment, calculated in mere seconds, when everything will change and we are dwarfed and mortified by our incompetence and impotence. And such a moment came at 5:02, Newfoundland Standard Time, on the afternoon of November 18, 1929.

DEEP below the north wall of the Laurentian Channel, a vast slab of the planet's brittle shell, along what scientists call a strike-slip fault, jerked violently.[1] The earth's crust, a series of solid plates, floats on a thick fluid mantle almost two thousand miles deep. It's mostly stable because the plates are usually stuck together, but now and then, they slip, let go, creating the sudden jolt of energy we call an earthquake.[2] Most of the time, the result is noticeable only to people who read seismographs. But the slippage off the coast of Newfoundland in November 1929 created an unmistakable surge of energy, unleashing a disaster that would unfold in real time and unexpected ways for decades.

There were actually three slips in a period of twenty-seven seconds: a major lurch on a fault line running to the northeast, followed by two lesser jerks along nearby fractures. And then a momentary stillness while the pent-up seismic energy shot out in waves that caused a violent shifting of the silt and sludge clinging to the sides of those sub-sea ravines and canyons. And suddenly, a submarine landslide was tumbling down the southern edge of the continental shelf, gathering speed and sludge and water, racing down the continental rise and, flushed finally from the canyons and the valleys, fanning outwards onto the vastness of the underwater plain for hundreds of miles.[3]

The full scientific account of what happened that day presents a spectacle we can only imagine—and even then, of dimensions that stagger the mind of the non-scientist. The impact of the disruption deep in the earth's crust shook up an area of the continental slope about the size of Israel; it sent the equivalent of a mountain range of mud and sludge tumbling to the ocean floor.[4] The avalanche, moving at more than sixty miles an hour, soaked up water as it slipped downwards, gradually turning into a heavy, soupy underwater wave that would continue moving for more than thirteen hours, redistributing what had been shaken loose over the unseen world below the ocean.

But it was what was happening along the way that would capture the attention of scientists and engineers for decades. All telegraph communication between North America and Europe in 1929 passed through cables that criss-crossed the continental shelf and slope and the adjacent deep-sea basin.[5] The earthquake's epicentre was in the middle of this dense network. Six cables lying at depths of between 150 and 1,800 fathoms were snapped immediately. The breaks continued in a sequence that could be precisely timed by onshore communications stations until the relentless current severed the last one thirteen hours and seventeen minutes after the initial shock. There were, in total, twenty-eight breaks in the twelve affected cables on the slope and in the ocean basin. It would take almost a year to repair the underwater damage.

On the nearby land, unsuspecting families were about to experience an onslaught that would mark them for a lifetime.

ONE

The Quake

1.

THE day had been a blessing, a relief after a stormy weekend, with all the inevitable predictions of a long and gloomy winter. Until shortly before five that afternoon, the sun was shining. There was a chilly breeze.

According to Cecelia Fewer, the telegraph operator in St. Lawrence, the weekend storm had knocked out communications with St. John's. But for the ten thousand people living on the far end of the Burin Peninsula, the silence didn't matter much.

St. John's was a distant world, in many ways irrelevant, except when it came to pricing fish, which were the economic staple for everyone who lived in the remote, sparsely populated island nation, Newfoundland. There was no road between the capital and the southern peninsula called the Burin. France was closer than St. John's—the French islands of St. Pierre and Miquelon were just twenty miles away. The people there were fiercely French. But they mingled, married, did business—officially and unofficially—with the nearby Newfoundlanders.

In many ways, the people of St. Lawrence, while their roots were mostly Irish, related more to the United States, where so many of their friends and kinfolk lived. For many years, the two radio receivers in the town of about nine hundred brought news and entertainment mostly from America During the thirties, Gabriel

Heatter would become a media personality in St. Lawrence. At nine most evenings, people would gather round the privately owned radios in town—one in the rectory and one at Louis Etchegary's house—to listen to the news from WOR in New York. The only Canadian presence on the airwaves was CJCB, from Sydney in Cape Breton, two hundred miles to the west.

Monday, November 18, had been a perfect washday. Clotheslines were flapping and crackling in a light breeze. This break in the late-autumn weather was a bonus for the housewives, who were busy all that day. The sunshine couldn't last. The weatherwise were already warning that there was another storm blowing up the eastern seaboard.

Bertha Slaney was temporarily living with her parents, Gregory and Mary Turpin, while her husband, Rennie, was off on the west coast of Newfoundland scrabbling for wages in the new pulp-and-paper industry, based in Corner Brook. He and his older brother, Arcule—a name that echoed their French connections—fished together, and the fall season that year had been productive, though the prices seemed to be unsteady worldwide.[1]

They were an odd pair of brothers, Rennie and Arcule. Rennie was younger but intensely curious and gifted at communication. Rennie, they would say, had a way with words. Even when he was relatively young, people took Rennie Slaney seriously. Arcule was quieter. People would defer to him for a different reason—unlike his younger brother, who was about five foot ten, normal stature for a Newfoundlander then, Arcule was huge, at least six four and near three hundred pounds. Gentle, though, as so many large men are, and powerful in a boat or on a codfish trap.

Most fishermen turned to other work in the gap between the end of fishing in the fall and the onset of winter—weatherproofing homes, cutting firewood. For the lucky and the venturesome, there were wages somewhere, in the offshore fishing fleet, the annual seal hunt. Rennie needed cash immediately. He and

Bertha were building their own home, across the harbour from the in-laws. So after fall fishing, Rennie went away.

Bertha missed her husband, but she understood the need for wages. And she would have acknowledged that just three years earlier, he had given up a paying job—he'd been a cook on the coastal vessel SS *Glencoe*—to marry her and try to live a normal life on land. Bertha would have been reminded of all this by a garment hanging in a closet at her mother's house—a suit, now rarely worn, that Rennie had purchased for their marriage from a haberdashery in Brooklyn. The wedding ring she now wore had come from Boston.

They were mostly self-sufficient. There were always fish. Rennie and Arcule were successful fishermen, and the catches for the last three years had been abundant. They would never starve as long as they could fish. And there were game birds in the barrens. Almost everybody had a cow or two for milk and butter. Most people in St. Lawrence had horses and oxen for heavy work and transportation. They kept pigs and sheep and hens. Rising above the town and the houses and the boats and the small businesses—the stores and fishing sheds, wharves and rickety racks for drying fish—were meadows where the animals grazed in the good weather. Yards around the squared-off tidy houses were secure behind tight picket fences that kept the kids and chickens from straying far from home.

Bertha Slaney already had two toddlers and another baby on the way. It would have neither daunted nor surprised her to know that she would in time bring fourteen children into a world that was, in her lifetime, hurtling through unimaginable changes. Large families were normal in mostly Catholic St. Lawrence. At five o'clock on the evening of November 18, 1929, however, she could not have imagined that for her and her husband and her children—for her whole community—the beginning of a transforming change was only minutes in the future.

~~~

GUS Etchegary was five and a half years old, but he'd started to grow up swiftly when his mother died just six months earlier. His mom had been Rennie Slaney's sister. In a photo taken before she fell ill, she is serene and solemn. She was quite beautiful and only forty-five when she was taken by tuberculosis, which had become a plague across the entire Dominion of Newfoundland.[2]

Gus's two older sisters had adapted quickly to running their father's household. Louis was away frequently, at sea or doing business in St. Pierre or the United States. Gus was too young to understand or care about his father's business ventures, beyond the fact that they produced an enviable stability at home, even when it seemed that everybody else—other than the Farrells and the Giovanninis, who were successful merchants—was struggling.

Not that there wasn't occasional anxiety among the Etchegarys when Louis was away for longer than seemed normal. And there would even be an anxious couple of weeks when, according to the local gossip, Louis, along with about a dozen others on a local boat, the slyly named *Which One*, was arrested somewhere in the territorial waters of the United States. Smuggling, the rumour had it. Gus and his sisters would soon find out that their dad and all his shipmates were indeed in jail, somewhere in New York City.

Gus and his sisters went to church every evening then and prayed for their dad's deliverance. And the prayers were swiftly answered, thanks to faith in the divine and a resourceful Yankee lawyer who was on the payroll of the famous New York gangster Charles "Vannie" Higgins. Soon Louis and his shipmates were back in St. Lawrence, celebrating freedom and the triumph of American private enterprise, not to mention justice.

Just before five on the evening of November 18, 1929, Gus was lurking in the family kitchen, waiting for his supper. His sisters had been frying sliced potatoes on the stove. Then they busied themselves with other preparations. Gus was hungry and now the fried potatoes were just sitting there. It was approximately two minutes after five.

He was staring longingly at the potatoes when, to his amazement, the frying pan began to tap-dance across the stovetop. Pots and pans were rattling, and there was a clatter in the cupboards. And Gus realized the whole house was trembling, creaking. Doors slamming. Loud and unfamiliar sounds from outside; wooden structures suddenly stressed to the limits of design, twisting, shuddering, threatening to fall. There seemed to be a sudden wind.

Across the harbour, on the east side, his aunt Bertha and her mother were running towards a china cabinet to brace the doors, which were threatening to swing open and send the precious dishes crashing to the floor. In the Giovanninis' west side fish shop, fifteen workers paused their cutting, gutting, beheading to steady themselves. The building was on wooden posts hanging out over the harbour. It was sturdy, but obviously imperilled by this extraordinary motion. The owner of the business, Adolph Giovannini, later told the St. John's *Evening Telegram* that he and his wife, Dinah, were at home, settling in for a quiet evening, when they felt the shudder passing through their house.

The peculiar movement and the unfamiliar sounds subsided, and all was quiet once again—even quieter than before, as people stared silently into each other's faces, seeking reassurance, some explanation for what had just happened.

Or did it really happen? Might it have been a freak of the imagination in the gloom of an early evening not long after Halloween, just before the prayerful weeks of Advent?

But the blank expressions and the silent questions in the eyes of parents, children, siblings, husbands, wives would have confirmed for everyone that, yes, it really happened. An earthquake had just happened in their town.

~~~

LATER that evening, after supper, Adolph and Dinah Giovannini decided to check their property for damage. It was close to half past seven. They put on their coats and stepped outside. They lived close to the shoreline and the shop, and they immediately noticed an unusual tidal action in the harbour. The water there was churning, swirling, menacing.

From the now-darkened lanes and pathways throughout the town, the sound of voices. People on the move, word spreading. Something ominous was going on.

There were people gathering near the Etchegarys' house. Gus and his sisters, too young to be afraid, stepped outside. They started walking towards the voices. There was a familiar murmur on a nearby veranda. The sound of women praying. The rosary.

They had already survived something potentially disastrous. But this new phenomenon, the disturbance in the water of the harbour, seemed more dangerous. It wasn't like the momentary shuddering of hours earlier. This peculiarity seemed to be continuing and growing.

Because it was a Monday, the people praying on the veranda would have been reciting the joyful mysteries. Even at the age of five, Gus would know that. And that the rosary was structured into themes called mysteries—joyful, glorious and sorrowful. How Catholics experienced life itself. The sorrowful mysteries were later in the week, on Tuesday and again on Friday.

2.

~~~

FAR west of there, in a different time zone but the same marine environment—the vast Gulf of St. Lawrence—a girl named Alice Donohue, not yet in her teens, was milking cows. Milking was women's work in many northwest Atlantic places with deep Celtic roots, like Bay St. Lawrence, on the northern tip of Cape Breton Island, where young Alice lived. Like the gulf, it was named for St. Lawrence—martyr and patron saint of comedians, cooks and miners. In such isolated communities, the Irish connection was still unmistakeable. Though growing dim in the memory, it survived in the speech, the politics and the traditions.

These northern Cape Bretoners felt at home in both Newfoundland and St. Pierre. They were foreign countries, but that didn't matter much to fellow islanders, people who had small regard for borders, liberated as they were by a wary knowledge of the sea. They travelled where they had to go. Borders were invisible and easy to ignore. In St. Pierre, they freely traded livestock for merchandise they couldn't buy at home, including rum.

Alice Donohue was fascinated by the small gold stud in her grandfather's earlobe, a permanent reminder of an early trading trip to St. Pierre. Equally fascinating to her was that Granddad never seemed entirely sure how this little bit of gold became implanted there and grew impatient whenever he was asked about it.[3]

For Cape Breton fishermen and sailors, like the people on the south coast of Newfoundland, the eastern and southern sea lanes were more relevant and better known than the vast continental territories to the west and south, with all their westbound highways and railroads, and all the broad lakes and rivers, with their thriving trade and traffic.

Quietly milking in a cavernous barn on that November afternoon in 1929, twelve-year-old Alice Donohue had many questions in her busy mind—and there was soon to be another. She was looking forward to her thirteenth birthday, less than a month away, in the middle of December. Suddenly, at 4:30, Atlantic

Standard Time (half an hour behind Newfoundland time), the cows all started to stagger. It was frightening. And then Alice realized that everything around her, beneath her, was moving, wobbling. Farm equipment in the barn was shifting, rattling. Dust fell from rafters and from the hay stored in the loft above her. There were ripples in her milk pail. The cow that she was milking had turned to stare at her with its huge liquid eyes.

And then everything was still.

Alice was well read and curious, and she knew that this was a moment she would never forget. This was something she'd read about. An earthquake. Perhaps, hopefully, a once-in-a-lifetime moment—a moment of potential disaster that had passed as a brief dramatic episode in an otherwise quiet pastoral existence. And indeed it was, for a short while, the talk of the community. Nature flaunting incalculable power. Maybe God reminding them to be aware of their innate vulnerability. Not to forget the fragility and transience of mortal lives. All worth serious reflection, a quiet prayer or two. A few decades on their rosaries before retiring for the night. But then, devoid of tragic consequences, the incident passed quickly into the private memories of those who had experienced it.

There was almost greater excitement at the shore later in the evening—an extraordinary tidal surge that Alice Donohue's father, Jack, a fisherman, attributed to the unusual fullness of the autumn moon. The phases of the moon were important in the lives of the farmers and fishermen who eked out a marginal existence from the land and sea in Atlantic Canada. Many aspects of their lives were determined by the moon.

Each autumn in November, the fishermen in northern Cape Breton would drive a stake in the shoreline, well above the high-water mark for normal tides. When the sea rose to the stake, it was a signal that the autumn moon was at its zenith, and that it was time to slaughter the pigs and superannuated cattle. It was also an ideal time to get a haircut—hair grew back more slowly on the waning of the moon.

These customs were rooted in beliefs drawn from centuries of experience, and while there might not have been scientific validation for the practices, logic was irrelevant. It was what they did because they had always done so.

When Jack Donohue returned from the shore that evening, he remarked that the tide had been extraordinary, even for a full moon. The incoming sea had surpassed the stake by a considerable distance and had even flooded over the deck of the wharf, raising the possibility that boats would end up stranded there and damaged as the tide receded.

But they were lucky: the tide dropped almost as quickly as it had surged. There was no damage to either the wharf or their boats. In the days and weeks and years to come, the people of Bay St. Lawrence would learn precisely how lucky they had been, sheltered as they were by the brooding mass of Cape North, which stood between them and a natural catastrophe unfolding beneath the sea more than two hundred miles to the southeast.

At 198 Young Street in the North End of Halifax, Frank Lowe was sitting in front of his kitchen range with his feet warming in the oven, possibly looking forward to November 30—the day Prohibition would end in Nova Scotia and alcohol consumption would no longer be a crime. Suddenly, at 4:34, Atlantic Standard Time, the house began to shake so violently it moved the stove.

A few blocks away, on Kane Street, a frightened family began moving furniture outdoors, while throughout the North End there was panic building as people recalled the December 6, 1917, explosion that had wiped out the entire neighbourhood. That disaster, after a munitions vessel collided with a freighter in the harbour, killed almost two thousand Halifax residents, many of them in the North End, and injured an estimated nine thousand others.

On this day, the weather was nasty. Just as a ferocious blizzard had added to the suffering on the day of the explosion a dozen years before, a severe snowstorm—the first of the winter of 1929–30—would soon be pounding the people of Halifax and the rest of the Nova Scotia mainland. As the storm moved on towards Newfoundland, the snow was followed by heavy rain driven by a thirty-six-mile-per-hour gale. Frank Lowe had good reason to have his feet in the oven on such a day.

The Halifax *Chronicle* reported the next day, November 19, that there had been widespread confusion in the downtown business district "as streams of men and girls rushed to the street. Reminiscences of the tragic explosion of 1917 were in the air. Several girls fainted including one on the way out of the Roy building and three at Simpsons."

At the post office, pictures and calendars hanging on the walls moved, and many clattered to the floor as the stone building shook. Clerks were afraid the walls and ceilings were about to collapse on top of them. The clock on the customs building wobbled but did not stop.

Telephone operators worked heroically at their switchboards, though several of the "girls" became hysterical and, according to the local evening paper, were removed, their places being filled immediately with extras. The phone lines were so busy just after the disturbance that the system crashed temporarily.

In Sydney, Cape Breton, a witness testifying at a trial in the Supreme Court passed out when the tremors hit. Throughout the city, chimneys cracked and toppled. In nearby rural areas, barns collapsed. Coal miners emerging from the pits in Glace Bay and in Pictou County, on the mainland, reported feeling the earth moving, while those still working underground remained unaware of the drama on the surface.

Lighthouse keepers reported that mercury slopped out of containers as the silent coastal sentinels rocked briefly. Ships at sea, south of the Grand Banks, suddenly were wallowing and vibrating, as though their propellers had been damaged. The SS *Nerissa* reported feeling the quake on one of her regular runs between New York and St. John's.[4]

Captain Frank Thornhill, sailing from Fortune to St. Lawrence with a cargo of lumber, later recalled the moment when "the boat and all started to tremble." He said, "We were off Lamaline then. It was right calm, calm as a clock. And I didn't know what the trouble was."[5] Moments later, when normal progress had resumed, the puzzled captains speculated that they'd struck uncharted underwater hazards.

At a sawmill in Lower River Inhabitants, Cape Breton, John MacLeod decided to leave work early and visit friends. It was a decision that may have saved his life.[6]

A SEISMOGRAPH at Dalhousie University responded so violently that it failed to give an accurate measurement of what Professor J.H.L. Johnstone described to the Halifax *Chronicle* on November 19, 1929, as "the greatest shock since installation." It would later be established that the earthquake registered 7.2 on the scale of magnitude, and that the first shock recorded in Halifax caused a measurable "disturbance" that lasted for two and a half hours, with a dramatic aftershock registered at 7:03 that evening. Instruments recorded the event in Montreal and Toronto, New York and Bermuda. People felt the tremors along the Atlantic seaboard as far as South Carolina.

Scientists in Halifax first calculated that the epicentre was somewhere in Labrador. Their initial guess was a mistake. The epicentre was, in fact, 165 miles south of Newfoundland's Burin Peninsula, about 375 miles east of Halifax, and the actual seismic shifting was more than twelve miles below the ocean floor.

At the time, there were no seismographs or tidal gauges in Newfoundland to create a scientific record of what had happened, just a multiplicity of human observations that would take days to coalesce into random snapshots of unimaginable destruction.

3.

~~~

THE town of St. Lawrence had 135 families, a population that was almost entirely dependent on the fishery like virtually everybody else on the south coast. The town's main businesses, run by families named Farrell and Saint and Giovannini, were at the mercy of the sea and the international market for salt fish. These merchants were accustomed to the whims of weather and of traders in St. John's, the United States, the Caribbean and Western Europe.

But nothing in the remembered history of the south coast could have prepared the people of St. Lawrence and all the other vulnerable communities—from Burin in the east to Lamaline in the west—for the chain of catastrophes that would begin at approximately seven thirty on the evening of a perfect late-autumn day in 1929.

The earthquake had been a dramatic but mercifully brief diversion—a perfect memory, a brush with disaster, but without apparent consequences.

Adolph and Dinah Giovannini were relieved to find that the shaking land had left their business undamaged. At approximately seven thirty, they were standing just outside the shop when Dinah noticed that the water in the harbour, which had been rising rapidly, was now receding, dropping even faster. Soon she and Adolph could see the bottom. It was uncanny—staring at a place you knew about but thought of, like certain parts of the human body, as private, never to be publicly exposed. It was shocking.

They were speechless for a moment. Then Dinah made what would turn out to be one of the most important declarations of her life: she urged Adolph to tell the fifteen men working inside the shop to immediately leave the flimsy structure, which was now hanging out over the edge of the naked shoreline. Everyone should head for higher ground. And quickly.

And everybody did.

It was surprising that on November 18 and in the days immediately following this epic geological event, there was hardly any public reaction from the capital, St. John's. In the city, people were startled and confused, but not terribly bothered by what seemed to be nothing more significant than a brief shudder.

Eloise Morris, a sixteen-year-old schoolgirl, would remember clearly that she'd been waiting for a friend at five in the afternoon, near the gates of the college residence where she was living.[7] A lamppost across the street from where she stood was swaying like a tree in a high wind, its lights switching violently.

And then it was over. Eloise thought briefly of her family back in Collins Cove, near Burin, where her father was the United Church minister, but it would be days before she, or anybody else in St. John's, heard details of how the earthquake had affected people on the south coast. It would be nearly a month before she got to see the consequences for herself.

One immediate concern in the island capital was a rumour that there had been a serious accident at the iron ore mines on Bell Island, but that was quickly ruled out. Reports from Bell Island and Fogo indicated nothing out of the ordinary. Bay Roberts did report a break in a submarine cable somewhere between Newfoundland and New York, but this wasn't considered serious—at least not immediately.

From the south coast of the Burin Peninsula, there was no news at all. Perhaps the capital was unaware that communication with the area had been disrupted by a storm on the weekend before the earthquake. But given the reassuring news from other places on the island, nothing of significance was read into the silence from the south.

For the moment, Newfoundlanders who were aware of the earthquake seemed grateful to have been spared yet another calamity in the island's long history of grief: the great fires that ravaged St. John's in 1846 and 1892; the lives lost on the sea and on the ice; the national catastrophe on July 1, 1916, at Beaumont-Hamel in France, with 233 young Newfoundlanders dead, 386 wounded and 91 missing, all in a single encounter. The First World War, still vivid in the psyche, had robbed this small, remote dominion of the lifeblood of a generation.

But there were even greater, if less remembered, calamities. Canada's deadliest natural disaster happened off the east coast of Newfoundland on September 12, 1775, when more than four thousand people lost their lives at sea and in coastal communities during a cyclone that has been ranked as the seventh-deadliest hurricane in recorded human history.[8] A brief contemporary account of that event noted that "for some days after, in drawing the nets ashore, they [Newfoundlanders] often found twenty or thirty dead bodies in them; a most shocking spectacle."[9]

That epic disaster was overshadowed by other world events—notably the beginning of the American War of Independence and a storm that had obliterated much of North Carolina just days earlier.

And now, late in 1929, there were other challenges to be concerned about. For most of Newfoundland, the earthquake on November 18 was, for at least a few days, little more than a distraction. As always, there was an immediate preoccupation with the imperatives of livelihood, and how it might be affected by larger and equally unmanageable external forces, such as global economics and the ever-looming peril of man-made catastrophes like war.

The closing months of 1929 were dark with speculation about hard times to come. Bad things could happen in remote communities and hardly anyone outside would notice—or having noticed, care for long. Rural communities throughout Newfoundland, which was at the time a nominally independent country—just like Canada, Australia and the other members of the British Commonwealth—depended heavily on the sea for transportation, food and cash.

On November 18, the people struggling to manage Newfoundland were, by bedtime, quickly moving on from a momentary interest in what had seemed to be a minor spasm somewhere deep in the bowels of the planet. The price of dried salt cod had fallen by half, and salt fish exports were in free fall. Relief rolls and dole payments were soaring. Starvation was a looming prospect for the vulnerable, the unlucky and the unwise.

The world economy was falling down around them. Newfoundland, utterly dependent on markets in the United States, Europe and Asia, was facing a real existential crisis. The brief tremor might have been an omen, but in the absence of immediate consequences, the public and the establishment in St. John's returned to worrying about the realities in front of them—the possible collapse of their economy and their democracy.

ON the northern tip of Cape Breton Island, twelve-year-old Alice Donohue climbed into her chilly bed that night with the drama of the earthquake already buried under layers of more recent memories. Her father's description of the tidal surge mingled with the trivia of other gossip from their community. Her most significant birthday to date was only weeks away. Christmas hovered just beyond. Special days.

In Cape Breton and Halifax, and along the eastern Atlantic coastline as far south as the Carolinas, the brief disturbance of the late afternoon would be permanently etched in the collective memory. But for young Alice, the more immediate excitement of soon becoming a teenager was the greater impediment to sleep.

She would turn thirteen on the fifteenth of December. That fact was paramount. But she could not have known that thirteen years later—an unimaginably long time to a twelve-year-old—she would begin her married life in St. Lawrence, Newfoundland, a community that, while she waited for the beginning of her dreams, was being devastated by a horrifying wall of water.

TWO

The Wave

4.

~~

BEFORE the distraction of the internet and television broadcasts, long before the infinity of social media amusement, there were cards. Sometimes the card games were community events with modest prizes for the proficient and the lucky. Sometimes they were to raise money to improve a school, a church basement or a hall. More often, they were simple, spontaneous gatherings in kitchens where the only prize was the right to boast until the next occasion. Amid the loud commentary on strategy and the thudding of emphatic fists on kitchen tables, there would be news and gossip, fragments of old stories.

In Kelly's Cove, St. Lawrence, Lord's Cove and Point au Gaul, card games were in progress in the early evening of November 18, after the supper dishes had been cleared away. It's easy to imagine what would have dominated the conversations. An earthquake. Who was standing where; what would have been observed, spoken; how certain individuals reacted. Rosaries and Bibles had been deployed. Might the extraordinary moon have caused the astonishing trembling of their world that afternoon? Was it an omen of some kind? Would it influence approaching winter weather? Affect cod prices, which had been in worrisome decline?

Testimonials about reactions to the earthquake, recounted from memory over the subsequent years, are woven from common threads of recollection: dishes clattering on shelves and smashing on floors; pots rattling on stoves; frightening sounds from cupboards and closets, or from upstairs, like "people jumping in their sock-feet."[1] Some people wept. Many prayed. One frightened mother, sprinkling what she thought was holy water on the head of her child, realized that in her panic, she'd grabbed cod liver oil.

Ernest Cheeseman of Port au Bras, near Burin, in a letter he wrote two days later to his brother Jack, who was living in St. John's, described "women screaming and praying" while "men stood silent and scared."[2]

Mary Anne Counsel was learning to spin wool and was making what she thought was great progress. But late that afternoon, she was having difficulty. The wheel seemed to have grown sluggish, stubborn, even perverse, breaking and entangling the strands of new-spun yarn. Frustrated, she swore aloud. "I wished the devil would take the [spinning] wheel."[3] The words were hardly out when "the big trembling came and the house was shivering, the dishes were dancing, the glasses rattling and I was frightened to death. I thought the devil was coming for the wheel."

And then the shimmering moonlight, the eerie calm, once the spasm had passed.

For about two hours, the coastal people on the Burin Peninsula would have been relieved. People who had felt the earth tremble that evening would resume the routines of an ordinary day, grateful that at least one potential disaster had given them a pass.

But the jiggle that had lasted just twenty-seven seconds, plus or minus, was only the beginning of a greater and more catastrophic drama. A hundred miles away from where they sat or worked or chatted over cards, a submarine monster had been disturbed, had begun a rampage, was already causing havoc on the ocean bottom and was now surging in its epic fury towards their shores.

The people out on the end of the Burin Peninsula and the nearby French islands, those closest to the earthquake's epicentre, would in time tell a story unlike the other anecdotes of momentary curiosity, of swinging lampposts in the city. It would be a different story altogether, an account of an event more harrowing than that experienced by most people on the eastern Atlantic seaboard that afternoon and evening, or ever in their lifetimes.

But it would take a while to get the story out. Intercontinental communication had been severely compromised. Nature had conspired to cut off the south coast. There were hardly any road links between the fifty-two communities on the peninsula, so in addition to being virtually isolated from the rest of the world, they were isolated from each other.

5.

ON Great Burin Island, twenty-three-year-old Louise Emberley was looking forward to a special treat at suppertime— her mother had been baking apple dumplings and the house was full of the aroma. There was a sudden noise. It seemed to be coming from the stove. And they realized everything was shaking.[4]

The drama was quickly over, but the questions lingered, so after supper, Louise walked along the shore, over a flimsy gangway made from planks, across the little wharves and working platforms, called stages and flakes, then up a hill to the telegraph office to see what she could learn.

There were already people there. Helen Darby, the telegraph operator for Great Burin Island, was also the local source for news. She made notes about events unfolding in the world in a "news book" and left it out for other islanders to read. For those who were illiterate or preferred to listen, she'd read her news reports aloud.

There was a small crowd, including an Englishman named Sidney Hussey, who kept the lighthouse. He was familiar with earthquakes, and he commented that from what he knew about them, when the epicentre of an earthquake was below the ocean floor, the event was usually followed by a tidal wave. It was an interesting observation, but the quake had happened nearly two hours earlier and the sea was calm and flat, a full moon rising over it, casting a reflection that resembled fire. Surely nothing bad could come from such serenity.

GEORGE Bartlett, a prominent Burin merchant and member of the Newfoundland House of Assembly, was in his office when he experienced what he later recalled as "a tremendous roar and vibration."[5] Customers in his general store rushed out into the street, but then sheepishly returned when it seemed to have been a passing shudder and a lot of noise.

Later that evening, people in Burin would remember and remark upon the fullness of the moon, the reflection of moon and stars on an unusually placid sea. As one would later ruefully observe, "There was no indication of the wrath to come."

NAN Hillier, who lived in the tiny community of Point au Gaul, on the southern tip of the Burin, twenty miles west of St. Lawrence, spent most of November 18 baking pies and cakes. The Ladies' Orange Benevolent Association was holding a meeting and tea that evening in Lamaline, three miles away. She and her husband, Herbert, along with her sister Jessie Hepditch and

Jessie's husband, David, planned to attend. Nan had committed to providing sweets for the occasion.[6]

The sisters had children—Nan had four, Jessie three—and the babysitting had all been arranged. Their parents, Henry and Lizzie Hillier (almost everybody in the place was named Hillier), would take care of the Hepditch kids. Herbert Hillier's brother Chesley, who lived with him and Nan, would take care of their four.

There was a third Hillier sister in Point au Gaul—Jemimiah. She was married to Josiah Hillier, and she had also planned to attend the meeting, but she was feeling unwell that day and the three-mile walk would have been more than she could manage.

At around four thirty, Nan and Herbert set off on foot for Lamaline. Jessie and David Hepditch would follow a bit later. It was a challenging walk. Although the landscape between the two communities was relatively flat—Point au Gaul occupies a kind of basin on low land, face on to the sea—the journey to the nearby town over what was essentially a cart track was rugged at the best of times.

Nan and Herb were about halfway to their destination when the earth began to tremble beneath their feet. They stopped and steadied each other. Telegraph wires were vibrating above them, creating an eerie musical hum. Ice in ditches crackled. Herbert hesitated. He'd been in the war, had travelled widely. He was familiar with earth tremors, and this is what he told his wife to reassure her. It was nothing. They kept on going. There was yet another Hillier sister, Rachael Bonnell, who lived in Lamaline, and they stopped at her place for a visit on the way to the Orange Hall. She decided to attend the social with them.

AT the Orange Hall, people were abuzz, sharing their reactions to the memorable happening. Nobody could recall such a sensation—the earth suddenly in motion, shaking up their houses, the contents of cupboards tumbling. Strange noises from places that were usually silent.

In Lamaline, as in many of the communities along the southern shore, people of deep religious conviction sensed foreboding in the strange incident—perhaps the end of time. Herbert Hillier, however, was assuring people he spoke with that the event was over, the danger past.

Just before seven thirty, as the buzz about the earthquake was beginning to subside, someone noticed an event more mystifying than the trembling of the earth: the water in Lamaline harbour was slowly draining away, and it continued doing so until the rocky seabed lay before them, utterly exposed.

At home in Point au Gaul, people were staring at the same bizarre spectacle—the dry harbour bottom. There had been about twenty horses grazing on a point of land near the entrance to the harbour when the earth shuddered earlier that afternoon. Startled, the horses raised their heads and looked around, then ambled inland and up a gradually sloping hillside. Now they were huddled there, as if waiting, as if they had anticipated this new strangeness.

Douglas Hillier was equally surprised to see a herd of sheep nervously milling around in his neighbour's yard. "They knew something was happening."[7]

In Great Burin at that moment, Louise Emberley was among a small crowd of men, including the prescient lighthouse keeper, Sidney Hussey, staring at the harbour, suddenly drained of water, Mr. Darby's dory at the wharf now high and dry. They started moving up to higher ground.[8]

MARION Kelly lived in Kelly's Cove, about twelve miles east of St. Lawrence (as the crow flies—there was no road then). She was thirteen years old and at a neighbour's house, helping an elderly woman write a letter to relatives in Boston. The letter was only partly written when the house began to shake. Marion was confused and frightened, excused herself and went home.[9]

Everything seemed normal there. She ate her supper with her mother, Frances Kelly; two brothers, Curt and Elroy; and her sister, Dorothy. Her dad, Vincent, like a number of the local men, was away from home, cutting firewood for the winter fuel supply. After supper was finished and the dishes put away, Marion sat down at the kitchen table to do her homework.

Carrie Brushett and her kids were also home alone in Kelly's Cove. Like Vincent Kelly, Carrie's husband was off in the bush, cutting firewood. Pearl Brushett was only five, but she would remember that it had been a difficult day. Her sister Lillian was suffering with an earache and they'd been sent to bed soon after supper, Lillian with a heated plate to place beneath her ear to ease the pain.[10]

MARY Walsh of Lord's Cove, a village just to the west of St. Lawrence, would normally have been in St. Pierre, where she'd spent previous winters helping out a family with small children. But she'd returned home in May to help her father, who was a fisherman and a widower. She was still at home on the afternoon of November 18.

Later that evening, with the memory of the earthquake already fading, she had put on her coat to go visiting and was in the doorway of her home when she saw an extraordinary sight: where the harbour had been just moments earlier, there was only rock and seaweed.

By then, word was spreading through the community and people were stepping outside to see what was causing the commotion. A small group had gathered on the road in front of Mary's house. Her father, Jim Walsh, was there. Her neighbours, the Harnett brothers. Paddy Rennie, another neighbour from down the hill, closer to the cove, along with his two boys, Albert and Martin.

The spectacle had interrupted a card game at the Harnetts'. Pat Rennie was a regular there, a feisty little Irishman who made a decent living, like almost everybody else in Lord's Cove, as a fisherman. Pat had left home earlier in the evening, after the earth tremor and his supper. His wife, Sarah, had put two of the kids—four-year-old Margaret and Patrick Junior, who was seven—to bed. Nine-year-old Rita was lingering downstairs. The baby in the family, Bernard, one year and eight months old, was strapped into a high chair near the kitchen table while Sarah was busy at her sewing machine. It was a clear moonlit evening, and from where he stood, up near the Harnetts' place, Pat could see his house just beyond Eastern Cove Pond, behind the beach where he would spread his fish on the rocks to cure in the summer sun.

Mary Walsh would not forget the moment: neighbours standing around, watching, when suddenly the emptied cove was full again, and rising above it, a towering, curling wave, racing straight at Patrick Rennie's home. She would remember his panic-stricken cry—"Look, there's my house! My wife and my children are in it."

The raging sea picked up his house, tossed it around, then dropped it on the beach as it withdrew, grumbling, seemingly exhausted.

And then the sea rose up before them once again. The wave was massive. "It was like it was coming out of the sky."[11]

TOM Pike was someone everybody knew in St. Lawrence. He was a veteran of the First World War and had lost an arm in the trenches of France. One of the small rewards for his service overseas was a partial livelihood as a customs collector and relieving officer, the man responsible for handing out the welfare chits to desperate people once a month—$1.84 per person per month, once their needs and means were proven. For many, the dole, pittance though it was, became the narrow margin between starvation and survival.[12]

The needy came to Tom Pike from as far away as Lawn—an eight-mile walk—and on dole day, Tom's wife, Agnes, and her household helper would bake multiple loaves of bread to hand out for sustenance on the weary walk back to distant homes. On the evening of November 18, she had bread in the oven while her husband engaged a group of neighbours in a friendly game of poker at the kitchen table.

The house Tom and his family shared was at the end of Shingle Point, a narrow strip of land that jutted from the western shore towards the middle of the harbour. The house was in a vulnerable spot, but it had been built sturdily because of its exposure to offshore gales and tides.

At about seven thirty, the poker game and the baking were interrupted by a townsman who arrived in a state of breathless panic. Something ominous was going on outside. Someone went out to check, then rushed back in—the tide was rising rapidly, he said. A tidal bore, almost like a wave, was surging down the harbour, straight towards Tom Pike's house. Cards were dropped. There were three children in the Pikes' house, little girls between the ages of one and twelve. Tom and his fellow card players grabbed the children and, with Agnes close behind them, ran across the open shingle strand for the safety of the meadows on the hill that rose above the town.

The water rose up again, cresting as a ten-foot wave, then spilling forward, breaking against the Pikes' house, then surging past it towards, and then well past, the end of the harbour. The house was still firmly on its foundation as the sea withdrew, dragging with it boats, debris from shattered wharves and staging, fishing gear. The water retreated seawards—only to return, now littering the shoreline with the remnants of what, just minutes earlier, had been the livelihood for a community.

And then Tom Pike could see his barn teetering as it floated down the harbour, and he could hear a furious racket coming from inside, the sound of battering. The door swung open and Pike's little Newfoundland pony leapt into the swirling water, swam to shore, clambered out and galloped away. Three days later, he returned.

In Lord's Cove, ten miles west of St. Lawrence, the first surge had carried Pat Rennie's house off its foundation and dropped it on the beach, where it grounded. The second wave lifted it again, and this time dragged it seawards, into the middle of Eastern Cove Pond. All around it, the wreckage of wharves and staging, small buildings, one nearly upside down.[13] And then the raging sea came back a third time, smashed against Pat Rennie's house again, rose up to the second-storey windows and retreated. Finally.

And then a ghastly silence. The evening was unnaturally serene again. A high, luminous moon. The air still. There would be stories from all along the coastline—stories and images permanently etched into the collective memories of the small communities that had, for these few horrifying minutes, been united by catastrophe. Stories from Burin, Collins Cove, Kelly's Cove, Stepaside, Port au Bras, St. Lawrence. Stories from Lawn, Lord's Cove, Taylor's Bay, Point au Gaul, Lamaline. Stories from a dozen other smaller places, and the ten thousand people whose future had just washed away.

There would be memories, undeniable even if imagined, of lamplight flickering in the upper windows of houses that were now afloat, still moving on the suddenly exhausted tide; images of the bays and harbours, drained and then filled up again with debris; exaggerated impressions of rogue waves up to eighty feet high, scouring flimsy man-made obstacles from their path. The flakes and stages smashed to kindling; the dories and the schooners tossed up on land or keeled over on the bottom of the bays; the homes, trustingly established near the workplace, now demolished. Winter food and fuel supplies, gone irretrievably.

In Lord's Cove, the deathly momentary silence would have felt like endless minutes. And then it was broken by a cry from the middle of the pond, from Patrick Rennie's house. An awful sound to the ears of any adult—the appeal of a small child in distress.

Jim Walsh and two Harnett brothers, Maurice and Clement, found an undamaged dory and launched it.[14] They attached a rope between the dory and a capstan on the hillside. Having seen three massive waves already, they would have been foolish not to anticipate another. Jim Walsh had lit a candle and planted it in a link in a chain that was attached to the capstan. It was a holy candle with special meaning in the Walsh family—last lit beside his wife's deathbed some years earlier.[15] He would credit that act of faith with the fact that his property, home, fishing gear, capstan and dory had survived unscathed while so much other property was shattered and washed away.

Walsh and the Harnetts persuaded Pat Rennie to stay behind with his two sons while they rowed out to his sunken house. Clem Harnett also stayed behind, by the capstan, in case of an emergency.

Jim's daughter, Mary (later in life, Mary McKenna), watched her father standing, nervous, at the bow of the little boat as it slowly approached the submerged Rennie home. The dory halted near an upstairs window, and Jim Walsh peered in. Then he broke through the glass and climbed inside. And then climbed out, carrying a small bundle.

The bundle was a child, Patrick Rennie's four-year-old daughter, Margaret. She was drenched, barely conscious, covered in muck and seaweed. There was nobody else. The water was nearly up to the second floor. The little boy, Patrick, who should have been in bed, was nowhere to be seen.

When day dawned on the nineteenth, Mary Walsh watched as the men towed the Rennie house back closer to the land. She watched the water pouring out. And the menfolk venturing inside.

The toddler, Margaret, would know about that night only from the memories of others. She would survive into old age—she died in 2015—and throughout her life, she was sought out frequently by folklorists, historians and journalists and asked to repeat her story, even though she remembered almost nothing. There were many embellishments by other people, but for Margaret Rennie, particular details—the facts that really mattered to her, passed on by survivors—would remain consistent.

"They found Mom and the children downstairs. Mom was found in under the table. She was sewing at the table with the sewing machine. Patrick was upstairs in bed earlier. I suppose when he heard the noise he came downstairs. Poor Patrick, he was found in under the couch. Rita was around there somewhere, I suppose. The baby, Bernard, was tied in the high chair."[16]

Throughout the remainder of his life, her father, Patrick Rennie, seemed unable or unwilling to talk about that night. His surviving sons were similarly silent. Martin's daughter, Sarah Brake, could not recall her father or her uncle Albert or her grandfather ever talking about that terrible event.[17] She remembered Patrick Rennie as a wiry little man who worked hard and kept his memories inside. He was missing two fingers, but she had never heard an explanation for how he lost them—perhaps because, in the years that followed, missing fingers would be the least of his concerns.

Patrick Rennie's life, just a few years later, would take another turn into the unknown, and eventually into a dark place that eclipsed even the memories from the night of November 18, 1929.

After that terrible night, he would abandon what had been his life from boyhood, the sustenance of family for generations. He would turn his back on the fishery, on the capricious ocean. And four years later, he would become a hard-rock miner in St. Lawrence.

6.

~~~

I T would be decades before the word that technically describes what happened on that night came into common local usage. Tsunami. For Newfoundlanders, through the years that followed, the simple phrase "tidal wave" was a more visual and comprehensible description of what they had experienced. In fact, the Japanese word now used to describe the phenomenon simply means "harbour wave," which is basically what Newfoundlanders have been saying all along.

Taylor's Bay, just a few miles west of Lord's Cove, was unusually vulnerable to the sea and offshore disturbances. It's a marshy landscape, open to the North Atlantic and the relentless winds from the southeast. In November 1929, the coastal road through Taylor's Bay passed over a ridge of sand and gravel that blocked the sea from a pond and a saltwater marsh where heather grew in abundance.

The tsunami "wave" in Taylor's Bay crested at nearly twenty-five feet, crashing on land with a momentum that drove it far beyond the shoreline and up a slope to a height at least forty feet above sea level, inundating almost every building in sight.[18]

The community would never recover from the onslaught.

~~~

ON the Burin Peninsula, the extraordinary waves surged down long narrow harbours, devastating everything before them. A slump near the epicentre of the earthquake had set the sea in motion—at first imperceptibly, in a long, broad swell travelling hundreds of miles an hour. But then, like any wave approaching shore, it lost momentum, fought the rising seabed, curled up, breaking forward and spilling towards the land; releasing incalculable energy in a devastating assault on any obstacle before it; running wildly until the energy exploded in a crashing surge against a wall of rock, or dissipated to exhaustion inland, far beyond the shoreline.[19]

The human consequences of such a force are dictated by decisions people make: a considered choice of where and how to build a house, or instinctive responses when a house or life is threatened. In Lisbon, Portugal, in 1755, people terrified by wide crevices opening in the streets and squares of the city centre rushed towards the harbour, only to discover that it was dry. Boats sat stupidly on the harbour bottom amid the rocks and weeds and litter. And then the sea returned.

Estimates of the death toll from that earthquake, the fires it caused and the tsunami that followed range between twenty thousand in Lisbon alone and eighty thousand throughout western Europe and Africa.[20]

What if the tsunami of 1929 had swept towards Halifax or Boston or New York, and not a sparsely populated coastline? The consequences of human failures—wars, environmental hazards, plagues—can be avoided or mitigated by the better impulses of human nature. Creativity and common sense. But when nature inflicts a calamity, there can be no mitigation except in reaction. And among the most sensible and useful reactions is planning—for the next time.[21]

The potential for destruction is now quantifiable. The 9.1 magnitude earthquake in the Indian Ocean, off the coast of

Sumatra, on December 26, 2004, released the energy of twenty-three thousand atomic bombs, and the tsunami that followed killed an estimated 163,000 people.[22]

What if the winter storm that struck the south coast of Newfoundland on November 19, 1929, had arrived a day earlier? Ten thousand people in the forty most vulnerable communities would have been sheltering in their homes.[23] In bed early. Preoccupied with the challenges of staying warm and dry. Cocooned and careless. How many lives were spared by the providential occurrence of a calm, dry moonlit night, when people were on the move, socializing, busy at last-minute chores outside, alert?

7.

I N Taylor's Bay, between Lord's Cove and Point au Gaul, Dinah Bonnell was still wearing the pretty rose-coloured dress she'd put on that morning to visit her sisters in Lamaline.[24] According to the 1921 census for Taylor's Bay, there were eighty-two people living there. There were forty-four named Hillier and twenty-three Bonnells. In all, there were seventeen houses in the community.

Dinah would survive for many years, and her memories were vivid and consistent with other, more perfunctory accounts of what happened to her family.

She was sixteen, the youngest daughter among ten kids in the family of Cyrus and Mary Ellen Bonnell. She lived at home with her parents. Her fifteen-year-old brother, John, and an older brother, Bertram, and his wife, Elizabeth, were living in the same house. Bertram and Elizabeth also had three young children of their own—Bessie, who was eight, three-year-old John, and Clayton, only seven months.

The earthquake that afternoon had been frightening, but by seven the community was peaceful and the momentary panic had passed. Then, at about seven thirty, they heard "a terrible roaring noise" outside, and as it was registering inside, an uncle dashed in shouting, "Run!" Dinah looked out and saw what she later described as "a huge, white, foaming wall . . . bearing down."

She ran, joining a growing crowd of men, women and children, sheep, cattle, horses—all desperately trying to outrun the wave. Her mother, Mary Ellen, was still in the house. Her movements were slow and painful because of arthritis, so she told Dinah's brother John to go on without her. He was barely out the door when the first wave crashed against the house.

Mary Ellen made it through the door, but only to be picked up and swept away by the retreating surge. She disappeared in a growing debris field of wood from shattered houses, sheds, dories, stages. Bertram and Elizabeth were still inside the now-disintegrating house trying to save their three kids. Elizabeth had shoved eight-year-old Bessie out the door behind her husband's teenaged brother and they had fled. Now, with the rest of the frantic crowd, the two children scrambled for a place beyond the grasp of the first wave, which had already swept up the bay, over the coastal road, through the pond and into the distant marshland.

Bertram, meanwhile, dashed upstairs, grabbed his sons, John and Clayton, wrapped them in a quilt, and raced back downstairs and out—into the grasp of yet another wave, which knocked him down and swept the boys away.

A similar horrifying scene had been unfolding in the house next door, where Bertram's brother Robert was living with his wife, Bridget, and their four children. Robert made it out with his son Gilbert. Bridget shooed two of the kids—Cyrus, who was two, and four-year-old Amelia Alice—into what she thought would be a safe place, a little alcove behind the stove. Then she ran upstairs to save her baby, Mary Gertrude, who was one year old. Bridget was rushing down the stairs when the second wave struck. She and the infant vanished.

Miraculously, Amelia Alice and Cyrus survived the night where their mother had left them, deeply traumatized but still alive.

Dinah could have known none of this as she huddled among her neighbours on a low hillside, watching as the sea calmed down. In the moonlight for as far as they could see, it was an ocean of wreckage. The beach was littered with the bodies of animals caught in the tsunami because they had been confused, terrified or slow. Of the seventeen homes in Taylor's Bay, only five were left. Among the few buildings that survived, the little one-room school was still intact. The townspeople ventured off the barren hillside and took refuge there. Someone gathered fuel and lit a fire.

The dawn would reveal the measure of Dinah's loss. Her father's house was gone. It seemed likely that her mother had gone with it, but Mary Ellen emerged, wet, half-frozen, in the daylight. She'd survived the night clinging to the wreckage of the local wharf.

Dinah's brother Bertram and his wife, Elizabeth, were numbed by the loss of their two little boys. It would haunt them for the rest of their lives. Eventually, the body of Clayton was found underneath a barrel, among turnips that had been stored for the winter, in Jacob Bonnell's kitchen. Survivors would search in vain for the body of his brother.

Robert's wife, Bridget, and the baby, Mary Gertrude, were nowhere to be found. Their bodies were discovered in the inner pond, tangled in the kelp, nearly two weeks later, on December 1.

The grief in Taylor's Bay was far from over. One-month-old William Piercey would die from exposure that day in the house of Jacob Bonnell, his maternal grandfather.[25] Amelia Alice Bonnell would never fully recover from the violence of the night;

she died four years later, at the age of eight. Her brother Cyrus, who huddled with her through that long, cold, terrifying ordeal, died seventeen years later, when he was nineteen.

Bertram and Elizabeth left Taylor's Bay with their surviving daughter, Bessie. Bertram, according to family members, never fully recovered emotionally from the horror of losing the two little boys—of having saved them, only to see them swept away in the violence of a single moment that he would never cease to relive in his imagination. What if? What if I had not wrapped them in that quilt? If I had held them closer, tighter? What if I had waited inside? Turned this way outside? Or that way? An infinity of what-ifs to consume a miserable lifetime.

8.

As Dinah Bonnell shivered in the darkness on a gentle slope above Taylor's Bay, two couples from the community just west of there, Point au Gaul, were hurrying home from the Orange Hall in Lamaline to face their own family disaster.

The social evening sponsored by the Ladies' Orange Benevolent Association that had brought them to Lamaline had barely started when nature interrupted.[26]

First the sea withdrew from the Lamaline harbour, leaving it suddenly—shockingly—dry, and then it came roaring back in three surges, destroying everything that stood before it as people watched aghast or scrambled to reach higher ground.

Nan and Herb Hillier had brought pies and cakes, their contribution to the social gathering. Suddenly everyone was heading for the exit. Now there was but one thought in their minds: home. Herb grabbed an unclaimed cake as they were leaving—a treat for the waiting kids.

The Hilliers and the Hepditches were at least a little reassured by the fact that as far as anybody knew, there had been no loss of life in Lamaline. It would later be confirmed that an elderly man, James Lockyer, who lived on Allan's Island, just beyond the harbour entrance, had died of shock. But they didn't know that yet.

With their seven children in the care of grandparents and an uncle, all four parents felt they were in good hands.

Just the same, it would be a long, hard journey home through coastal bogs and brooks where roads and bridges had been washed away or damaged. And maybe it was just one of those perceptions that form only in retrospect—it seemed that there was something driving Nan's sister Jessie and her husband, David Hepditch, a primordial anxiety that spurred them onwards. They were walking quickly and in silence, and soon they were out of sight, lost in shadows looming in the silvery darkness of the moonlit night.

And maybe they were praying silently that somehow their village had been spared—that this freak of nature had been visited exclusively on Lamaline. But it became obvious as they neared the village that the devastation had been even worse at Point au Gaul. For as far as they could see, the ocean was littered with wreckage. Boats and houses floating freely on the tide. Just outside the village, a man stopped them, urging them to go no farther. They ignored him. They met a woman who was moving slowly, oblivious and weeping.

As they neared home, Herb's brother Chesley rushed out to meet them, barely able to restrain his distress. "Where are the kids?" Nan asked, now nearing panic. Chesley told her that her kids were okay. He'd taken them to his and Herb's parents' house, which was farther up the hill. But Nan shouldn't try to go there, he said, because there was a bridge washed out along the way. She should wait at her own place while Herb and Chesley went up the hill to fetch the children. She should wait inside and put the kettle on.

As soon as Nan was in her house, Chesley broke the news to Herb. It was worse than either couple had imagined in their darkest fears. The sea had claimed Nan and Jessie's mother. She was gone. The entire house was gone. And Jessie and David's three small children. And young Irene Hillier, a daughter of Nan's ailing sister, Jemimiah. Irene had been visiting her cousins and her grandmother. All gone.

Nan was boiling water for tea when her brother Thomas walked into her kitchen. Even before he spoke, his face would have told her everything she didn't want to know. "Mother is gone," he said simply. "Father's house is gone."

He was, at that moment, too shaken to offer more than the grim basics. Whatever relief Nan had been feeling from the news that her kids were okay instantly evaporated. Her mother? Dead? And her sister's children?

And then Jessie and her husband burst into the kitchen. Where they had left their children, there was nothing now. The house and everybody in it. Gone. Jessie was hysterical—screaming for her babies. Earlier that day, she'd been nursing the youngest, Betty, who was only eight months old.

In a matter of minutes, while she was absent, she and David had lost their home and their belongings, their three young children and her mother. Her father, Henry, had survived only because he'd been attending a meeting of the local temperance society when the tsunami struck and carried off his family and home.

THERE was little time for grieving—at least not then. Even in the darkness, survivors were combing through the wreckage and the seaweed on the shore, searching for the missing. Searchers found three-year-old Henry Hepditch, in his pyjamas, at midnight. He was in a boat, clinging in his death grip to a corner of the engine cover.[27] Nan and Jessie's mother, Lizzie, and the remaining two missing Hepditch children were tangled in the seaweed and wreckage littering the beach.

By the light of the following day, even the weather had turned malevolent. The temperature dropped and the southeast wind picked up, battering the village with wet snow. Survivors picked through the debris, searching for the missing and whatever personal belongings they might be able to retrieve.

Eight days would pass before Josiah Hillier found the body of his and Jemimiah's daughter Irene, who was ten years old, lying on the shore. By then, there were stories to last a lifetime and beyond—stories of other tragedies in the little village.

Thomas Hillier, who would have turned forty-four on November 21, had been enjoying a card game with his neighbours when someone noticed the peculiarity outside—the harbour drained, its rocky bottom revealed, boats dangling at the wharf or lying on their sides among the rocks. Thomas dropped his cards and dashed to the wharf to save his boat. He was struggling to get it to a safe place when the tsunami struck, probably crushing him between the boat and wharf. He left a pregnant wife and four young children.[28]

Judy and Basil Walsh lived next door to Basil's mother, Mary Elizabeth, a widow who shared her house with her late husband's elderly sister, eighty-year-old Mary Anne Walsh. Judy and Basil were newlyweds, having married in April that year. They heard the tsunami before they saw it, a sudden roaring sound coming from the sea.[29] There was no wind, no apparent reason for the growing rumble, which made it all the more frightening. Basil went out to investigate while his wife rushed next door to be with the older women. The tsunami struck. Basil managed to escape its grasp, but a retreating wave carried off both Walsh houses.[30]

Basil's house floated away but remained intact, and he eventually towed the building back to shore—and relocated it farther inland. His mother's house was wrecked. Searchers found Basil's aunt, Mary Anne, on the shore at Point au Gaul just after ten that night. They carried her to the church hall, which had become a morgue. Basil found his mother on a distant beach three days later.

Judy Walsh survived, but her daughter, Sheila, would graphically describe her mother's condition to an interviewer many years later. When they found Judy, "she was naked, bruised and delirious." In the days that followed, she lost her hair because of stress, the trauma of the deaths of loved ones and the near impossible struggle to put her own life back together.

Robert Hillier, who had helped recover the bodies of both Mary Anne Walsh and little Henry Hepditch, would observe, many years later, that it seemed to be a hopeful sign that though eight people perished in Point au Gaul that night, two new lives began the same tragic evening—a baby born just moments before the wave struck, and one just after.[31]

9.

~~~

T HE urgency was real and personal. Each individual in the forty small communities directly affected by the waves faced the same grim necessity—recover. Live for those who still lived. But there was also the reality of grief. The communities were all extended families, and the families, spread out along sixty coastal miles, were all linked by blood and marriage and the common challenge of survival in a harsh and unforgiving place.

November 19 was too soon for grasping the totality of loss, the larger picture. The death toll. The sum of damages and material destruction. It was too soon to take such information in. And even for those who wondered what had happened outside the narrow scope of what they could see and feel after the disaster, when so many were now homeless and hungry, soon to be lashed by snow and the moaning southeast wind and the stinging spittle from the ocean, there was no way of getting news from other places in the same predicament. Not right away.

And even if they could, the "big picture"—twenty-seven dead, hundreds suffering and traumatized, $1 million in damage (a massive economic blow in 1929)—would have missed the even greater reality of what had happened, and what would happen in the coming years and decades.[32]

THE tsunami crashed against Newfoundland's south coast at about seven thirty on a calm, dry moonlit Monday evening. It would be nearly noon on Thursday before anybody beyond the isolated world of the Burin heard about its impact there.

The Burin Peninsula had been cut off days before the earthquake by a storm that brought down the single telegraph wire linking the Burin communities to St. John's. There was no road between Burin and St. Lawrence, and the links between villages as far west as Lamaline were little more than trails and cart tracks.

There had been three coastal steamers tied up at the wharf in Burin on Monday afternoon and evening, but two lacked wireless radios, and the third, the customs cutter *Daisy*, had a wireless but nobody on board at the time with the expertise to use it.[33] It's likely that stormy weather the following days prevented the *Daisy* and the two other vessels from venturing towards Argentia, across Placentia Bay, or even all the way to St. John's, to spread word of the disaster. And even before the storm arrived, the crews had other priorities, trying to retrieve what had been washed away, saving people trapped in houses that were now afloat, salvaging what could be recovered from the destruction.

Early on Thursday, November 21, an unsuspecting Captain Wes Kean of the coastal vessel *Portia* rounded the point leading into Burin channel on a routine visit to the town. It would take him a while to absorb the spectacle before him—a floating field of buildings, many still intact, and debris for as far as he could see.

10.

IN St. John's, just before noon on Thursday, Sir Richard A. Squires, prime minister of the Dominion of Newfoundland, had probably forgotten the momentary distractions of the geological disturbances on Monday afternoon and evening.

He had bigger issues on his mind. Newfoundland's economy was almost completely dependent on fish exports. The island was getting ferocious and successful competition from Norway and Iceland in European fish markets. One of the country's most lucrative markets, the United States, seemed to be going through some turmoil in the stock market—three gut-wrenching drops in stock prices on Wall Street in the preceding month. Pessimistic analysts were warning there was worse to come.

The ever-imperious Dominions Office of the British government in London had been obsessing over and would continue to complain about the island's finances—the potential damage to the credit of all the dominions in the Commonwealth caused by a default in this one. It was as if none of the dominions had been broke before. What about nearly bankrupt Australia? And wasn't the mother country herself up to her eyeballs in debt? It was as if the British didn't understand that this island was a country, just like all the others in the empire, at least the way Richard Squires saw things. It was as if the Commonwealth had forgotten that this small dominion had raised a regiment for the recent war, and that it had cost Newfoundlanders dearly in both blood and treasure—costs that continued to weaken a fragile economy.

Squires could actually find some comfort in the various political pressures he was under from outsiders. Never mind the agitation in Ottawa and London—it reassured him that the United Kingdom and Canada would view it as not in their own best interests to let him sink beneath the considerable burden of debt the country had amassed through no fault of its own. He could take shelter among the vagaries of the world economy. And the world would have to understand what he was up against at home: primitive infrastructure; an economy grossly dependent on a single staple; a small, scattered, unsophisticated populace.

The barriers to progress and prosperity were numerous. Corruption? It was a word that kept cropping up in editorials and political polemics, but it was, in his opinion, a red herring, a perennial distraction in the ongoing drama that informed the politics of Newfoundland, where today's ally was tomorrow's deadly foe, as implacable and chilly as the summer fog. The last thing Squires needed was bad news. But as that Thursday morning crept on, bad news was on the way.

His first official word came via the wireless from the coastal steamer *Portia*. Captain Kean hadn't taken long to realize that he was a first outside witness to the aftermath of a disaster. He would quickly transmit an urgent note from the magistrate in Burin, Malcolm Hollett, under the alarming subject line "Earthquake Calamity on South Coast." Before Squires finished reading it, he was reaching for his telephone. Almost simultaneously, the telegraph wires and phones in the south coast communities, down for days, were back up and humming.[34]

The superintendent of postal telegraphs, George J. Veitch, received a similar message from his Burin operator. Two justices of the peace in Lamaline were soon elaborating for the media on the human tragedy in nearby Point au Gaul, Taylor's Bay and Lord's Cove, offering sketchy details of what had happened to Mrs. Lizzie Hillier and her four grandchildren, the Bonnell family, and Sarah Rennie and her three children.

Sir Richard Squires was a paradox of contradictions. He preached austerity but indulged an appetite for style and luxury. At a time when people with steady jobs could live on $600 a year, his lifestyle cost an estimated $15,000,[35] a sum well beyond his salary, not to mention his personal resources. He was a fierce Orangeman who cultivated strategic political alliances with Catholics; a social drinker who supported Prohibition; an opponent of women's suffrage whose wife, Helena (who also opposed the suffrage movement), would become the first elected female in the parliament of Newfoundland. He was a staunch Methodist with the appearance and confidence and eloquence of a preacher—he seemed the embodiment of personal integrity. And yet he was prosecuted for corruption (income tax evasion) and was the subject of a royal commission that upheld charges he had taken kickbacks and misappropriated public funds, including money meant for veterans of the First World War.

It was like water off a Cape Ann hat. Even after proven charges of personal corruption, he easily won his second term as prime minister of Newfoundland in the general election of 1928.

Whatever the contradictions in his character, Sir Richard would demonstrate, on November 21, 1929, perhaps his greatest strength in politics: decisiveness. It might have been sparked by self-confidence—his dramatic win, against the odds, in the recent general election. Or it could have been just another manifestation of his well-known eagerness for spending public money. Whatever the reason, Squires moved quickly over the noon hour.

By early afternoon, he had created an emergency committee of senior politicians and bureaucrats. By mid-afternoon, there was a ship at dockside in St. John's taking on relief supplies for the stricken communities of the south coast. By nine thirty that evening, the SS *Meigle* was sailing through the Narrows, bound for Burin.

Along with the relief committee, the *Meigle* carried five elected politicians, a cadre of doctors and nurses, and an impressive load of supplies to meet any human need: nearly nineteen tons of flour; a ton each of sugar and butter; half a ton of tea; one hundred barrels each of beef and pork; four hundred bags of hard bread; and nails, window glass and putty.[36]

Among the doctors and nurses, politicians and crew on the *Meigle*, there were no members of the news media. The newspapers had asked to put a journalist on board but were perfunctorily refused. "It would be inexpedient," was the brief response to an official request from the St. John's *Evening Telegram*.

BY Friday—even without a single professional correspondent on the scene of the disaster—the media were accurately reporting that the death toll from the tsunami stood at twenty-seven. Amelia Alice Bonnell from Taylor's Bay would become the twenty-eighth victim,[37] after a lingering four-year illness caused by the trauma of cowering with her little brother in a battered house as her mother and baby sister were swept away.

Based on interim reports by officials on board the *Meigle* and interviews with people who'd travelled to St. John's from the afflicted area, property damage was being estimated by the weekend at $1 million ($14.5 million in 2018 dollars). It was a staggering amount in the context of the time and circumstances of the small, hand-built communities in a sparsely populated, debt-warped island country.

AS THE *Meigle* carefully approached the Burin waterfront at three thirty on the afternoon of November 22, the politicians, bureaucrats and doctors aboard thought they had a fairly clear idea from the local magistrate of what they should expect.[38] If anything, he'd understated things.

There had been a great deal of damage to shorefront property, but because of the depth of Burin harbour, the tsunami hadn't crested and crashed the way it had, with devastating consequences, in most other places. And yet, even at the entrance to the harbour, the *Meigle* encountered what, in the days ahead, would become a drearily familiar sight. Entire buildings afloat. Crates and barrels and drifting storage buildings full of necessities that had recently been set aside for use in the winter, which was only days away. There were people picking through the ruins, and buildings being towed back into bays and anchored. On the shore, wreckage and destitution; from everyone they spoke to, stricken stories of survival, shocked accounts of human loss.

Several of the hardest-hit communities were not far from Burin, and two of the most tragic were Kelly's Cove and Port au Bras. In one of his earlier communications with St. John's, Malcolm Hollett, the magistrate, had reported the stark details to the minister of justice:

> Seven dwelling houses in Port au Bras were carried to sea with a loss of seven lives.
>
> Four houses at Kelly's Cove and Stepaside disappeared to sea in an instant with loss of two lives.
>
> None of the bodies yet recovered; there are many hair-breadth escapes and many people are suffering from shock and privation.[39]

The particulars from the mouths of the survivors were more chilling, and the memories, even decades later, would confirm that in the aftermath of a human tragedy on any scale, numbers can never accurately capture the personal reality.

~~~

WHEN she was living in a seniors' home in St. John's seven decades later, Pearl Brushett would still remember events vividly:

> The first wave took our house from Kelly's Cove beach over to Bartlett's Island. It grounded there . . . The first thing I remember after they [her mother and older sister] woke us up was looking out the window. All the flakes and all the stages were down in the harbour. The harbour was all debris. I remember that.
>
> Then the second wave came and took us back to the beach. Not exactly where [the house] came from but near. That's when Mr. Ben Hollett and his wife, Beatrice, came down and got us out through the parlour window . . . Then we took off and went higher on the hill.[40]

The next wave carried the house to sea. In her child's memory, "the cat went crazy," scrambled from the drifting house through a window "and swam to shore," then promptly disappeared. A swimming cat? Or a parent's comforting image after the event for a grieving little girl?

THIRTEEN-year-old Marion Kelly, in Kelly's Cove, was doing homework when she heard the roaring sea. She looked outside. Her little brother, Elroy, was three and a half years old. She grabbed his hand as she went out the door. They dashed around the house and climbed a fence. The water was already at their feet.

As they climbed the fence, Marion looked back in time to see her house lifting off its foundation. Her mother, Frances, appeared in the yard. She hesitated. There was another daughter, Dorothy, who was ten. She wasn't with them. Frances turned back.

The house shuddered, then drifted off on the retreating wave, a burning lamp still visible through a window. Marion Kelly's mother and sister were never seen again.

There was a fourth child, a boy named Curt, but he'd been visiting an aunt and was safe. Marion's father returned with the firewood a week later, unaware of what had happened while he was gone. He and his neighbours would search in vain for the bodies of his daughter and his wife, who was just forty-two years old.

November 18, 1929, was the last day of Marion Kelly's childhood. It would fall to her, from that day on, to run her father's house and raise her younger brothers.

AN elderly couple in Port au Bras, eighty-one-year-old Billy Allen and his wife, Louisa, eighty-two, were also caught inside their house when the tsunami lifted it and started dragging it away. Billy escaped with the help of a neighbour.[41] Days later, a local boy, eleven-year-old Benjamin Abbott, found Louisa's body floating in the wreckage underneath a wharf owned by a local fisherman.

BILLY Allen's neighbour, Thomas Fudge, watched, aghast, as his own house lifted off and sailed away on the retreating tide. Inside, his wife and three young daughters were screaming for help as he scrambled to launch a dory in an effort to catch up with them.[42] The parish priest in Burin would, days later in St. John's, describe the awful spectacle: the frantic fisherman had almost reached his drifting house but was blocked at the last minute by another floating building. And then there was another wave, and his house was gone.[43]

The bodies of his wife, Jessie, and one daughter, nine-year-old Harriett, were found two days later, still in the house, now beached on the shore three miles away. Fifteen-year-old Gertie's body would not turn up until the spring of 1930. Seven-year-old Anna was lost forever.[44]

In the final report of the South Coast Disaster Committee, in the summer of 1931, there was a footnote that could only

62

refer to Thomas Fudge and the terrible memories that must have haunted him in the days and nights and weeks—if not years—that followed. Among compensation payments, there were allotments for "unusual and pathetic circumstances," including one to an unnamed man in the Burin district who had "lost his wife and three children in the disaster and as a result became badly depressed."[45] The relief committee had set aside $1,000 to "domicile" him but stipulated that the title to his new house would be assigned, in trust, to the Burin magistrate—the assumption being that for the foreseeable future, the individual could not be entrusted with the management of his own affairs.

In the 1935 census for Port au Bras, Thomas Fudge, widower, was still in the community, living, presumably in his new house, with his teenage son—whose name was Job.

FIFTY-EIGHT-year-old Mary Ann Bennett was a widow. Her late husband, a schooner captain, had, several years earlier, been lost at sea near St. John's. Her brother, Henry Dibbon, ran a store down by the waterfront in Port au Bras, and when she realized what was happening, she rushed down to his store to make sure that he was safe—only to be caught up in the same wave that was carrying her brother and his business off to sea.

Henry's body would never be recovered. Mary Ann was found by searchers on November 20, beneath the government wharf in Port au Bras.

THE Cheesemans were a prominent family of merchants in Port au Bras. On November 20, Ernest Cheeseman wrote an anguished letter to his older brother, Jack, in St. John's. Jack was John T. Cheeseman, the former MHA for Burin. He was well known in the commingled worlds of politics and business in Newfoundland. Because his birthplace, Port au Bras, was still quite cut off from the rest of the world, his brother, known in the family simply as Ern, composed a letter to his influential sibling. "Dear Jack," Ern wrote. "I hardly know how to begin but here is the gist of what happened Monday evening at five-twenty. We had an earth tremor . . ."[46] He then described the "twenty-foot" waves that swept into the harbour a couple of hours later:

> You could hear the poor humans who were caught, scream-
> ing, women and men praying out loud. Oh God, Jack! It
> was terrible . . . Everyone is miserable, nervous wrecks and in
> need of help immediately. All people who had food for the
> winter lost it in their stores. We must have flour, sugar, tea,
> molasses, beef and pork immediately. The government will
> have to send relief as soon as possible. Everything we have is
> gone and we are ruined.

Jack would undoubtedly have known all this before the letter from his brother reached him. In fact, there were five local members of the legislature on board the *Meigle* and heading towards Burin the night after Ern sat down to write. By late afternoon on the twenty-second, the *Meigle* was tied up at the Burin wharf, offloading even more supplies than Ern had asked for.

On that grim Saturday, November 23, the assemblyman for Burin East, J.A. Winter, visited his constituents in Port au Bras. The weather had turned miserable again, with high winds and thick blowing snow. As he reported to the *Daily News* on November 27, 1929, survivors were picking through the debris on the shore "endeavoring to salve wreckage . . . [Fish] traps were torn to shreds and floating in all directions . . . As yet the people do not seem able to realize their losses and are dazed and stunned."

By Monday, the storm had once again knocked out telephone and telegraph communications between the Burin Peninsula and the capital.

11.

~~~

C OMPARED to Taylor's Bay, Lord's Cove, Point au Gaul, Port au Bras and Kelly's Cove, the community of St. Lawrence got off easily. While many of the houses were flooded out, few were seriously damaged. There was no loss of life there. But the town was devastated just the same. Businesses destroyed. All the infrastructure that supported life—roads, wharves, bridges, fish-processing facilities, boats—was gone. Cecelia Fewer's telegraph office was in the middle of the harbour, and she had narrowly escaped.

Adolph and Dinah Giovannini and their fifteen fish proces-sors had hardly left their shop when the tsunami tore it down and carried it away.

People who lived closest to the shore had escaped to higher ground. Gus Etchegary and his sisters, hearing the commotion outside, headed out to investigate the cause of the excitement. They were afraid and, as panicked people often do, ran towards the danger. Their neighbours turned them back.

And when the sea had settled down again, the bewildered people drifted towards the safest place they could think of—the church.

Augustine Thorne was more than the parish priest for the Catholic population of St. Lawrence—he had a secular authority that few in any religious denomination would have questioned. And he took charge that night, leading prayers and organizing citizen committees for the hard work of recovery—a task he knew would have to start with the first light of the day.

His equal in the aftermath of the disaster was a woman he would have known only from a distance and by reputation—but someone about whom he would probably hear more in the days that followed.

Her name was Dorothy Cherry.

TO COLONIAL SECRETARY—from H. M. (Harris) MOSDELL (MHA Burin West, Chairman, Newfoundland Board of Health)—Nov. 23

The Florence Nightingale of the earthquake and tidal wave disaster on the Southwest coast is Nurse D. CHERRY of the Nonia Centre at Lamaline.

At every point the Meigle has called we have heard stirring tales of her courage and devotion to the interests of the survivors. Starting her work of mercy immediately after the occurrence of the catastrophe, she has known no rest day or night since then and has been without assistance of any kind until the arrival on the coast of the doctors and nurses of our relief expedition . . .

The weather was intensely cold with snow falling almost all the time. Her ministrations proved nothing less than providential to terror-stricken women and frightened women and children . . .

All day yesterday the Meigle sheltered at Lawn. A southeast storm with high seas and driving rain rendering communication with the shore almost impossible. Towards evening, that rain turned to sleet and there was nothing to do except wait until the dark and tempestuous night had passed.

During the lull in the storm of the morning Nurse Cherry was taken on board. She was found almost in a state of collapse after her strenuous and self-sacrificing efforts . . . Despite her objections, the expedition kept her with them and have taken her as far as Burin to enable her to recuperate.

(Sgd) Mosdell [47]

12.

~~~

AND who was that heroic woman, Dorothy Cherry? Without a doubt, her "courage and devotion" helped save many lives. And yet beyond this factually brief testimonial, we know little of her efforts. In this, her destiny was not uncommon. That the death toll from such a natural catastrophe remained low, relative to what it might have been, was thanks to the bravery of countless people—those who survived and those who didn't. The chaos of the event left most of them anonymous.

We know from sparse official records that Nurse Cherry worked herself almost to death, struggling through the worst of the devastation, from Lamaline to Lawn, on horseback and on foot. We know something of what she encountered because the medical team on board the *Meigle* kept a rough account of what they found in the days after she had passed through the blizzards and the wreckage and the suffering. Had there been journalists on board the *Meigle*, or had reporters independently made their own way to the place, we'd probably know more particulars about the human drama, including Dorothy Cherry's powerful story. She'd have become one of the great human-interest stories in the larger narrative.

What we do know is that she came to Newfoundland from England, and that seventeen years after the tsunami, the list of Newfoundlanders named to the Order of the British Empire included "Dorothy Cherry, a district nurse."

But Dorothy Cherry's story, like the catastrophe itself, would fade into the relative anonymity of local anecdote, soon to be overwhelmed by another wave—a gathering tsunami of politics and economics and scandal that was about to wash across the island. Nurse Cherry, whoever she was and whoever she became, would, like the small communities she served, slip back into an obscurity that would hide more suffering in the years to come.

~~~

SIXTEEN-year-old Eloise Morris was at school in St. John's, studying music, among her other courses, when she felt the trembling of the earthquake and saw the streetlight swaying, swinging wildly.[48] Like most people in the city, she didn't hear news of the consequent tsunami for days.

Her father's parsonage, back in Collins Cove, was on high ground and so had escaped the brunt of the devastation. But like many others on the south coast, Eloise would soon discover that there were other costs, other damages that might not be revealed for quite some time.

She left St. John's on the coastal steamer *Portia* on December 15, bound for Burin. It was after dark when she arrived. The mail boat was waiting to take her across the harbour to Collins Cove.[49] The men were quiet as they rowed, but when they neared the wharf below the parsonage, the boat crunched against the gravel bottom, still a short distance from dry land. One man grabbed the mailbag and her suitcase and climbed out into the water. The second man picked her up as if she were a child and carried her to shore. The wharf at Collins Cove, like all the other man-made structures on the waterfront, was gone.

She'd been looking forward to the holidays, the festivities, the Christmas break, when her family and the church would be at the centre of merriment and celebration. But it was different this year. It would be a sparse and quiet holiday—but most distressing for Eloise was the change she found in her father. He'd grown old. He was exhausted and depressed. It was clear that the stress of the preceding month had aged him immeasurably. Survivors in the communities along the south coast of the peninsula were struggling with the same condition, a malady both physical and psychological that would permanently compromise their lives.

For Reverend William J. Morris, his status as a community

leader and source of spiritual reassurance would have made the burden seem unbearable. He was obviously ill that Christmas, and it was confirmed soon afterwards that his heart had begun to fail him. He would linger for nine more years and die at the age of sixty-four.[50]

DEATH is the usual metric for the severity of disaster. But the true measure of a tragedy lies in how its impact will disfigure the emotions and the lives of the survivors. There were twenty-seven dead, but there were thousands who were still alive and facing an overwhelming challenge—recovering from exhaustion, injury, grief and related illnesses. Rebuilding lives when there was nothing left to work with. These people made their living from the sea, but the sea had turned against them savagely, smashed their boats, swept away their nets and traps, their stages, storage shacks and homes.

In the aftermath of the devastation, John Cusick, from St. Lawrence, surveyed the wreckage on the shore. He would soon discover that there were unseen, lasting consequences well beyond the shore. The fishery was gone indefinitely. He had no choice but to move on. Start again, somewhere else. His wife, Nora, was pregnant with their first child. They moved to St. Pierre, and John started a new career—rum-running, serving the unquenchable demand for alcohol wherever it was being thwarted by the law. For him and many like him, the only relevant authority in 1930 was the imperative of need.

John Cusick would never cease to be a Newfoundlander, but he and his family (with the exception of one daughter) would call St. Pierre home for the remainder of their lives.

THE survivors had to continue living. But the sea, for centuries a benefactor, would soon grow sullen and barren, and many would abandon it for different occupations in other places, including nearby St. Pierre, which had somehow escaped the devastation that befell the people of the Burin.

There are no formal records that document a migration from the Burin Peninsula to the French islands after the tsunami. But it might be significant that during a period in which the population of St. Pierre mostly shrank, available statistics show a 7 percent bump between 1926 and 1931.

Much later in life, Gus Etchegary would still remember mournful scenes of people packing up and leaving. In an interview in 2006, he was wistful about the events of 1929 and 1930, and the hard times that followed. "It brought about an enormous change in the economic life of those people and they wound up, a lot of them, leaving, having to leave, to take jobs in New York, Boston, fishing out of Lunenburg, out of Nova Scotia or out of other places in Newfoundland."[51]

In time, these migrants would count themselves among the lucky.

13.

SOMEWHERE in the city of St. John's, sometime in 1929—just before the Western capitalist economies began to crumble and a tsunami wiped out entire communities on Newfoundland's south coast—a local businessman named William Taylor was bragging to a visitor, a twenty-seven-year-old accountant from New York.

The Newfoundlander had a dream, a vision of great wealth built upon an asset he had recently acquired—licences that permitted him to exploit mineral resources in an area the young New Yorker had never heard of. Those minerals were in the

Burin Peninsula, beneath some remote fishing villages, one with the intriguing name of Lawn, and a neighbouring community with a name that, given the geography, would have been easier to remember—St. Lawrence. The St. John's businessman planned to start a mining industry in St. Lawrence. He owned rights to dig up a mineral known as fluorspar, which was abundant there and an essential element in the making of everything that mattered in a modern economy—steel, aluminum, chemicals.

It was providential, in a way—a kind of epic symmetry. The unfolding of the universe had left the earth's crust unstable and human lives vulnerable to earthquakes and volcanoes, avalanches and tsunamis. But the same prehistoric mechanisms had also left a legacy of great wealth. And rocky Newfoundland was a beneficiary: vast quantities of iron ore, rich pockets of copper and, on the south coast, fluorspar.

A geophysical calamity would create terrific hardship in Newfoundland. But now two businessmen, quite undaunted by the instability inherent in the universe, were speculating about the potential of geology—specifically, the fortuitous discovery of fluorspar—to enrich the lives of ordinary mortals, especially the two of them.

The American was intrigued. Fluorspar? What the heck was that?

But this meeting, given the prevailing international circumstances, was auspicious, at least for the American. It was a fluke that he was there at all—a minor business matter. And it was by chance that he had encountered the visionary Mr. Taylor.

There is no evidence to suggest that the young New Yorker, whose name was Walter Seibert, was either superstitious or especially religious. But when, some months after the great financial crash of 1929, Taylor showed up at Seibert's office in Manhattan, his finances and his dream by then in tatters, the accountant might have thought that this too was destiny in action. He listened sympathetically as Taylor elaborated on the sudden downturn in his prospects. And Walter was only too happy to help the unfortunate Newfoundlander by taking the precious asset off his hands for, it is reported, the modest sum of three hundred and fifty dollars.[52]

On its face, this small transaction would signal the beginning of recovery, a promise of a new economic vitality in at least part of a region that had, since the men's meeting in St. John's, been devastated by a natural calamity. But there would be, as always, strings attached.

THREE

Legacy of Chaos

14.

FROM where he stood just outside his glebe house on that grim Tuesday morning, even Father Thorne, for all his deep faith and fortitude, would have been daunted by the sight that he now saw clearly in the watery light of the new day. The wistful southeast wind was already whistling, and there were large, soft snowflakes settling on Cape Chapeau Rouge at the harbour entry. Before the day was out, there would be another storm. He could feel it in his weary bones, feel the damp southeaster gusting on his face.

The working part of what had been, the day before, a struggling but entirely viable community now lay shattered, scattered on the shore, littering the landwash at the head of the harbour, up to and well past the road to Little St. Lawrence.

The church and rectory were safely up the hillside east of Great St. Lawrence harbour. Most of the houses in the community had been beyond the reach of the tsunami. But he could see where two homes had been, now empty spaces. It might have been much worse.

The house where Tom Pike lived with his family, on the end of Shingle Point, had survived the full force of the sea. That Tom and Agnes and the little girls got out of there alive was miraculous. The water had inundated the first floor of the house. He

75

could imagine the bread Agnes said she'd left baking in the oven. Sodden dough, the colour of death. Pike's barn was gone. As was Adolph Giovannini's fish store. Wharves and stages and the flakes where they laid fish out to dry in the summer sun—all shattered.

Most of the homes were undamaged. Thankfully, there had been no loss of life in St. Lawrence. But the people were understandably afraid. Many refused Father Thorne's encouragement to go home. They stayed with friends on the higher ground. Some slept in barns. Many didn't sleep at all.

The priest might have briefly wondered about the neighbouring communities. Lawn. Lord's Cove. It would have been hard to imagine that people in those places were worse off, and it would be a while before he knew the terrible reality. The death. Almost every home in Taylor's Bay destroyed.

For now, he had enough to think about, right in front of him.

It had been a long night. Even as the first wave was retreating, people came straggling up the hill for the sanctuary of the church, the glebe, the convent. They had arrived, white-faced, some nearly overwhelmed by panic because a spouse or child had gone missing in the confusion. They came to him carrying those who couldn't walk, the elderly and sick. They came to him for the reassurance he could offer, his connection with a power that was greater than the sea, and certainly more merciful. Many of them would be reluctant to go home.

He was a reassuring figure, Father Augustine Thorne. A holy man, but also manly. Stocky. Strongly built and—as he demonstrated from time to time on the soccer pitch—fit as any of the local football fanatics. It was one of the delights he discovered in St. Lawrence when he'd arrived six years earlier. The passion for sports. And for education—nurtured by the nuns who had run an admirable school here since 1871.

He was now forty years old. Who knew what lay ahead of him? But he could happily spend the remainder of his priesthood here, among these worthy people. They were, in his opinion, a cut above the average for the island's baymen, thanks to the school and the steely character nurtured by athletic excellence.

Like many clergymen of many denominations in small, isolated places, Father Thorne projected an authority that ran well beyond the symbolism of the collar and a powerful institution, but it saddled him with responsibilities that he might have felt woefully unqualified to handle. And he knew that he was now staring at another one, perhaps a greater challenge than he would ever face again. Rebuilding a community's economy from scratch. He would meet the challenge because he knew his people better than they knew themselves, and he knew that he could mobilize and motivate them.

But on this morning, so full of menace from the weather, so soon after the catastrophe, they were coping with the shock of what had happened to them. He would give them time, at least the morning, while he was busy taking stock of what they would have to do to get through and beyond this crisis.

As the day progressed, the storm intensified. But he was able to persuade the people who had moved in with relatives and friends to go back to their homes, to begin the cleanup. The wave had interrupted normal household routines. Supper dishes left on tables. The smaller children snatched from beds. Cards dropped where they'd been dealt. The vandal sea rampaging through kitchens and parlours left filth behind with all the shock and wreckage. In the aftermath of fear, it would be easy to succumb to anger, bitterness. Or worse, the numbness of defeat. But there was no time for that. No time for weakness. It was time to face the mess, restart the clocks.

Father Thorne was able to convince his people that in the litter strewn along the shoreline, there was material to be salvaged, lumber to be used to restore the wharves and the stages and the fishing stores, and if for no other useful purpose, to be reduced to firewood for the hard winter days ahead. Fuel supplies had washed away along with winter food—the salted fish and beef, molasses, sugar, flour. All the essentials for their self-sufficiency. Tons of fish, stored for later shipment, later income. All gone.

Among the immediate requirements was communication with the world beyond the harbour, Burin and St. John's, even nearby places to the west. The waves had knocked out the telegraph. He could now see Cecelia Fewer's office squatting lugubriously in the middle of the harbour. Lines and poles were down.

ON the evening of the nineteenth, Father Thorne summoned the townsfolk of St. Lawrence to a meeting and gave a rousing speech about resilience, about the power of faith, not just in the Almighty but in themselves. By the next day, according to the *Daily News*, he had teams of St. Lawrence men at work, starting to recover and rebuild.

Miss Fewer and the postmistress, Mrs. Sylvia Fudge, had managed to climb through an upstairs window in the floating telegraph office and salvage the equipment they'd need to restore communications. Quite amazing people, these St. Lawrence women. Strong men raised the poles, restrung the wires. And within a few days, they got the word out. They were in deep trouble. By then, they would have heard about the other places. They were beginning to get the full measure of the calamity. The death and scale of the destruction along the shore, from Burin all the way to Lamaline. The awful news from other places would have come—after they'd recovered from the shock—as reassurance that they were not alone. Ten thousand people in at least forty nearby communities like theirs were now at risk of an added peril—the relentless and inevitable winter. St. John's couldn't help but notice. The world would notice.

And they would have been comforted and reassured by the prompt attention of important people from outside—politicians and senior civil servants; doctors and nurses, comforting the sick and injured; the steamship *Meigle*, replenishing supplies. Newspapers in St. John's telling their stories—second-hand, of course, but preferable to not at all, which was often how city people reacted to distress in smaller places.

The drama of the immediate relief effort would understandably have generated expectations. Their needs were long term, with emotional and physical aftershocks that would require attention well into the future. It would have been hard to imagine, in November 1929, that the attention they were getting would be transient.

Living in the reality of destruction, it is difficult to see the drama from the point of view of an outsider, even the most highly motivated visitor. How could such dramatic spectacles, so deeply etched in local memory, ever fade from the mind of anyone who had seen them, even briefly? How could such indelible impressions so soon be overwhelmed by the imperatives of fresh events, by new demands on limited reserves of empathy and money among strangers?

This, within a few months, would be the greater challenge facing the people of St. Lawrence and the entire south end of the peninsula. When it came to the hard work of long-term recovery from the catastrophe, they were on their own.

15.

FATHER Thorne would have been among the first to learn of the young visitor from New York in the summer of 1931. Not much of importance could ever happen in St. Lawrence without the knowledge and approval of the priest. The visitor had a vaguely German name. Seibert. Walter Seibert. Undoubtedly a Protestant.

And so, while there is no formal record of an encounter, future circumstances would indicate that Father Thorne, whose opinions mattered definitively in the town and far beyond, was an early advocate for Walter Seibert's plan. A mining venture. Mining fluorspar, a mineral so ubiquitous it practically defined St. Lawrence—its brilliant outcroppings catching sunlight in unexpected places. A mineral now in great demand, even in the midst of a depression, by industrialists near and far. In exchange for the right to exploit this resource, the young American was offering another commodity, something priceless, something in short supply no matter where one looked for it in Newfoundland in 1931: optimism.

At this early stage, the particulars, the nitty-gritty business details, didn't really matter. Aubrey Farrell, young and shrewd, from a solid family and a devout parishioner, had nothing but compliments for Mr. Seibert after he went back to New York. Young Aubrey was enthusiastically buying into his proposal, putting credibility and money on the line.

That was good enough for Father Thorne, and Father Thorne's benediction was good enough for Aubrey Farrell—and eventually everybody else in and near St. Lawrence.

And yet—even for a priest, an educated man who viewed temporal hardship through a long spiritual lens—there would have been a nagging wariness, a hint of scepticism. There might have been a whiff of fishiness about Mr. Seibert and his project, which local cynics were already calling his "fluorspar empire."

Seibert was young, not yet thirty, too young to have acquired the experience and wisdom to justify the kind of trust he asked for, the confidence he projected. The confidence, perhaps, in a worst-case scenario, of a shyster.

Oh, well. As they say, beggars can't be choosers. Any port in a storm. Etc.

He was good-looking, this Walter chap. He was slick. Articulate. He was fun to be around. They say he was the life of the party, even played a piano passably. He was, at first blush, a typical well-heeled American. He was, above all, persuasive.

Between July and December in 1931, six local prospectors employed by Seibert wandered the barrens, evaluating the resource and locating new deposits of fluorspar at Iron Springs, Hare's Ears, Lord and Lady Gulch—for no remuneration.[1] It seemed that Mr. Seibert, while he projected a confident prosperity, was actually strapped for funds. But wasn't everyone in these chaotic days? It was a temporary situation, surely. And in the short term, it wouldn't cost the local people much to help him get a start. They had no money, but they had time, a far more precious asset.

In 1932, Walter Seibert paid a second visit to St. Lawrence, and this time he was candid. He was having trouble raising capital. This would have come as no great surprise, the money situation being what it was. But he had succeeded in scrounging $2,000 to buy some second-hand equipment that he'd located in Cape Breton. He would bring it in on a boat. He hoped the local men would volunteer to help him drag it from the dock to a location half a mile northeast of town, where he planned to launch his mining project. It would allow these idled fishermen to make a start at something else, something new and modern. Something with a future.[2]

And so they did.

He had a contract with people who were prepared to buy a first consignment—two thousand tons of metallurgical-grade fluorspar, to be delivered by the spring of 1934, paid for on approval by their chemists. It would be a shoestring start, to be sure. But desperate times called for ingenuity and sacrifice. They'd be starting on the Black Duck vein.

Black Duck. The local people shrugged. They knew Black
Duck. It was in the woods, out behind the graveyard. People
had been prospecting around Black Duck for decades. This was
encouraging. A beginning. They understood the elusiveness of
money.

BY the spring of 1933, Seibert had installed a full-time manager, another American named Dr. Warren Smith. He was a
friendly, approachable geologist, smart and likeable, and almost
immediately he was known far and wide as Doc.

And before long, Seibert's man, Doc Smith, had twenty
more St. Lawrence men working for him.[3] It was back-breaking
labour, using picks and shovels and two dilapidated jackhammers
to dig up rock, using wheelbarrows to carry it away for rudimentary processing and grading. That nobody was getting paid
in money—just chits to take to Farrell's store for groceries—
would probably have raised eyebrows in a more materialistic
populace, but this technicality didn't seem to bother anybody
in St. Lawrence.

Father Thorne and Aubrey Farrell, and thus almost everyone
in town, had suspended judgement, suppressed their scepticism.
Rennie Slaney would have typified the local attitude. He and his
brother, Arcule, had pretty well given up on the fishery. The
goddamned fish were gone. Ever since the tidal wave. Rennie had
a growing family. He was among the first to sign on to the Seibert
project. Arcule signed on not long after his younger brother.

What other options did they have? Ever since the tidal wave,
the fishing was a waste of time. The majority of people in the
town were on the dole. To turn down a job—even if there was no
immediate compensation, just a vague promise that they'd be paid
at some future date—would have jeopardized their entitlement to
even minuscule relief.

Pat Rennie, originally from Lord's Cove, was now living in Little St. Lawrence, down the road a mile or two from the Black Duck site. Most people by then would have heard of Pat Rennie's tragedy the night of the tidal wave. Wife. Three kids. All gone. But he had a new wife now, Lucy Clarke. The Clarkes were one of the founding families in the area. He and Lucy had started a new family. And Pat Rennie was, with Rennie Slaney, among the first to sign on for the effort to make Seibert's "fluorspar empire" a reality.

Odd as the arrangement with Walter Seibert was, the people of St. Lawrence, though isolated from St. John's, might have taken certain fundamental things for granted. They might have assumed that they had the protection of laws and regulations to prevent unacceptable exploitation. They might have assumed that there were safeguards enforced by government officials—that people higher up the chain of public responsibility would be looking out for them.

There was a dominion government in St. John's. Surely there were laws. Surely, haywire as the dominion political establishment seemed to be, the politicians and bureaucrats were good for that—for enforcing rules, for oversight.

In that assumption, they were all mistaken.

The mining project would, in the beginning, feed on the desperation of a shattered people who were living in communities willing to suspend basic human rights as part of a unique, and in many ways naive, investment in their future. Their investment would eventually transform a small part of the Newfoundland economy and introduce a tenuous prosperity, but at a human cost that would eclipse the memory of what the people of the Burin lost on November 18, 1929.

They could not have known or understood, in 1932 or in 1933, that the real peril of the undertaking in St. Lawrence, when all was said and done, would arise from the reality that for many years, there would be no protective agency to look after them, no collectivity, union or bureaucracy that mattered to their working lives.

The government in St. John's was a facade. The dominion's nominal democracy was effectively dysfunctional. The details of the breakdown would have been vague to anyone who wasn't closely following the complicated political contortions at the time. And to make matters worse, the people of the Burin were more attuned to events in Canada and America and St. Pierre. That was where most of their news came from. Those places mattered more than St. John's and its crazy politicians.

It would soon become clear that those places, too, were irrelevant. If the people of the Burin were to survive, they'd have to build a future for themselves. And in the long run, they would have to learn to fight for basic rights—dignity and health and life itself.

16.

THE fist came out of nowhere. Sir Richard Squires was sure it was a fist. He hoped it was a fist and not something potentially more lethal. And now the prime minister of Newfoundland was being helped to his seat, no longer sure where he was or where he was going. This much he now had in common with the common people.[4]

The impact of a fist on one's face—the unique sensation of soft tissue mashed between the moving bone of knuckles and the rigid bone of jaw or teeth or skull—can be, for someone who is introspective, a moment of enlightenment.

It isn't painful, not right away, but it is disorienting. And in the uncertainty between initial confusion and the eventual, inevitable pain and outrage, there is a flash of objectivity about what could have led to this surprise—perhaps a moment of educational self-doubt.

It must be said, however, that introspection and self-doubt are not necessarily assets in a successful political career. And in the long, miraculous political career of Sir Richard Anderson Squires, either quality would have been a handicap.

It is tempting to speculate that on that late Thursday afternoon, Sir Richard might have entertained a brief reflection on the corruption of his own behaviour, his dubious leadership over the past four years of this, his second term as prime minister of the Dominion of Newfoundland.

It is more likely that his resolute self-righteousness remained unshaken. And he might legitimately have harked back to his finer moments during the months of November and December 1929. For surely those were the days when he, like many other Newfoundlanders, had revealed a capacity for decisive, precise, unselfish and effective action in the face of a crisis—a crisis not of his design. An earthquake. A tsunami. A natural disaster.

It would be too much to expect that this reflection would have led him, or anybody else in the Liberal caucus there in that sanctuary of democracy, the executive council chamber in the courthouse on Duckworth Street, to ask a relevant question: Where had the qualities of leadership, so ably demonstrated in those tragic days, been hiding in the years since then? Years of disaster of a different kind. No less a humanitarian crisis. Man-made, this time. Politically driven. No less catastrophic.

Sir Richard's hand was bleeding and now his head was sore, and he was, to be quite truthful, uncertain and afraid.

~~~~

THERE was no real mystery about the fist. The man attached to it—never specifically identified but possibly named McGrath, Furlong or Kelly[5]—had been trying to get the attention of someone in the government for days. He'd been patient, right up until he, or someone with him, finally ripped a piece of banister from the stairway outside the chamber, where they'd been waiting all afternoon, and smashed it through the window in the entranceway. After which, he and his fellows barged into the room, where the Liberal Party was holding a private caucus behind locked doors.

The sight of this group of relatively wealthy politicians, their shocked surprise and the disdain in their expressions, would have challenged the limits of his patience. He was without work. He was living on $1.80 a month. Dole was often provided in the form of a voucher with which he could acquire food from a list prepared by government. Flour. Fatback pork. Beans. Cornmeal. Split peas. Cocoa. Twelve ounces of cocoa for a month. These cockroaches. How long would one of these last on $1.80 a month? Two pounds of beans?

Peter Cashin, until ten days earlier, was a member of this odious assembly of crooks, their finance minister, until the burden of their infamy became too much even for him—and he quit. And then he blew the whistle on their corruption.

Sir Richard had seemed undaunted by the defection of his finance minister and the political crisis that followed, and he seemed undaunted now in the presence of this motley gang of agitators. But as he raised a hand to wag a finger, opened his gob to remonstrate . . . well, it all became too much. And suddenly Sir Richard was staggering, grabbing on to something, and now there was blood on his hand and he was being supported by his accomplices.

There could be no backing down now. Now was the time to escalate the level of the threat and to reinforce the principal demand: the dole must be increased at once. Or else.

Sir Richard, hand swaddled, face bruised, huddled briefly with his mates. The conversation was intense, but with surprising speed, it seemed to reach a resolution. We can safely presume that much because of what happened shortly after his consciousness returned, and with it his renowned instinct for political survival.

He capitulated.

Sir Richard rose to his feet, stepped forward, faced his adversaries. And he quietly agreed to bring forward a motion that would increase the dole—mind you, to nowhere near what a body needed to survive. But every little bit was a penny further away from the ugly, constant presence of starvation.

A CRISIS can be a godsend, especially a crisis caused by a natural disaster, one in which human responses are uncompromised by feelings of responsibility and blame—humanity united against nature in a struggle to survive. In man-made catastrophes, it's man against man. A lot of energy and talent and material wasted in conflict, finger pointing, guilt and recrimination.

That was the political beauty of the crisis of November 1929, when cruel nature broke the communities of the south coast, tried to break the people but failed because the people came together, and not just the people of the Burin—all of Newfoundland; all of Canada; all of the mother country, England; and all of the adopted country for so many Newfoundlanders, the United States. People everywhere united by this reminder of their vulnerability, the common peril. Nature.

Faced with an assault by nature, humanity has no alternative but to mobilize a unified response. This is when the better aspects of humanity prevail, when we must find within ourselves the qualities that God withheld from heartless Mother Nature— generosity and mercy. And we survive if we succeed. We survive as individuals, as communities, as a species.

The immediate political response in November 1929 had been impressive. The resilience of the communities affected had been inspirational. Ordinary people in Point au Gaul, Taylor's Bay, Lord's Cove, St. Lawrence, Kelly's Cove, Port au Bras—picking up the pieces of their lives, literally, helping one another through grief and hunger and exposure to the sudden onset of relentless winter weather. Ordinary people throughout Newfoundland and Canada and England and America, digging into depleted pockets and coming up with more than $250,000 in contributions to the relief effort.[6] Inspirational generosity. And above it all, inspirational leadership.

But that was yesterday. Nobody in government in 1929 could have anticipated yet another natural calamity—the total failure of the fishery. And by 1930, there was an overarching preoccupation with new challenges, an awareness of the possibility of a new catastrophe, a man-made calamity. The Dominion of Newfoundland was, for all practical purposes, nearly bankrupt—a looming prospect that was exacerbated by political paralysis and would quickly overwhelm whatever humanitarian concern remained for the particular challenges of small places in the hinterlands and bays.

The political and commercial elites of Newfoundland, almost all concentrated in St. John's, should have seen that violent confrontation in the executive council chamber coming. They surely would have understood the origins of this man-made fiscal crisis. They would have known where it was coming from and where it would terminate if it weren't stopped.

And they might have stopped it because they understood it, and they understood it because, in so many ways, they had caused it. But unlike the response to a natural calamity, the reaction to a man-made disaster is rarely unified because there is blame, recrimination, defensiveness. It is war. Maybe minor, metaphorical and bloodless. But as war is the supreme man-made calamity, all lesser calamities of human failure are a form of war.

17.

I N Newfoundland by early 1931, there were two new disasters looming. One was caused by nature, perhaps a consequence of the tsunami.[7] Nobody seems to be entirely sure. But for years after the tsunami, the fishery went flat all around the island country. There was hardly an outport that was unaffected. Nowhere were the effects more vicious than on the Burin Peninsula, however, where people had been deprived by the tsunami of the basic necessities of survival.

They would have still been struggling even if the times were prosperous. No boats, no fishing gear. In many cases, they were still striving to establish homes, grieving for lost and ailing kin. Spirits, if not broken, badly crippled.

All along the coast, people like Patrick Rennie, Thomas Fudge, David Hepditch, standing on the shore of what had been a workplace, the senseless ocean now lapping at their feet like a large domestic animal that had misbehaved, gone berserk and wrecked the house, killed the children and the parents and the grandparents, and was now remorseful. But not so remorseful that it could offer compensation. No. The fish were gone, and the way they saw it, the collateral catastrophe was because of that brief rampage.

There would be financial compensation to help buy new boats and gear and houses. But there was no way to bring the fish back. Only the sea and God could accomplish that. The omnipotence that took it all away.

And now, two years later, the people of the south coast were just part of a larger systemic emergency, and the collapse of the fishery in the 1930–31 season was just part of the existential challenge facing government and the country's future. Undeniably, the fishery was an issue, but it was clear the greater problem was that Newfoundland had nothing to fall back on but borrowed money.

And so, you really had to sympathize with the confused and now almost useless politicians. They were, for all their posturing and speeches, at the mercy of the banks. The solutions to the challenges of the years 1930, 1931, 1932 were in the hands of bankers who were located in Canada. The larger issue facing Newfoundlanders was that Canadians and bankers, like people everywhere, had problems of their own.

And it has to be recognized that one of the problems bankers had in common with ordinary people, the idle fisher folk in the outports and the angry urban poor, was a lack of confidence in the political leadership of Newfoundland.

The country, from the perspective of the bankers, was a mess. Fish had drawn people to the forbidding island centuries before. The island was essentially a fishing platform. A global appetite for fish had motivated people to try to live there—and they had succeeded, after a fashion. The majority always poor, always vulnerable to the double jeopardy of hunger and the weather. And—truth must be told—vulnerable to the interests of the minority of settlers who were not poor; people who were well-to-do and educated, who had power and knighthoods. People like Sir Richard Squires, self-improved through study, determination, work and luck—but now more at home in London, New York or Montreal, where accents were refined and the conveniences reliable, where physical assault on public figures was mostly unheard of.

The Canadian and American and British bankers and the politicians in Newfoundland were all in basic agreement on one important point: there had been, for far too long, too great a dependency on fish as an economic staple. But efforts to diversify the national economy—while costly and ambitious, if not grandiose—had been mostly unsuccessful, and had led to hubris and corruption. And now that too was a factor that was affecting the confidence of bankers.

And finally, on the afternoon of February 11, 1932, they had the spectacle of a fist connecting with the jaw of the first minister in the government of Newfoundland, in the centre of decision-making power, the executive council chamber in the courthouse.

THAT day, February 11, had started ominously, darkened by the wearying frustrations that everybody was accustomed to. Crowds of dole recipients gathered on the waterfront to discuss their difficulties, the impossibility of their hopeless situation. They decided to speak directly to the prime minister himself and marched together up to Duckworth Street, where they knew the most important politicians were assembled.

They asked for Squires. They were told that Squires was unavailable. They went away. The frustrations didn't go away, but instead metastasized to anger, which was, by afternoon, boiled off to rage. Now another crowd, numbering about twelve hundred, marched towards the courthouse once again. This time the place was locked.

The protestors stood around all afternoon, waiting for someone of importance to emerge, to talk, perhaps to listen. Nobody did. The meeting under way inside, in the executive council chamber, went on and on, it seemed. It began to look as though the people waiting outside were being stonewalled by their representatives.

This time, they were disinclined to go away.

Even the thickest idiot among them, even the man who swung the fist—even the shocked bankers and the bureaucrats in Montreal and England who would soon hear all about it—would have understood the outrage and the symbolism, would have seen the future in that moment.

18.

~~~

I T wasn't just the dole. If Sir Richard and the members of his cabinet had been sharing the hardship—if they had been leading by example, with resolve, participating in the sacrifices—maybe Newfoundlanders would have been forgiving, more inclusive in their allocation of responsibility and blame. Maybe they would have pulled themselves together, as they had shown themselves so capable of doing in 1929, and improved the prospects of their survival as a country. But things were different now, and nobody was in a better position to appreciate the differences than Peter Cashin, the minister of finance.

He was a tall man and had a history of decisiveness and valour. He was a veteran of the First World War, had risen to the rank of major in the revered Newfoundland Regiment and was seconded to the British army as a machine gun corps commander. He had a physical demeanour that was, for many, intimidating. For those who admired him, he was eloquent. For others, a volcanic blabbermouth.[8]

He was born and raised in a political cauldron—his father, Sir Michael Cashin, was finance minister prior to the First World War and, briefly, prime minister of the dominion. Peter Cashin seems to have inherited his father's mercurial temperament—Sir Michael's political affiliations shifted frequently, and invariably with great drama.

Major Peter Cashin had what ordinary people might have called a bad streak—he was talented but unpredictable and, he later would acknowledge, a heavy drinker. A bad combination in a politician inclined to speak and act out of principles and personal interests, rather than from an overarching team commitment. The army and the war should have knocked some of that vanity out of him, but they clearly didn't, and the years in which he served as finance minister, 1928 to 1932, must have been uncomfortable for Sir Richard Squires.

But Squires depended on Cashin, on his gifts. He had a mind that was just as sharp as his tongue, and woe betide the man (for they were all men in the assembly, with one exception—Lady Helena Squires) who rose to take him on. And he was a Catholic. Squires was not, and this mattered in a place where Catholics were numerous and unpredictable.

How often Peter Cashin must have bit his tongue in 1930, when it was still possible to pretend that the country had the resources and the character to avoid what, for many, was an inevitable reckoning after years of political mismanagement and wasted opportunities. It was still possible, in 1930, to look on the bright side, tout the resilience so well demonstrated in the war, in the aftermath of the tsunami.

And Peter Cashin would have remembered his own cheerful voice in the chorus of optimism as the island's politicians persuaded bankers to keep the money flowing in 1930. Like all governments, Newfoundland lived on credit, and the confidence of bankers was a matter of survival.

And then it was 1931 and the optimistic eloquence of the political elites was fooling nobody, least of all themselves. The little country had a debt of $90 million and it was growing. In 1931, the assembly passed a bill authorizing another trip to the money markets to raise another $8 million, part of which was earmarked to pay a $2.2 million interest bill that was coming due on July 1 that year.

The notices went out—the big investors were invited to bid on another issue of Newfoundland government bonds. It was routine. It was how governments everywhere paid the bills that came due daily. But this time would be different. The invitation to grab a piece of what should have been considered a perfectly safe investment was met by—silence.

The deadline for submitting bids was May 22. The deadline passed without a nibble. On May 23, there was confusion. This never happened, but it just had. The message was clear: Newfoundland didn't just have a bad credit rating. It had *no* credit rating.[9]

ST. JOHN'S is a garrulous place, and over the course of that long holiday weekend, the rumours were flying. The *Evening Telegram* had the scoop but wouldn't run it. The potential consequences were too dire. In any case, the word was on the street, and on Tuesday morning, May 26, there was a lineup of worried clients outside the government-owned Newfoundland Savings Bank.

On May 27, the government dispatched a "most secret" telegram to London, where the attitudes at the best of times were those of anxious parents towards a wilful, mouthy child. The telegram essentially told London to ignore "mischievous and misleading reports" of an impending financial crisis.[10]

Two days later, there was another "most secret" telegram to London, assuring Whitehall that Newfoundland was considering a dire response to those "mischievous and misleading" reports. "In conjunction with cable companies, consideration is being given to possibility of taking action to prevent transmission of prejudicial and false reports by telegraph."

By then, Squires and Cashin were on their way to Montreal, caps in hand, to meet the bankers. But as one prominent Newfoundland writer would observe years later: "May 22, 1931, brought no catastrophic fire, epidemic, bank crash, fatal charge towards loaded machine guns, collapse of an industry, or sealing disaster, but it truly was one of the Dominion's blackest moments."[11]

And nowhere was the darkness more impenetrable than on the southern end of the Burin Peninsula.

～～～

As far as the people on the south coast were concerned, St. John's might as well have been a suburb of London, England, or on another planet entirely. In 1931–32, the prospect of starvation was a looming presence in the daily lives of thousands of people scattered through communities that had been devastated by the tsunami and the sudden collapse of the fishery.

Their lives were a grim continuation of November 18, 1929. All around them were the reminders of that day. For those who had rebuilt or repaired homes, there were the painful memories of lost children, parents, friends and cousins. Loud sounds from nature, from the normal turbulence of the ocean or the wind, now stirred anxiety. Over many generations, they had learned to live with nature in all her many moods, but now they knew she could never again be trusted.

They were living hand to mouth, fending off starvation on a meagre diet dictated by dole administrators, a recipe for malnutrition. And all the while being told by bureaucrats in London and St. John's that they were bankrupting the country, these able-bodied men who sat home doing nothing.

The particular plight of the south coast would have been far from the immediate concerns of the people running Newfoundland in 1931. The dole itself was under pressure. Canadian bankers and British politicians were squeezing the dominion government to cut back on relief or face dire consequences.

If they were at all aware of what Walter Seibert was up to in St. Lawrence, it would have been good news: the promise of jobs, wages to take pressure off the dole. The peculiar details of how he proposed to go about the project would not have mattered. He was launching his new industry in what would turn out to be a place where entrepreneurial initiative was unhampered by rules and regulations and red tape—a great advantage for an empire builder.

And from the point of view of an empire builder, the situation would get better, even more permissive, as things got worse for Newfoundlanders.

It took two nerve-shredding weeks in the spring of 1931, with much political string-pulling by Squires and Cashin, to persuade the Bank of Montreal to put together a four-bank consortium that would extend a short-term loan of $2 million at 5.5 percent interest to prevent default on July 1. The banks, essentially, agreed to lend Newfoundland just enough to pay the interest on money Newfoundlanders already owed the bankers. And even then, there were conditions.

On June 19, the British high commissioner in Ottawa notified London that the Canadian prime minister, R.B. Bennett, had been instrumental in putting together the deal, and that Sir Richard Squires, in a concession to Bennett and the banks, had agreed to ask the British treasury to send across a fixer who would help overhaul Newfoundland's woeful finances.[12]

After so much stress, Sir Richard Squires required a holiday, and in July he and Lady Squires set off for England for ten weeks of recuperation. But the time Squires spent in England wasn't wasted, and while in London, he was able to recruit his budgetary expert—a senior British treasury official.

Sir Percy Thompson, deputy secretary in the Department of Inland Revenue, agreed to spend some time in Newfoundland sorting out the island's finances. But he didn't come cheap, and he demanded first-class travel to the remote dominion for himself and his assistant, as well as Lady Thompson and their two daughters. His salary would be more than $18,000 a year.[13] And one of his first priorities, as the man now ultimately controlling the dominion's purse strings, would be to reduce the dole.

The irony was later noted in the legislature—Sir Percy pulling down $18,000 a year (in Canadian dollars) while "the poor mortals of people in the outports are forced to live on six cents a day." Squires was unsympathetic, retorting that the poor mortals should be grateful "that they had someone who could find six cents a day for them."

THE June bailout was obviously just a bandage, and the "most secret" wires were humming once again in November as another deadline loomed for payment of interest on the nation's debt. January 1 would prove to be another nail-biter for Peter Cashin, and he was working on it even in September, when Sir Richard was still in London recovering from the travails of the pinch in May and June.

Squires finally headed home in mid-September, but via New York, where he and Lady Squires decided to unwind for a few more weeks. Cashin had to go there to discuss what he saw as a steadily deteriorating situation in Newfoundland. Squires was sympathetic but really couldn't offer any fresh ideas.

ON December 21, ten days before what was looking like a catastrophic default, another wire came from London: "Not possible for HM government . . . to intervene."[14]

The telegram acknowledged that failure by Newfoundland to "meet obligations" would have "a serious impact on Empire credit," but the Brits had financial problems of their own, and in any event, a bailout for Newfoundland would set a dangerous precedent at a time when many of the Commonwealth dominions were facing financial difficulty.

It was December 28 before Sir Percy Thompson, now up to his neck in Newfoundland's affairs, was able to reassure his British colleagues that once again, at the very last minute, the banks had come together to save the hide of this prodigal pseudo-country. There were strings attached as usual, but the strings this time would begin the slow strangulation of Newfoundland's political autonomy.

Across the island, from St. John's to Port au Choix, from St. Lawrence up to St. Anthony, ordinary people were suffering. There were reports of malnutrition, even starvation. The government was broke, and some hard-liners in the British Dominions Office were complaining that a large part of the problem was malingering and laziness, an inability by the able-bodied common man to help himself because of moral failure, ignorance, weakness of character. It was not a good time for anyone who was struggling to survive on the Burin Peninsula, or anywhere else on the island, to expect help or even sympathy from people in authority.

Meanwhile, Sir Richard and Lady Squires had come home and moved into the Newfoundland Hotel, where they were conspicuously entertaining the better quality of Newfoundlanders at lavish dinner parties.

19.

I T was no secret that Peter Cashin was sick of Squires, his lifestyle and lackadaisical approach to the ongoing financial crisis, his long absences from Newfoundland, his unwillingness to consider new ideas for solving problems.

In October 1931, Cashin and two other members of the cabinet had bluntly told Squires that he should resign—that the only way to restore confidence in the dominion was to create a new coalition government under new leadership. Squires should quit. They should all quit. Hand the reins of power to someone else. Squires refused. There would be an election in 1932. Let the people decide who should run the country then. What's another year?

But another year was too much for the bankers and the British bureaucrats, and by the end of 1931, they, not Cashin and certainly not Squires, were calling all the shots. And now Peter Cashin discovered that Sir Richard had been using the public treasury as a private piggy bank, and he believed that Squires had altered cabinet records to conceal the fact.

Cashin had no choice but to resign. And he did so, on February 1, 1932. Squires accepted his resignation and ignored the uproar the major had incited in the assembly when, in his resignation speech, he hinted at systemic corruption in the government. But there was no way that Squires could ignore the common people forever—although he tried. He avoided public appearances. Holed up in his hotel. Occasionally he had to surface for urgent government or party business, however, which was how the people got to him on February 11.

On February 16, five days after the attack on the PM on Duckworth Street, Peter Cashin—now the former finance minister—went public with specific accusations in the assembly. The public galleries were packed and rowdy as he read out a litany of charges: misappropriation of funds, forged orders-in-council, deliberate deception of the parliament and governor, a criminal cover-up.

Squires just shrugged it off and stalled for time. But time, like money, was rapidly diminishing for Sir Richard Squires and Newfoundland.

By March 1, 1932, the finances of the dominion were, for all practical purposes, being managed out of London. Sir Percy was reporting to his boss, J.H. Thomas, British secretary of state for dominion affairs, who was reporting to his boss, the chancellor of the exchequer and future prime minister, Neville Chamberlain.

The budget for that fiscal year was bad news all around.

The deficit, according to Sir Percy's figures, would be just above $4 million, almost three times what he had hoped for. The cost of "able-bodied relief" would be $1,170,000. Sir Percy called that figure "the most disturbing item" in the budget and warned that it was only going to get worse.

Squires delivered the bad news in a budget speech that was obviously written by Sir Percy. It begged for private charity to relieve the public burden of the dole, "the help of neighbours and churches, local charities and local organizations, the settlement or the town . . . to recognize their responsibilities toward the distressed before the government is called to step in. The state should be the last and not the first resort."

It was an ironic twist, and galling for the neighbours and churches and charities that would have known about Sir Percy's salary and were reading in the social columns of the newspapers about the first family's dinner parties in the Newfoundland Hotel—reports that included guest lists and menus in mouth-watering detail.[15]

Sir Percy was aware that while the public purse was empty, well-off Newfoundlanders were sitting on about $25 million in private bank accounts. He implored them to dig down and cough up a substantial share of what he was calling "a prosperity loan" to the Newfoundland government—essentially a loan of $2.5 million to themselves, which he termed "a safe and profitable investment."

The public was sceptical, and the call for lenders seemed to be falling on deaf ears. The "prosperity" appeal sounded like desperation.

There was, around this time, a bizarre proposal, briefly entertained, to import Scotch whisky from the UK, reduce its alcohol content to zero, then export it to the dry United States, where, presumably, enterprising Americans would find a way to restore the original integrity. It would create jobs in Newfoundland and a windfall in import duties, proponents said. Sir Richard laughed at the idea: "I don't think that it is a scientific or potable proposition," he declared in the assembly.[16]

There was also a half-hearted attempt by Squires to sell Labrador to Canada, but he wanted $100 million. Ottawa declined.

Sir Percy finally cut a deal with Imperial Oil Ltd., in which the mainland company agreed to underwrite the prosperity loan to the tune of $1.75 million and to make annual cash advances to the treasury in exchange for a fifteen-year monopoly on the sale of petroleum products on the island. Well-off Newfoundlanders then came up with the balance.

It all helped, but it was crisis management at best, and in the long run, the financial and social burdens would be borne mostly by ordinary people—new taxes on food; increased taxes on income, profits, sales; and so on. In 1932, there would be a drastic cut in civil service salaries and a 25 percent reduction in the salaries of cabinet ministers—convincing evidence of desperation—and most incendiary of all, cuts in the pensions of war veterans and the widows and orphans of the war dead.

There was an instant outcry and Squires was forced to back down, at least on veterans' pensions—especially when he was confronted with the fact that one of the pools of public money he'd been pilfering was funded by war reparations from Germany. But it wouldn't be the end of the controversy. The protests would continue and get worse.

20.

THE first paragraph in the story on the front page of the *Daily News* of St. John's on April 6, 1932, neatly summed up the crisis that now paralyzed the government of Newfoundland.

"Every window of the Colonial Building is glassless: the Prime Minister practically a refugee, the law of enforcement of the city turned over to the authority of ex-servicemen, as the result of discord which marked the culmination of weeks of protest and dissatisfaction with maladministration of the government."

At a rowdy public meeting on the night of April 4, a parade of speakers from among sixty platform guests vented public outrage over the budget and the allegations of corruption.[17] One war veteran at the gathering declared that if Squires had been convicted of such charges on a battlefield, he would surely have been shot by a firing squad.[18]

The meeting resolved that there should be a protest march the next afternoon, assembling at the Majestic Theatre on Duckworth Street and timing its arrival at the assembly, about a mile away, as the members were beginning their daily sitting at three o'clock. The protestors would present a petition demanding action on the Cashin accusations.

By 2:15 the next afternoon, the Majestic was packed and Duckworth Street was "a mass of moiling humanity," according to the April 6 *Daily News*, waiting for the start of the "parade." One of the demonstration leaders, the prominent lawyer and sometime politician J.A. Winter, from Burin, begged for order. There was music from a military band. The "moiling" crowd was estimated at eight to ten thousand men, women and children.

They set out along Water Street on a staggered course that avoided the most daunting hills of downtown St. John's. They eventually swarmed up Cochrane Street, past a hotel rumoured to have once given hospitality to Leon Trotsky, past the palatial home of the Newfoundland governor and onto the grounds of the parliament. There were thirty policemen, four on horseback, waiting when they reached their destination.

After half an hour, and as the grumbling of the crowd became intimidating, the military band struck up the dominion anthem, the "Ode to Newfoundland," and it seemed to calm things temporarily. As the *Evening Telegram* reported on the following day, "Every man and youth in the vast assembly stood with a bared head until the piece was finished. It was a most impressive sight."

Finally, four leaders, including Mr. Winter, were admitted to the assembly to present their petition. Squires listened, then rose and, obviously stalling—a tactic that often worked for him when faced with peril—began another tedious discussion about procedure. How to handle the petition and its insinuations.

Outside, the protestors, many of whom were hungry and impatient, were growing restless again. There was shouting at the front of the crowd, causing those in the rear to press forward to find out why the people at the front were yelling. Tension built. Mounted police officers blocked the steps to the entrance of the building. Several demonstrators ran at the police and tried to drag them from their horses. Almost got one down, tore his cape off. The band struck up the national anthem once again. Once again, the struggle ceased. Men and boys dutifully doffed their caps. But as the last stirring strains of the anthem faded, the crowd renewed the struggle. A Union Jack at the entrance to the parliament was torn from its flagstaff.

The four petitioners, who were inside listening to the politicians talking about procedure, heard the racket, rushed outside, begged for order. But by now the crowd was beyond persuasion. Young men at the front attacked the entrance. The police retreated inside, blocked the doors and held them shut. Someone outside found a five-foot iron bar and used it to smash through the panels in the door.

The police, from inside, used their nightsticks on the people closest. But their effectiveness was limited. They were inside, reaching out, weakly threatening the nearest demonstrators. Then, as the *Evening Telegram* reported the next day, the besieged police "threw off their overcoats and with flailing batons, rushed outside and charged the crowd." It went downhill from there. Someone threw a rock. Soon there was a hail of rocks and other projectiles. Windows, doors and doorframes were shattered. A crowd of citizens became a mob.

The mob was soon inside. Someone tried to steal the ceremonial mace, symbol of the authority of parliament. Another stole the sword of the sergeant-at-arms. A piano was hauled outside and demolished. Offices were ransacked. Two young men found four bottles of White Horse whisky. Shared the liquor with their mates. There were two attempts to set the place afire.

The ruckus lasted all night long. Inevitably, hidden supplies of liquor were discovered. Posses of war veterans took over the policing duties and patrolled the streets, doing what they could to safeguard lives and property. Miraculously, nobody died in what was now officially recorded as a riot.

Days later, on April 9, Sir Percy Thompson, in a chatty letter to a high-placed friend in the Dominions Office in London, blamed the riot on young men—numbering between 100 and 150—who had been waiting at the legislature before the main body of protesters got there. "There is considerable evidence," Sir Percy wrote, "that this crowd of youths had been organized and instigated by certain politicians to create a disturbance with a view to forcing the resignation of Squires."[19]

Certainly, the one man whose life was most at risk that night was Sir Richard Squires. He kept out of sight for as long as possible. But when he tried to leave the building, protected by an ecumenical brigade of clergy and loyal politicians, someone spotted him. Every way he turned, his path was blocked. The crowd, barely restrained by pleas from senior police officers, hurled abuse.

The stalemate lasted for an hour. Squires was cornered. Now the crowd seemed uncertain what to do, milling mindlessly around the preachers, the police, the politicians, the prime minister. Some were loudly "advocating violence," according to the press reports on April 6. And then Squires and his protectors made their move—headed for the sanctuary of a nearby private home, the Connolly residence at 66 Colonial Street.

Once inside, Squires wisely kept on going, straight through the ground floor of the house towards the back rooms. A clergyman, according to the *Telegram* reporter on the scene, "had the premier make his exit from the back of the Connolly house to come over fences to a Bannerman Street house [a short block away] and without delay placed him in a taxi."

It was an image that would endure: the prime minister of the dominion scurrying through the darkness, through backyards, clambering over fences, to escape the wrath of the people who had elected him and who now blamed him for their idleness, their poverty, their hopelessness.

Thus the political autonomy of Newfoundland entered a death spiral from which it would not recover for seventeen years. Any hope of continued nationhood died in the crush that afternoon.

WHATEVER sense of obligation towards the devastated communities of the south coast still existed at the end of 1929, it had, by April 1932, been overwhelmed by the more immediate financial crisis in St. John's. Now the spectacle of a mob attacking the Colonial Building—smashing windows, looting offices and liquor depots, systematically demolishing a piano in Bannerman Park—would, in the minds of bureaucrats and bankers and politicians, overwhelm whatever images remained from nature's rampage through forty vulnerable villages, twenty-eight months earlier.

While those earlier events, described by one anonymous Newfoundland writer as the "gaunt tragedy" of 1929, might have bolstered the moral strength of the dominion's position in the Commonwealth, there is no evidence that the particulars of the south coast disaster factored into the appeals for help from the banks or the governments of Canada and Britain in 1932.

The death, the injuries, the illnesses; more than a million dollars of damage to productive property; the devastation of the island's most important economic resource, the fishery; more than a third of the population now directly dependant on relief—all human factors that somehow failed to figure in the fiscal and political equations. Instead, there was consistent hectoring about the dole, invariably framed in moral terms—economic help-lessness rising from an absence of initiative combined with low intelligence. Newfoundlanders, according to one contemporary politician, didn't have the brains to recognize political talent even when "a good man" stepped up to help them.[20]

At the Imperial Economic Conference of Commonwealth leaders in Ottawa in 1932, the earthquake and tsunami didn't seem to merit a mention as factors in Newfoundland's grim financial situation. The overwhelming preoccupation of Sir Richard Squires and Peter Cashin, of Sir Percy Thompson, J.H. Thomas and Neville Chamberlain, was the confidence of banks and the credit ratings of Commonwealth dominions. And tactics.

It was the beginning of the end of self-government for the island.

And it could be that in the context of fresh memories about the most savage war in human history, a collapse of Western cap-italism, and rampant poverty and unemployment throughout the developed world, it was easy to ignore twenty-seven (soon to be twenty-eight) deaths and the suffering of ten thousand people in a place that never made the news, that nobody important ever had to think about.

By the end of 1932, Squires's political career was finished. His government had been replaced by a perhaps potentially more honest, but seemingly more confused and impotent administra-tion, led by . . . it didn't really matter anymore. Moses, Jesus and

Muhammad would have been equally perplexed by the challenges facing this remote society. One prominent Newfoundland politician, publicly and quite seriously, called for the emergence of a Mussolini. "If a man with a soul encased in steel, experienced and not under forty years old, appeared on the political horizon in this country today as a Mussolini, I would support him with all my strength."[21]

In the absence of a Mussolini, Newfoundlanders got a committee of bureaucrats and recycled politicians—an appointed commission of government, effectively controlled from England. For fifteen years, Newfoundland would be governed by seven unelected people, four of them (including the chairman) from the British public service. The attitude with which the British commissioners approached their task was encapsulated in a comment recorded in the Dominions Office in London on September 2, 1933, as the political future of the island was being hammered out: "The political life of the island was corrupt from top to bottom, as the main object of the individual politician and the individual elector was to get what each could out of the public till."[22]

SIR John Hope Simpson arrived on the island in February 1934. A former British MP and civil administrator, he had been comfortably retired when he heard about the crisis in Newfoundland. All the former British colonies seemed to be having problems— financial problems from the First World War, the Great Depression. But this remote dominion was facing bankruptcy. And that was a threat for everyone, including Britons.

It was a challenge that a long-time loyal public servant could not resist. He was to become commissioner for natural resources, potentially one of the most influential positions in the new government. For him, the only hope for Newfoundland was to find ways to diversify the economy to reduce the dependency on fishing. It was fairly obvious to him: build up other economic sectors, like agriculture and forestry. There also seemed to be a limited but strong mining industry with significant potential for expansion.

Sir John felt the long-term solutions to the problems in Newfoundland should have been obvious to anyone with knowledge of public service systems and familiarity with backward places—new industry for sure, but equally important was a renewed spirit of industrious resolve by ordinary people.

Newfoundlanders were a proud, potentially heroic folk, as they'd demonstrated in the Great War. The best of British stock. Democratic politics had failed them. What the people needed now was competent administration, which educated Englishmen were very good at, as they had demonstrated masterfully in the Indian subcontinent, where Sir John Hope Simpson had spent nearly twenty useful years.

But his long career in the British foreign service—India, Palestine, Greece—would have stamped what was fundamentally a "liberal" tendency in politics with certain prejudices about people and their needs. He was compassionate, but also a strong believer in traditional virtues, like enterprise and pluck.

There were many reasonable explanations for the failure of the dominion. But failure never justifies a feeling of defeat. This was the challenge facing Sir John and the other members of the new commission government. Rekindle confidence. Get the ordinary dole-corrupted Newfoundlander off his ass.

And perhaps if he'd had twenty years to spend in Newfoundland, Sir John might have made a difference. But he'd be there for only thirty months. He would become familiar with entrenched and crippling poverty and its awful consequences. Malnutrition. Illness. Tuberculosis was rampant. To catch it was to die. The death rate from the disease was by far the highest rate anywhere in the so-called developed world. There were also recorded deaths from starvation. Rickets and beriberi were commonplace, especially in the more remote settlements. These were some of the reasons why one-third of the population was on the dole, with no immediate prospects for getting off it.

For Sir John, home would be, for the duration of his stay, the Newfoundland Hotel. His wife, Lady Mary Jane (known to acquaintances as Quita), was much impressed by their accommodations ("heavenly" linen and "rose du Barry silk eiderdowns"). "We are," she enthused, "much more luxurious than at home."[23]

The physical grandeur of the island was, of course, inspiring. But the poverty, seen up close, was profoundly distressing. They'd have to have been senseless not to notice the sight, the sound, the smell of it. You couldn't miss it, especially in St. John's, where the poor were more conspicuous and noisier.

And on the day they docked from England, mingling with the dignitaries waiting to receive them, they saw "a crowd of poor folk—pitifully poor and half starved, they looked." Lady Hope Simpson was aghast. "The accounts of the condition of the people are simply appalling. They are so apathetic—they have suffered for so long that there seems to be no energy in them."[24]

The time she'd spend in Newfoundland would only reinforce her first impressions. "Work among these people is most disheartening. They have been practically serfs and have no traditions—no moral impetus. They are apparently charming to meet—very friendly, but there it ends."

Sir John and Lady Hope Simpson would eventually find small grounds for optimism. They toured the scenery. They made friends. And they might have been intrigued had they met another married couple, young people, Americans still in their twenties, also drawn to Newfoundland by a belief that the island's natural resources could transform the place.

Donald Poynter, an engineer from New Jersey, had arrived a few months earlier and was settling into a little town on the south coast, a place the new commissioner would soon get to know and, however briefly, see as part of a solution to the economic problems at the core of Newfoundland's political collapse.

The town was St. Lawrence. And the project that brought Donald Poynter to the place was exactly the kind of venture the new commissioner would be encouraging while he was there. A mining operation.

It was already up and running. That was a spot of good news. But St. Lawrence was a long way from St. John's, and the commissioner would be halfway through his mission in the distant island before he'd get to see, at first hand, what was really going on there.

FOUR

The Cooperation

21.

~~~

For a couple of Methodists fresh out of Nutley, New Jersey, it must have been a scene straight from the Middle Ages, this Roman Catholic performance. The mournful singing; the timeless weathered faces gazing raptly on the man at the front, magisterial in purple vestments appropriate for a commemoration of the dead; back turned to the people; wheeling and gesturing, genuflecting, rising, holding above him the totems of the faith, the round white disk, the golden chalice; all the while muttering as if he were alone, in a private world, communing privately with God.

The two Protestants didn't recognize the words but assumed they were Latin. They knew that much about Catholics and their rituals. There were gruesome scenes of torture and crucifixion on the surrounding walls. Candles flickered, casting eerie shadows on the lurking statuary.

Donald and Urla Crammond Poynter knew vaguely why they were there. Fascinated, they had listened at the Giovanninis' boarding house, where they were living, to quiet references to the event that was being mourned at this commemorative Mass.[1]

And their astonishment was even greater when this priest, this Father Thorne, finally set his things aside, strode to the pulpit and acknowledged that they were all there together with a single purpose—to remember twenty-eight dead people and thousands

who were ill and grieving and suffering the aftermath of an earthquake and a tidal wave. But they were also there in the spirit of
thanksgiving, that their own community, St. Lawrence, had been
spared the loss of life. Property demolished, yes, but as anyone
could see around them even after just four years, property can be
replaced.

How could the Poynters not have heard? An earthquake?
And then they had a renewed and deeper understanding of the
isolation of this place, their new home, the distance they had
travelled from the thriving precincts of Brooklyn, from dizzying
Manhattan, from the bucolic gentility of the countryside and small
towns of New Jersey. Another world entirely, this New-Found-
Land. How could they not have known about the suffering of
this place, now so vivid to them, so recently, in 1929?

And yet, strange to say, the tragedy that had struck four years
before they got here was now partly theirs by virtue of their par-
ticipation in the communal grieving, which was also a celebration
of recovery—a rebirth in which Donald A. Poynter was determined to play a major role.

After the Communion, after the members of the congrega-
tion, with the exception of the two Protestants, shuffled to the
cloth-covered railing at the front, knelt, received a wafer from the
priest, mumbled gratitude, rose, turned and made their way back
to their pews, Poynter recognized many of the faces. Hard, craggy
faces temporarily softened by the sacrament, the memories of lost
loved ones. Men from the mine. Or to be more candid, as he was
in private moments with his new bride, from the glorified trench
that he, Donald Poynter, would help, hell or high water, to turn
into a mine.

How long had it really been since their arrival? Just over two
months? It felt like a lifetime, and in a way, it *was* a lifetime, since

they had travelled through time to a place that seemed to be a century removed from Nutley and everything they remembered from the United States, to this frontier country, the entire dominion with a population only two-thirds that of Jersey City.

No roads. Everything by water. There was a railroad, if you could call it that, but even to get to the train you had to take a boat. Getting to St. Lawrence had involved what seemed like an endless boat ride along the coast, stopping at small places on the way. Charming little places with romantic names and friendly people who gathered on the docks to see the strangers on the boat, to collect their parcels and their mail. François. Hermitage. Belleoram. Lamaline. Donald Poynter loved boats, and he would have enjoyed the journey more if he hadn't been in such a hurry to get to the destination, to start the work, to turn Walter Seibert's dream into a reality.

And what a destination it was. St. Lawrence, Newfoundland. A speck of a place on the end of a boot-shaped peninsula thrusting southwards in defiance of the unforgiving North Atlantic. Population nine hundred, give or take. No streets, but a few roads and cow paths between quaint houses crowded round the harbour. A few stores. A school. Glowering over the whole scene, this cavernous church.

And all around, the knobby hills, rocky barrens softened by ponds and streams and soggy bogs, gale-stunted evergreens. Pale green lichen and grey moss mottling the outcroppings of granite. Here and there the sparkle of fluorspar, pink and purple. But all-defining rock, everywhere you looked—you couldn't survive here for any length of time without becoming as rugged as the rocky landscape, unyielding as the ocean. It was something he would have to keep in mind, this insight into the local character.

He studied the faces of the men returning from the Communion rail. He would soon know them all—the names, the families, the family connections—for the venture at Black

Duck mine was starting small. Just thirty miners, if you could call them that. Fishing had been their occupation for centuries before this slump, which was caused, as far as they could tell, by that tsunami and that other, greater earthquake originating back near where Donald Poynter came from: Wall Street. As foreign and mysterious to him as Newfoundland, and as challenging to him as mining was for these south coast fishermen.

Donald Poynter was an engineer. And an athlete. He'd gone through Bucknell University in Pennsylvania on a football scholarship. He wasn't much interested in high finance—only what financiers could do for (or to) the people who depended on them. He'd learned that lesson bitterly. His father's lighting business back in the States had gone under thanks to the calamity on Wall Street in 1929.

A weird coincidence: the earthquake, the tsunami, the market crash, he and Urla being here now, in this unlikely place. And an even weirder coincidence—how he'd come to be involved with Walter.

It had been through their mothers. They shared a German heritage, and after the two women met some years back, in Brooklyn, they stayed in touch. Their sons were close in age. Walter had embarked on a career in high finance. Donald wasn't happy in his engineering work. When their mothers introduced them, he was with a company that was building a boardwalk for visitors to Staten Island.[2] It was a job that, in his mind, was literally going nowhere. He quickly became enthused when Walter explained the industrial importance of fluorspar and described his potential mining properties, out on a rocky place in the middle of the Atlantic, past the edge of North America.

Poynter was keen to go there, and the young woman he was about to marry, Urla Crammond, also saw the move as an adventure and a way for both of them to escape their overbearing families. It came as no surprise to them when their families

Above: Louis Etchegary's family in 1929, likely early autumn, shortly before the tsunami transformed their town and their future lives. *Front row, left to right*: Louis Jr., Florence (later Mrs. Donald Poynter), nephew Bobby Pike and (in white cap) Gus Etchegary, then five years old. *Back row*: daughter Kathleen Etchegary (*left*) and Ellen Slaney, sister of Louis's recently deceased first wife.
COURTESY OF LISA (SLANEY) LODER.

Left: Father Augustine Thorne, St. Lawrence parish priest and community leader in the aftermath of the tsunami and the early days of the mining industry.
COURTESY OF ST. LAWRENCE MINERS' MUSEUM.

Patrick Rennie, Lord's Cove. On the evening of the tsunami, Patrick and his two sons, Martin and Albert, were playing cards at a neighbour's house. His wife and four other children were at home. His wife and three children drowned in their house. Four-year-old Margaret, asleep upstairs, survived.

COURTESY OF SARAH BRAKE.

Lord's Cove, days after the tsunami. The Rennie home, where Patrick Rennie's wife and three of his children died, is slightly in the background to the left of the building in centre-frame. After the disaster, Patrick and his sons became fluorspar miners in St. Lawrence.

PHOTO BY DR. HARRIS MOSDELL, CHAIRMAN OF THE NEWFOUNDLAND BOARD OF HEALTH AND PART OF THE RELIEF TEAM ON SS *MEIGLE*. COURTESY OF PUBLIC ARCHIVES OF NEWFOUNDLAND AND LABRADOR (PANL), COLLECTION MG 1011, ITEM A 86–90.

Waterfront, Burin district, post-tsunami.

One of eleven photographs of the Burin area taken by local parish priest Father James A. Miller. Six of his photos were published in the *New York Times* on December 8, 1929.

The iconic post-tsunami photograph, by Father James A. Miller of Burin, that many mistakenly believe shows a schooner towing a house. In fact, research by Alan Ruffman of Geomarine Associates Ltd., Halifax, a leading authority on the tsunami, reveals that the house, from Port au Bras, was discovered by its owner about a mile offshore and towed back to Little Burin Harbour, where it was then tethered to the anchored schooner, the *Marian Belle Wolfe*. COURTESY OF PANL, PARSONS FAMILY COLLECTION, ITEM A 2–149.

St. Lawrence, Newfoundland, east side of the harbour, early 1930s.
COURTESY OF ST. LAWRENCE MINERS' MUSEUM.

St. Lawrence, Newfoundland, west side of the harbour, mid-1930s, at the beginning of fluorspar mining. COURTESY OF ST. LAWRENCE MINERS' MUSEUM.

Black Duck mine, mid-1930s. COURTESY OF ST. LAWRENCE MINERS' MUSEUM.

Sir Richard Squires, prime minister of
Newfoundland, 1919–23 and 1928–32.

Major Peter Cashin, First World War
veteran, minister of finance in the
1928–32 Squires government. He eventually brought down the government by
levelling charges of corruption against
the prime minister and his cronies,
setting in motion the final chapter in
the collapse of democratic government
in Newfoundland—which would leave
the colony in the control of appointed
bureaucrats until 1949.

Sir John Hope Simpson, outside Buck-
ingham Palace on June 3, 1925, the day
he received his knighthood from King
George V. Sir John was commissioner
of natural resources in the unelected
government of Newfoundland for two
years, 1934–36.

Walter Seibert (*left*), an accountant from New Jersey and New York, arrived in St. Lawrence *circa* 1932, to launch what local people would soon ironically refer to as "Seibert's fluor-spar empire." COURTESY OF ST. LAWRENCE MINERS' MUSEUM.

St. Lawrence merchant Aubrey Farrell (*centre*) was an early backer of the mining venture but soon grew disenchanted with the business practices of its American promoter, Walter Scibert. COURTESY OF ST. LAWRENCE MINERS' MUSEUM.

On April 5, 1932, an angry crowd, estimated to number nearly ten thousand people, marched on the Newfoundland legislature, the Colonial Building, to confront members of the Squires government, which they viewed as corrupt and ineffective. The gathering quickly morphed into a full-blown riot. COURTESY OF PANL, COLLECTION MG 592, ITEM A 19-22.

Lady Mary Jane ("Quita") Hope Simpson, with her two daughters, Mary (*left*) and Greta, in June 1904. The extreme poverty she discovered in Newfoundland while living there between 1932 and 1934 was frequently described in journal entries and letters to her then-married daughters and a son, John (Ian). Her personal correspondence from Newfoundland, and that of her husband, Sir John, has been compiled by historian Peter Neary in *White Tie and Decorations* (University of Toronto Press, 1996). COURTESY OF THE HOPE SIMPSON FAMILY.

"St. John's Urchins," from a photo album assembled by Albert J. Wallace, from Collingswood, New Jersey, *circa* 1937. Newfoundland, at the time, had possibly the highest rates of infant mortality and child poverty in the western world. COURTESY OF ST. LAWRENCE MINERS' MUSEUM, WALLACE COLLECTION.

Children photographed in St. John's "from a poor section of the city," *circa* 1937, by Albert J. Wallace, an American businessman. COURTESY OF ST. LAWRENCE MINERS' MUSEUM, WALLACE COLLECTION.

strenuously opposed the move to this godforsaken place—which, from what they could learn about it, seemed to have a lot in common with Siberia. Urla, they insisted, was too delicate for such a risky venture.

The couple packed up and headed off anyway. The ocean voyage from Brooklyn to St. Lawrence was a kind of honeymoon.

NEWFOUNDLAND was, the climate notwithstanding, a warm and exotic place. From the moment they had disembarked they'd found friendly faces, unselfish curiosity, an English dialect that was curiously accented and peppered with vocabulary and expressions and syntax that defied immediate interpretation. The people of the south coast were obviously poor, and now that he knew more about the recent history, Poynter was amazed by the forbearance, the absence of complaint. He was determined that as he and Walter Seibert prospered, so too would these worthy people.

Seibert's project was evolving slowly, but the vision was impressive. It was large and it was audacious in the tradition of America's most successful enterprises. It demanded a certain pioneering perseverance and conscientious ruthlessness. But Seibert had persuaded him that the place was a perfect testing ground for the American pioneering spirit—approach all obstacles, be they geographic, environmental or human, as challenges to be surmounted by whatever means became available. That ethos would make everybody wealthy in the long run.

There was one persistent question, however, and it would return occasionally in the months ahead: Were they raising unrealistic expectations among these needy people? Poynter wondered if they were taking unfair advantage of a crisis to cut a deal with the people here that would have boggled the minds of just about anyone who heard of it back in the boardrooms of New York. Free labour for an indefinite period? Credit from the merchants to keep men working? It was reminiscent, in a way, of how the pharaohs built the pyramids. The people who were doing all the heavy work had no options. And when people have no options, they really have no rights.

However, from what Donald Poynter and his fellow American on the ground in St. Lawrence, Doc Smith, could conclude from what they knew, the local folks were going into this with open eyes. The goal was simple: dig up two thousand tons of high-grade fluorspar and transport it to the wharf, load it on a ship and carry it to a steel plant in Sydney, Nova Scotia. The chemists at the steel plant would evaluate the shipment. If it met their specs, the Dominion Steel and Coal Corporation would pay for it. And keep buying it. And paying for it.[3]

The value of the miners' labour had been established in a flimsy contract with a local merchant, Aubrey Farrell, and a hand-shake: fifteen cents an hour—a fraction of what miners were earning elsewhere in Newfoundland, but never mind. Seibert promised that the local men would soon catch up. Farrell's faith would be rewarded. He'd keep track of the hours they worked and give them credit at his store. It would all work out when Walter started earning money.

And Walter promised Donald that he'd eventually become a partner in the new company, the St. Lawrence Corporation of Newfoundland. He'd get shares when the business was up and running. The company would build a nice house in St. Lawrence for Don and Urla and the inevitable children. Doc Smith, who had agreed to work without a salary for a while, would not regret this investment of time and talent.[4]

All the deals were sealed mainly by trust, affirmed in an earn-est handshake and a steady, honest gaze. Weird, even by rough-and-ready pioneering standards, and in retrospect naive. It would take years for the miners' wages to match what miners earned in other places. Poynter never would become a partner. Doc Smith never would get paid. Aubrey Farrell and St. Lawrence would one day have reason to regret ever hearing Walter Seibert's name.

But it was a start.

AND what did Walter think? What did he think of this place, these unusual people? It was difficult to tell with Walter, he was so focused on the business opportunity. For sure he was enthusiastic about the fishing and the hunting. He'd make many visits to St. Lawrence just for those amenities. Walter was, at heart, a sportsman. You could see it in the way he approached a business deal. Warily and patiently. He recognized the potential wealth, an unused resource just waiting to be gathered up.

And the people—it was difficult to know just what he thought of them. Certainly, he loved their trusting attitude, their open-heartedness. That would be enough to start with. The times were anything but normal, and they called for imagination and improvisation and temporary sacrifice. Walter Seibert had the nerve and the imagination and a deep respect for sacrifice, especially by other people.

Progress, in the world that he inhabited, stemmed from a kind of marriage between enterprise and sacrifice. And he was nothing if not enterprising. From the little that we know of him, it's apparent that Walter Seibert was driven by his instincts: see opportunity where others don't; move swiftly, aggressively, creatively to exploit what destiny delivers. To start a mine from scratch in a remote part of a thinly populated island in the middle of the Atlantic, with no knowledge of the mining business and no money in the bank, during a global financial crisis—it would have daunted even a Carnegie or a Rockefeller.

And it would have failed without the unquestioning commitment of a rare community of trusting people.

Walter Seibert had made a crucial connection in Aubrey Farrell.

The Farrells were related by marriage to the other major merchant family in St. Lawrence, the Giovanninis—Aubrey's mother was a Giovannini. Almost everybody in the area depended, one way or another, on the Farrells and the Giovanninis. Eventually they'd all get to know the real Walter Seibert—but for the moment their trust and support were factors that, more than any other, launched the audacious New York accountant into the mining business.

He would eventually find investors willing to put up initial capital of $100,000, but that would take a while. His investment in equipment at the outset was laughable—$2,000 for mostly obsolete second-hand machinery.⁵ But he'd cleverly figured out a way to launch a labour-intensive project without spending anything on labour. That was the key to any prospect of success.

THERE were obviously no mining men available in or anywhere near St. Lawrence. Because of the recent earthquake and the tsunami and the collapse of the local fishery, people in the area were desperate for jobs, any kind of work, no matter how low the wages. But cheap labour wasn't quite what Walter had in mind. He wanted local people to make a real investment in the venture by working, at least in the beginning, for no wages at all. To work hard for a *promise* of payment in the future. Wasn't that the essence of doing business? Borrowing and promising repayment?

In this case, he would borrow sweat and time. When and if it all worked out, he'd pay the fifteen cents an hour. If it didn't . . . well, that's the nature of investment, a form of gambling.

He would present his scheme as an opportunity. The payoff for the workers was a lifetime of job security and steady income. It was, as Walter Seibert would explain it, a win-win all around. Even the parish priest, Father Thorne, seemed enthusiastic, at least in the beginning, and urged the local Catholics to have faith in the Americans. And when Walter Seibert had his venture functioning by mid-1933, it would have made him happy to discover that the local people were referring to his company as "the cooperation." They understood the spirit of the enterprise, and they embraced it. The St. Lawrence cooperation. The miners were his partners, just like Farrell, Smith and Poynter.

But there would be early signs of discontent among the workers and the merchants. These Newfoundlanders weren't as simple as they seemed. Sophisticated outsiders like Walter Seibert will sometimes mistake open-hearted simplicity for stupidity. Time, for the Americans, would be educational.

THE practical imperative was the production and delivery of two thousand tons of fluorspar to the steel mill in Cape Breton. And by March 1934, with their picks and shovels, antiquated drills and wheelbarrows, the men had pulled it off. The next chapter should have been straightforward, but as always seemed to be the case with Walter, events didn't unfold as expected. Seibert's company got paid. Seibert took his time—until late June that year, more than a year after everyone had started working—sharing the proceeds with his partners in "the cooperation," the merchants and the miners.

Part of Donald Poynter's job in St. Lawrence was to reassure the locals. Annoyances and disappointments, frequent as they would be, should be written off as growing pains. In time, Poynter would become good at troubleshooting, persuading when he could, playing hardball when he had to.

Those early days, late in 1933 and in 1934, would mark the beginning of a long and often awkward life experience for young Donald—caught between a distant, arbitrary boss and a community into which he would, in the coming years, slowly be absorbed socially and personally.

~~~~

It's difficult to imagine now what Donald Poynter thought his job would be when he and his wife disembarked from the SS *Portia* in St. Lawrence, Newfoundland, in mid-September 1933. His immediate assignment was to turn his engineering skills to surveying Seibert's mining properties, to work with local prospectors and to help Doc Smith with the early stages of the Black Duck development.[6]

It was both more and less than he had anticipated. And he must have felt some deep misgivings, watching as young Walter Seibert casually manipulated and reneged on promises while local workers busted their guts to hold up their end of the strange bargain they'd made with him.

But even if he'd wanted to turn back, even if his background had been mining and he'd understood just how much sweat and capital it would take to turn this Black Duck operation into a profit-making mine, Poynter seemed to realize from day one that he was beyond a place from which he could easily retreat.

There was a Depression on. Engineers weren't exactly in high demand. There were engineers lining up for free soup and bitter coffee all over America. There could be no turning back. Luckily, the athlete in Poynter's character enjoyed a challenge that pitted him against himself, against his limitations.

Getting to Black Duck involved a long walk from the Giovannini boarding house, on the west side of St. Lawrence harbour, along a route that passed the graveyard at the northeast edge of town. To Donald Poynter, a young man in his twenties, this mournful property, a resting place for strangers, would hardly have merited a second glance. But if he could have seen the future— the future names inscribed on simple stones above the future graves—a quiet voice within would surely have instructed him to turn around. Collect your things, your fragile bride, go home to Nutley. Forget Seibert and his scheme. Forget St. Lawrence, Newfoundland, and all the people you are yet to know here.

22.

RENNIE Slaney would in the future become one of Donald Poynter's in-laws and a boss in Seibert's mining venture in St. Lawrence. He would, more memorably, become the voice for local outrage, a whistle-blower. But in 1935, Rennie Slaney was just another Black Duck miner, facing what they all faced, sustained by the same sense of optimism and trust that, in the early years, kept everybody going, including Donald Poynter and Doc Smith.

Rennie Slaney was twenty-nine, married with five kids, the youngest nine months old. He'd been at Black Duck almost from the beginning. Gone were the days of ships and fishing boats. Now life was all about the rocks and rocky places, the brutal machinery to break the rock and, in doing so, often break the man who used it. He'd gone from the open air—an environment that was familiar, the sea, often a cruel place but integral to the culture he'd grown up in, the traditions he'd inherited—to this new and, in some ways, brutalizing struggle.

As the Black Duck pit became a mine, he and his fellow miners faced impenetrable darkness. Extremes of heat and cold. The recurring dread that crawls up from behind in an environment that all your senses tell you is unnatural, causing limbs and organs to protest. The lungs heaving. The heart racing. The legs stumbling in darkness. Wading through incessant water. Water running down your neck. Inside your boots. Dry one minute, soaking wet the next. Wet work clothes freezing rock hard on your body as you walk home hungry on a winter evening. The infernal drills, bone-jarring, deafening, hammering through granite, turning rock to dust, choking dust, plugging nostrils, infiltrating lungs.

These were conditions that they willingly put up with—Rennie Slaney and his brother, Arcule; Patrick Rennie; and in time, hundreds like them from communities all along the south end of the Burin. Men with long memories of worse: tragedy at sea, on battlefields. The fresh memory of a horrifying night in November 1929. Men still struggling to feed families, arriving at this hard workplace often hungry. They willingly accepted hardship for a greater benefit—the eventual autonomy that comes from honest work and steady pay.

That autonomy, in optimistic moments of reflection in 1935, was the better future they foresaw. It was what they had to see because there really wasn't an alternative anyone could realistically imagine.

IT WAS, in some ways, better in the beginning. The work was always hard, but in the early days they worked in daylight, breathing relatively fresh air. The weather was a problem, especially in the winters, and they might have looked forward to the day when the mining would go underground, unaware of the larger problems waiting there. None of them had ever worked in mining.

To know what really lay ahead would have been discouraging, but the anomalies and hardships of working in the St. Lawrence mines evolved in increments. Daylight diminished gradually. The dust became a greater problem as the men dug deeper; flooding increased below the water table. As a species, we adapt to incremental growth in hardship.

They bought relief from flooding by hand-digging a deep ditch, a thousand feet long, to drain Black Duck Pond, which was close to where they worked.[7] And for a while, it helped. But soon they needed high-volume pumps. The water came from everywhere, it seemed—from the skies, the surrounding bogs, the ponds. The rock itself oozed water.

Incrementally, the job became more difficult physically. They were manhandling awkward steel-wheeled barrows, loaded with a hundred pounds of rock, up a sharp incline. And when the slope became too long and too steep, they sank a shaft the way you'd dig any deep hole in the ground—picking and shovelling straight down, jackhammering, drilling, blasting. Rudimentary timbering to keep the walls intact. Their first hoist was a hand-cranked log and a long rope. Barrels once used for shipping pork, now used for lifting ore.

The company provided the bare necessities, the drills and jackhammers to break the rock when the men got past the relatively easy digging. A second-hand air compressor ran the drills. There was a rough road to Black Duck by the end of 1934. A couple of antique trucks. Beyond that, they were on their own.

They walked to Black Duck in their ordinary clothes, in whatever workwear they could find at home—being fishermen, they probably would have had rubber boots, sou'westers, whatever rain gear they'd used in boats. There wasn't a lot of choice. The company offered nothing but the opportunity to work. No frills like safety boots, hard hats, eye or ear protection. Most of the men working in those rough-and-ready early days would not have known such things existed.

When they were working near the surface, in 1933 and 1934, the wind would help to dissipate the dust and grit. They could see what they were doing, at least on day shift. But as the mine went deeper down, the workplace grew progressively darker and more confined, and the dust and blasting smoke became a problem that, for the first time, made a young man think about his health.[8]

Working in the woods or on the sea, you were constantly aware of danger, but it wouldn't have occurred to a sailor, fisherman or woodsman that he could get seriously and permanently sick just from being in the workplace. But this dust was overwhelming. The men tried covering their faces with cheesecloth to keep it out of their nostrils and their mouths. But exhalation carries moisture and the moisture captured dust, so within minutes, the cheesecloth would be clogged, the equipment operator gasping.

The drills were slung from the shoulder in such a way that the operator's face was unavoidably close to the drill hole in the rock. There was no way to avoid the dust. And there was no way that the miners could know what damage it would do. There was no hospital or clinic, no nurse or doctor, anywhere near St. Lawrence.

Sanitation at Black Duck was primitive. There were two privies on the surface, nothing underground. There was no place to wash. The miners ate where they were working. For drinking water, they'd slurp what seeped through fissures in the rock. In the winters, before the mining moved deep underground, they would huddle in a storage shed with their lunch cans while the wind and snow blew through the walls.

And there were more subtle costs, fundamental changes in lifestyle, the loss of a personal flexibility that once gave them time to plant a little garden, build a house or barn, hunt or fish for food. Time for the camaraderie that develops on the sea, between a father and a son, between brothers, friends and partners, working for each other, working for themselves.

Now they had invested time and sweat in growing a new industry, in work that left them emptied out at the end of a gruelling shift at Black Duck, or eventually, Iron Springs, Blue Beach, Tarefare, Director. It was a physical and ultimately cultural expenditure that would become quantifiable only at a future time, a bitter time when they would fully understand the price they'd unconsciously paid for this new industrial reality.

FINALLY, in 1935, the real mining started at Black Duck—when the shaft reached a depth of about a hundred feet, they began driving a long drift, essentially a tunnel, and large underground caverns called stopes into the belly of the ore body. Early access to the workplace was by ladders.

The Black Duck men were now real miners—but with none of the equipment, the protective gear, the lighting, the modern drills that suppressed dust and were commonplace in other mining operations. A five-horsepower blower helped control the dust, but minimally.

There were other open diggings now—Iron Springs, Blue Beach. There was widespread speculation circulating that there was a new mining venture on the horizon, a real mining company, perhaps, with real capital to spend on a modern operation. But in 1935, it was just speculation. For now, and the foreseeable future, "the cooperation" and Walter Seibert were the only game in town.

Rennie Slaney, writing about his experience at Black Duck years later, was vivid in describing those early days underground: "The further the drifts advanced, the dust and smoke became worse. Men were constantly vomiting. Those conditions were made all the tougher because of lack of suitable equipment with which to do the work. In the first days, since wages depended on production, there was never a thought of quitting. The men considered the mine as their own property."[9]

For Ed Stapleton of Little St. Lawrence, the job at Black Duck would have been an incentive to start a family near a place where he had roots, to avoid the out-migration and the loneliness of distant places that were large and alien. New York. Boston. Montreal. Families are happiest where there are blood and cultural connections. This was how many of the miners saw it. So many hard-rock mines were in the wilderness, where workers lived in rowdy camps. Seibert's mining "empire" was near the communities the men all knew well, where they had family. Hard though the workdays were, each man had a home to go to when the day was done.

Michael Quirke, at the age of twenty-eight, had returned to his hometown, St. Lawrence, for a job at Black Duck after working on a deep-sea diving tender for several years. The contrast between work at sea, in the fresh air, and the conditions he encountered in the mine—and the eventual toll those conditions would take on his health—convinced him early on that he'd do everything he could to create a better future for his son, Peter, who was two years old. He'd make sure of that—Peter would be spared the ordeal of working underground.[10]

It was the dream of many of the St. Lawrence miners—work hard and sacrifice to make a better life for the next generation. But for most of them, it was futile—the destiny of that next generation, including little Peter Quirke and Ed Stapleton's boy, also named Edward, was already being carved in stone.

Pat Tarrant became a miner at Black Duck at the age of thirty. In 1933, he had six kids and another on the way. It was the work that mattered—the hardships he encountered in the workplace were of transient significance, the peculiarity of working for a promise rather than a paycheque was mitigated by the sense of hope that Black Duck offered. A stable livelihood, a future for his kids and their kids. He, like everybody else there, had grown up with a sense of the inevitability of sacrifice. This was just another phase in a long history of hardship. But this time, there seemed to be a real possibility of progress and improvement.

WALTER Seibert had tapped into a tradition that he might not have known about had he not met Aubrey Farrell and learned a bit of local history. His formula for starting up his mining business was not unlike a long-standing practice in the fishing sector.

For Pat Rennie, who had moved to the area from Lord's Cove after his livelihood and four members of his family had been wiped out by the tsunami, it had always been, more or less, like this. It was how the business of the fishery had always functioned. Like it or not, the fisherman was in a cooperative venture with the merchants and the buyers. All the while he lived on credit, some years never seeing cash.

The system worked. But the problem in the fishery was that neither the fisherman nor the merchant ever quite knew what the bottom line was going to look like when the final tally was completed. With this new mining venture, you at least knew what your hours were worth. Fifteen cents an hour was a joke, even in 1933. They all knew that. But $1.20 a day was an improvement over dole—which was just $1.80 a month.

Nobody knew for sure when they'd actually see the money they were now theoretically earning. It would not have crossed their minds that compensation would be less straightforward than they'd been promised—that as always was the case, their wages would depend on distant market factors and the priorities of distant strangers.

23.

A UBREY Farrell was only twenty-six years old when he met Walter Seibert for the first time. It was mostly out of courtesy and at the urging of his younger brother, Howard, that he agreed to meet the New Yorker at all. But they hit it off. They were about the same age. The Farrells, Aubrey and Howard, who still lived at home with their siblings and their widowed mother, enjoyed the company of interesting strangers, and they gladly housed and entertained the Seibert party when Walter came to town in the summer of 1931.[11]

Aubrey's father, Aloysius Farrell, who had died seven years earlier, had been interested in the mineral potential of the area.

He'd loved wandering the barrens and prospecting, at which he became an enthusiastic amateur. Aubrey never shared his father's passion for the rocks. But he was quick to recognize a business opportunity. Seibert's plan was, potentially, a lifeline for a struggling community. And he was impressed and intrigued by this likeable young accountant who came straight from the heartland of sophistication and high finance, Manhattan.

For the first year of their relationship, Aubrey had no reason to doubt his instincts about the deal and about the man. But now, three years into what the townsfolk had been calling the cooperation, Farrell was beginning to have misgivings. He had delivered an able-bodied willing workforce, as he had promised. He cringed, at times, when he saw how hard the men had to work, the primitive conditions they had to work in. He was already hearing stories about men with breathing problems. The equipment they were using was appalling. He was only too familiar with their poverty.

The remuneration was ridiculous. It was as if the Americans had never heard of cash. And they seemed to have forgotten that the original arrangement—to withhold wages until the Seibert company was earning money—was supposed to be temporary. By 1935, the Farrells' business, a general store, was having an awkward time financially itself, largely because of Walter Seibert's cavalier approach to paying bills.

Aubrey Farrell and other merchants in St. Lawrence were depending on the patience of their suppliers to maintain their inventories; their bankers seemed to understand that the St. Lawrence merchants required a little extra flexibility because of Seibert's management of money, a juggling act that was showing little sign of ending. Bankers are not famous for patience with potential deadbeats, or elasticity in their accounting. But knowing what was at stake in St. Lawrence, bankers in Burin and suppliers in St. John's seemed to have been exhibiting a surprising tolerance. Even customs officers became cooperative, waving through an essential item (or covering the duty from their own pockets) when Smith or Poynter pleaded temporary poverty.[12]

Donald Poynter, instructed by Louis Etchegary, with whom by then he had a warm friendship, would sometimes have to smuggle crucial items—equipment, explosives—from St. Pierre, and sometimes he'd bring products that weren't quite so essential to the job but were vital for the quality of life (alcohol, cigarettes, cigars and chocolate). It was widely suspected locally that Father Thorne, another ally, would lend Donald Poynter his clerical garb to wear on smuggling runs—presuming, accurately, that a conspicuous priest on board a boat would deflect the curiosity of customs cutters.

Seibert's seemingly perpetual financial crunch meant paydays often had to be postponed when Walter decided that some other monetary obligation was more important than a miner's wages or compensation to a local merchant.

Aubrey Farrell had concluded, even before the end of 1934, that being Walter Seibert's business partner was grating on his nerves. It was challenging enough to keep a small family business afloat during the Depression—especially with the collapse of Newfoundland's staple industry, the fishery—without also having to worry about Walter and his fiduciary eccentricities.

There could be no more excuses for the missed paydays, the rubber cheques, the exasperated bankers in Burin. Walter, after all, was an accountant by profession. He knew what he was doing.

A MINER's paycheque, once normal paydays started, typically came to $7.20 a week. But the company would pay only $5.00, the balance being withheld as "back time."[13] Nobody, including Aubrey, was sure what this was all about, but it was a problem for the miner because, by payday, he'd have run up a bill at Aubrey's store for most of what he'd earned. Being arbitrarily docked about 30 percent of his wages made a problem for both him and Aubrey.

The cheques were supposed to be certified but never were, and the merchant knew from past experience with Walter that more often than not, the corporation (most locals had ceased calling it the cooperation) had insufficient funds to cover them. Aubrey honoured the corporation paper anyway. When a miner showed up at the store on payday with a dodgy corporation pay-cheque, Farrell would accept it at face value, even knowing that he might have to wait months before the cheques would clear the bank. At least the miner and his family could eat. And if there was a balance owing to the miner, Aubrey would issue him an IOU that the store would subsequently take back as cash.

By late 1935, St. Lawrence was virtually an economic sub-system in Newfoundland with a peculiar unofficial currency—IOUs, sometimes handwritten on scraps of wrapping paper. Aubrey Farrell was fed up with it, and he informed Seibert bluntly that, thenceforth, their relationship would have to be along the lines of accepted business practice.

Both Poynter and Doc Smith would have been aware of Aubrey Farrell's frustration, and would no doubt have sympa-thized. They had their own complaints—Smith wasn't getting paid at all, and Poynter had learned that he couldn't rely on Seibert to pay him when he was supposed to or to deliver on raises that he had promised.

By mid-1935, there were rumours circulating that both bosses were about to leave. Smith was running out of patience with Seibert's shoestring operation, but Poynter's situation was more personal. His wife, Urla, had returned to the United States late in 1934 to give birth. And in December, she and Donald had become parents of a little girl they named Barbara.

But mother and child weren't long back in St. Lawrence when it became apparent that Urla wasn't well. She had persistent headaches and they'd been getting worse. Tuberculosis was epidemic throughout Newfoundland, but she showed none of the familiar symptoms.[14]

The headaches became more severe. At times, her mind seemed to wander. There were signs of meningitis, perhaps a rare variety caused by tuberculosis. By early summer in 1935, Poynter was coming under pressure from Urla's family back in New Jersey to bring or send her home for proper medical attention.

The family's concerns were understandable, given that there were no medical facilities at all in St. Lawrence. There was a small hospital in Grand Bank, more than fifty miles away on a bad road. But the fate of someone living in St. Lawrence, suffering from injury or illness, was dependent on his or her own physical resources and the healing skills of neighbours.

After living among the Newfoundlanders for more than a year and half, Donald Poynter would have known enough about the island's political and economic circumstances not to expect improvement in the quality of life at any time in the near future. In July 1935, he had to make a hard choice between career and family.

24.

~~~

ST. LAWRENCE, NEWFOUNDLAND
TUESDAY, JULY 23, 1935

AUBREY Farrell, in a state of apprehension and relief, watched the visitors climb into Father Thorne's black sedan and head off up the hill towards the Lawn road that sunny summer morning.

The priest had the only car in the parish, and he had generously volunteered to drive the elderly couple as far as Lamaline. He wanted them to see the south coast communities that had been devastated by the tidal wave of 1929—an event they were obviously unaware of.

It had been a brief visit, an evening and overnight, but Sir John Hope Simpson, the commissioner of natural resources in the new administration, was interested in the Black Duck mining project. He'd actually insisted on seeing the place and being briefed on progress. It was a clear summer evening. He'd seemed unusually well informed. He'd mentioned Seibert. Spoke knowledgeably about the challenges. To read between the lines, he was unimpressed by the American. He was noncommittal on the mine itself.[15]

Did Aubrey know, as he watched them go, that it was Sir John's sixty-seventh birthday? Probably. Sir John's chatty wife, Lady Mary Jane, also known as Quita, would have let that slip in the context of describing her husband's commitment to his task in Newfoundland, and the amazing vigour he displayed in what had turned out to be a physically demanding schedule on their south coast tour.

She might have explained that very early on the previous day, they had started out in Marystown and driven across the peninsula to the community of Garnish—only about twelve miles away, but it took an hour to get there. They had been terribly impressed with Garnish, the people proud and apparently self-sufficient. No dole in Garnish. Ladies in hats with parasols. Garnish looked "so Somerset," Sir John had noted.[16] If Aubrey were sensitive, he'd have taken the high praise for Garnish as evidence of a less-than-positive impression of St. Lawrence. But no matter.

After Garnish they went on to Burin, where they seem to have participated in a brief but significant meeting that would soon result in establishing a little hospital there. Not good news for

St. Lawrence. With a nascent mining industry, the town needed doctors and nurses and, ideally, a hospital facility. But there was already a small hospital in Grand Bank, and now that the commissioners were approving a hospital for Burin, St. Lawrence wasn't going to be on their agenda for improved health care any time in the near future.

In Burin, the commissioner and Lady Quita had boarded the SS *Malakoff* for the voyage to St. Lawrence. It was significant that even after a busy day and a late arrival, Sir John seemed eager to visit the Black Duck project. That was more important than parasols and hats. Sir John was probably the most influential of all six commissioners now controlling the lives and destinies of Newfoundlanders. He seemed to be aware that Black Duck needed the support of government.

The pit was already so deep you couldn't see the bottom, and Sir John had commented on the rickety arrangement of ladders and platforms that vanished in the gloom. This was how the men got to and from the workplace? It looked dangerous. He was reassured that it wasn't, that the men were happy with the climb up and down.

Overall the project looked untidy, improvised. Ditches and dirt piles; shacks for storage; equipment that seemed worn out, although the place was new—all the signs of a struggling operation. But it wasn't necessarily a bad thing for Sir John to see the place in such a helter-skelter state. It was evidence of need but also of initiative, the hard work going into making the mine a success, the kind of resolute commitment that Englishmen admired and, hopefully, rewarded.

Surely he would see the worthiness and know the significance of this mining venture in a country that was desperate for new economic growth, in a rocky place with vast untapped mineral resources. Sir John seemed to know what fluorspar was used for— that it was a staple in production of steel, aluminum, chemicals and ceramics—and that was definitely something in their favour.

The car was hardly out of sight—on its way to Lamaline for another busy day there and up the bay in Fortune and Grand Bank—when the sky darkened. Late that day, the Hope Simpsons would rejoin the *Malakoff* and, they hoped, head for Port aux Basques. Sir John was looking forward to a leisurely voyage and some salmon fishing on the way—a small concession to the traditional felicity of a birthday, even if it was a reminder of advancing age.

But Aubrey would have recognized the beginning of a change in weather. It had been gloriously warm and calm and sunny for the past ten days. Now the clouds were gathering. He could feel the breeze, the subtle coolness that always warned of rain. A sudden gust of wind foretold a rough evening on the water. The *Malakoff* would not be going far that night, or maybe even the next day.

Sir John's sixty-seventh birthday would be memorable for discomfort, if nothing else. It took two and a half bone-rattling hours to cover the twenty-seven miles to Lamaline. It was another day of dreary meetings and tiresome tours, modest public buildings, mediocre public people, dilapidated public works—all needing public money.

By early afternoon, the rain was lashing down in horizontal sheets. Definitely not a day when he would or could have toured Black Duck, even if he'd wanted to. And clearly not a day for salmon fishing. Thank the good Lord that Sir John's visit had fallen on the Monday, when the weather was salubrious, and not on his birthday, when it wasn't. At least St. Lawrence had lucked out with the weather.

The sudden change in weather on that day, on the other hand, might later have been interpreted as symbolic of larger changes in the wind, of black metaphors—storm clouds gathering on the horizon, an approaching stretch of turbulence.

~~~

IT MIGHT have been a bit depressing for Aubrey Farrell and Doc Smith, who presumably had led the little party on the tour of Black Duck mine on that July evening in 1935, if they'd known more about the inner workings of Sir John Hope Simpson's mind.

Smith and Farrell had probably hoped that Sir John's brief visit to St. Lawrence would provide an important boost for the local project where it mattered most—in St. John's—and that the commissioner for natural resources would become an advocate for fluorspar development. But if they had been privy to the commissioner's frank opinions, which, by the time he was back in the capital, he was already shaping into a lengthy memorandum, they might have found a lot that, while they would agree with most of it, left them deeply disappointed.[17]

Before he visited St. Lawrence, Sir John had been fully briefed, in writing, by Doc Smith about Black Duck and other fluorspar mining prospects around the town. He had available to him the advice of a couple of first-rate geologists, one of them a bright young Newfoundlander named Claude K. Howse. And on top of all that, he had actually met face to face with Walter Seibert, talked to him at length and sized him up.

Sir John seemed to have been much impressed by Seibert's man, Doc Smith, for his professional commitment and expertise, not to mention his principled decision to work without a salary. Young Howse was knowledgeable and unafraid to speak his mind. The commissioner admired that. Walter was another matter altogether. The commissioner of natural resources wasn't quite so taken with Seibert. And this fact, while not explicit, would be a lingering challenge for St. Lawrence.

MONTHS before he visited St. Lawrence, Sir John had what he called "a long interview" with Walter Seibert. By the end of that meeting, the commissioner was convinced that Seibert was flying by the seat of his pants and, because of his fecklessness, was actually jeopardizing a potentially valuable resource.

He calculated that, properly run, St. Lawrence fluorspar mines could pump $200,000 a year into the Newfoundland economy. Seibert needed money badly—at least $150,000 to modernize his mining operation. The commissioner agreed with the estimated need for new capital. He even thought it could come from funds available in Britain. But he was less than confident that Walter could be trusted to make proper use of it.

By mid-November, Sir John had put his observations and his misgivings on paper for his fellow commissioners. Seibert was developing the resource "spasmodically," he declared. There was every reason to believe that he was ruining a potentially important opportunity. "He has no capital; indeed, he has been so hard put to it for money that his late manager, Dr. Warren Smith, worked for him for two years without salary on the off-chance of the mine being developed sufficiently in that period to afford him an adequate share of the profits."

But worse than this was "the inadequate and irregular payment of the miners." Sir John wrote, "Mr. Seibert employs men as he can afford it; perhaps it would be more accurate to say that the men undertake to work on the off-chance of their money being paid after the fluorspar which they mine has been sold by Mr. Seibert."

The situation was "not only unsatisfactory but unfortunate" because a potentially lucrative resource was being wasted. The solution, he thought, was to find another operator, or failing that, to come up with an arrangement in which the government would properly capitalize the operation and then take control away from Seibert for at least ten years.

It was particularly important to make this mining venture work. It was a rare example of potential in an otherwise bleak economic and social landscape. Newfoundland, in the absence of major new economic development, was, as Sir John Hope Simpson came to see things during his two-year sojourn in Newfoundland, a lost cause. "Taking the island as a whole," he wrote shortly before he returned to England in 1936, "it is fair to say that there is a low standard of education, a low standard of living, a low standard of housing, inadequate social life, a low standard of fishing and a low standard of agriculture."[18]

Beyond the walls of the Newfoundland Hotel, it seemed, there were no high standards anywhere.

The mining industry could, with proper stewardship, become vital to the long-term prospects of the island, Sir John insisted. But his specific proposals for taking more direct control of Black Duck—borrowing enough money from the British government to turn the shoestring operation into a modern and productive mining venture—seem to have gone nowhere. There is no evidence that either the commissioners governing Newfoundland or their political masters in London even read them.

OMINOUSLY, in 1935, even before Sir John's visit to Black Duck, the operation had been in the midst of a dramatic shift in leadership. Smith ceased to be the corporation mine manager in St. Lawrence. Before the year was out, he would be in charge of exploration for a group of new investors who were in the process of starting up a different mining venture. Donald Poynter had, as of mid-July, returned to the United States with his ailing wife. It was apparent to everyone who knew the gravity of his family situation that he'd not be coming back any time soon, if at all.

Seibert had recruited a new manager, an Irish American mining engineer named Cornelius Kellcher. Where Smith and Poynter had established cordial relationships in the town and on the job, Kelleher seemed to have, from day one, antagonized almost everyone who worked for him.

For the most part he was seen as a loner, a heavy drinker with a mean streak that he might have attributed to the fact that he'd been injured as a six-year-old in Ireland and had spent the next seven years in and out of hospitals. The injury left him with a permanent limp. His father died when he was just fifteen, shortly after the family had immigrated to New York. He found work in an office on Wall Street, where he met a wealthy businessman with mining interests in the west. With the help of this patron, Kelleher became a mining engineer with a degree from Columbia University. He had a promising career, but by the time he got to Newfoundland, it would appear the promise had dissolved in disappointment, which he couldn't help projecting on the people working for him.[19]

His personality and a confrontational approach to management would have a long-term impact on the Black Duck project. He would, in the three years and three months he ran the mining operations in St. Lawrence, effectively eliminate the last vestiges of "the cooperation."

THE problems in St. Lawrence had been building for a while. Besides the irregularity of paydays and the unreliability of paycheques that invariably stalled when presented at the bank, by late 1936 there was a new consciousness of the perils in the workplace. On October 24, 1936, Ed Stapleton of Little St. Lawrence—one of the early hopeful recruits to Black Duck—was killed in an underground explosion. He was thirty-two years old. His widow, Evelina, was twenty-one. Their little boy, Edward Jr., was two.

The Stapleton fatality—which was the first mining death for St. Lawrence—convinced Claude Howse, the government geologist, that Black Duck, now that it was underground, had become exponentially more dangerous. One year earlier, Howse had assured Sir John Hope Simpson that the mine was safe.

Since then, he'd lost his confidence in how the place was being managed.

EVEN if it had been nothing more than a charade, the concept of cooperation had for a while motivated and sustained an extraordinary achievement—the creation of an industry from sweat and sacrifice by labour with very little capital. Kelleher would put an end to the cooperative spirit that had made the effort possible. Whatever cautious goodwill Seibert, Smith and Poynter had fostered in 1932 and 1933, Kelleher totally exhausted it.

Urla Poynter's illness couldn't have happened at a worse time for the mining project. The people of St. Lawrence had welcomed the young Americans in September 1933. They seemed eager to become part of the community. The two Methodists had even bonded with the priest, and it was remarked that Mrs. Poynter had been seen on evening visitations to the parish church with Mrs. Giovannini, and that she, like Mrs. Giovannini, would light candles and sometimes kneel in prayer. The community even celebrated with them when they had a child. And then, suddenly, they were gone. It was awkward timing. The affable Doc Smith had been replaced by an ill-tempered bully. The deeper Black Duck went for ore, the more dangerous and difficult the mine became.

Either Seibert had no money or he had money he was unwilling to invest to mitigate the dangers and the difficulties in the workplace. Kelleher, who had become mainly an enforcer for the absentee owner, didn't seem to care.

Donald Poynter would eventually come back to Newfoundland to face an atmosphere of rancour that would inevitably bloom into bitter confrontation.

Urla Crammond Poynter would never see the place again.

FIVE

~~~~~~

Revolt

25.

CLAUDE Howse should have been in an optimistic, upbeat frame of mind when he arrived in town that morning. It was the beginning of summer. He was thirty years old. He had his masters in geology from Dalhousie University in Halifax. He was well regarded by influential people at Princeton University, where he might yet begin studies for a doctorate. But for now, he had a great new job—assistant government geologist for Newfoundland. He was in St. Lawrence for discussions with the principals behind a promising new mining operation in the area.

He was visiting a place he knew well. He'd been born in Burin. He'd lived in a number of small communities around the island, including Tilt Cove, site of Newfoundland's first major mining operation. He felt at home here on the Burin Peninsula, where he knew the people, understood the geology, was excited by the potential for mining.[1]

His father was a clergyman from whom he'd inherited a set of strong moral scruples and a capacity for outrage when confronted by unfairness. Before this day was done, his optimism would be sorely tested and his sense of outrage mobilized.

Claude Howse was familiar with the Seibert mining operation. He'd been a trusted adviser to the first commissioner of natural resources, Sir John Hope Simpson. He had the ear of Sir John's successor, another Englishman with little knowledge of Newfoundland and even less of the mining business.[2] His job was to help these important strangers, and that gave him a great deal of influence—or so he might have thought.

He'd always been candid in his assessments—Seibert was running a dodgy operation, sustained only by the willingness of local men to put up with conditions that would have been intolerable had they not been desperate for work of any kind. Seibert would have been chased out of Buchans or Bell Island or, when it had been operating, Tilt Cove—anywhere with any history in mining or any depth of expertise in how a mine should operate, how miners should be treated. But the people of St. Lawrence had given him the benefit of all their doubts—reasonable doubt having been suppressed by the urgency of need.

Claude Howse, like most people in St. Lawrence, was a realist. Until Seibert came along, the people who were now his miners had been idle fishermen. The timing couldn't have been worse for them—the fishery was flat, Seibert was too young to have the right connections for proper financing and, in any case, capital markets were chaotic.

There would be growing pains. Hiccups. There would be tension from time to time.

Looking on the bright side, which Claude Howse was temperamentally inclined to do, Seibert's representatives in St. Lawrence, Donald Poynter and Doc Smith, were reasonable and competent and had kept the job on track. Black Duck mine was still a mess, but there, and everywhere, you could see the potential for improvement. Iron Springs would benefit from what the managers and miners had learned in the early struggles at Black Duck. The fluorspar beneath St. Lawrence and its surrounding barren lands seemed limitless. If there was a cloud on the horizon, it was in the form and face of the Irish-born

American manager who had replaced Doc Smith in the operation, Cornelius Kelleher.

Kelleher had been on the job for more than a year, and Howse had become familiar with his style and personality. Kelleher had a severe limp, and Howse respected that he had overcome some daunting challenges to become a mining engineer.

Obviously, he knew the mining business. But there were apparent personal flaws that deeply troubled the young government geologist. Howse had no tolerance for alcohol abuse, and Kelleher was clearly a heavy drinker—even while on the job. People in town quietly referred to him as a drunk. People who worked for him thought he was a bully, quick to discipline and dismiss, always ready to remind a worker with a grievance, no matter how legitimate, that there was no shortage of people willing to replace him.[3]

Howse was hardly on the ground that morning when he realized that there was something seriously wrong.

He asked around.

The miners at Black Duck, who hadn't seen a paycheque for a month, had just walked off the job. June 1 was supposed to be another payday, but the miners had been informed that morning by Seibert's proxy, Kelleher, that they'd have to wait at least two more weeks for their money.

This was serious. Howse had known for a long time that Seibert seemed to consider wages an option to be exercised only when he had spare cash. It was well known that he paid his workers below the going rates for miners elsewhere on the island. It was scandalous that he routinely missed paydays, and that his cheques usually bounced or were held up at the bank for weeks at a time.

Howse decided on the spot to change his plan, which had been to meet with the people who were about to start a new mining operation in the area. Instead, he'd try to get to the bottom of what he now saw as a crisis at the Seibert project.[4] He spoke to many of the striking miners. He met with local merchants. He dropped in on Father Thorne. And he had a heart to heart with the mine manager, Cornelius Kelleher.

Kelleher was defensive. The miners, he told Howse, were being stirred up by the merchants. "But for the agitation of the merchants there would be no trouble with the men," Howse wrote, paraphrasing Kelleher's analysis.[5]

But even if they were troublemakers, the merchants had a valid point. "He [Kelleher] admits that cheques are issued before there is money in the bank to cover them. He believes that the men have no reason for complaint as their only alternative is the dole and they are better off working for the company than living on dole."

The merchants were indeed complaining about "what is to them an unjust charge on their accounts" because of the weird bookkeeping practices of Walter Seibert, who was, after all, an accountant and should have known better. He should have realized that sooner or later, his cavalier approach to paying bills would blow up in his face.

The men had grumbled many times before, even downed tools once or twice because of paydays without pay. This time, although they were disorganized, they were determined to change the intolerable situation. They had the backing of the merchants and the citizens. And perhaps to their surprise, they would find an outspoken advocate in young Claude K. Howse.

He listened to all sides carefully, and when he reported to St. John's on the uprising in St. Lawrence, he was unable—or unwilling—to suppress his anger. "[T]here are people in St. Lawrence today hungry, but with a month's work to their credit with the St. Lawrence Corporation," Howse wrote. "Five years ago, when the operations began, the men were prepared to accept reverses, hoping that conditions would improve. They have tried to help Mr. Seibert and have worked willingly with no prospect of immediate payment. However, conditions are quite as bad now as they were five years ago. The miners are going gradually in debt."[6]

Some of the harshest language in his report was directed at the mine manager, Kelleher—in particular, his boozing on the job: "I have seen the manager go underground only once during my whole series of visits, totalling over three months, and he was then revoltingly drunk.

"I have wondered if we should entrust the lives of our people to a man of such calibre," Howse wrote. Then he added a parenthetical reference to the recent death of young Ed Stapleton in an underground explosion: "There was a fatal accident in the Black Duck mine last fall which should never have happened if the miners had been instructed in decent mining methods."

He described women in church, praying for deliverance from Walter Seibert's hegemony in the local mining business, and for the success of the proposed new mining venture. "I have seen men in tears because they could not feed their families. I have seen a people generally lose hope, people absolutely at the mercy of an absentee owner who has held up the development of an important material resource and has kept a community in the depths of poverty, not because he could not get capital, but because his avarice dictated terms which no capitalist could accept."

Howse pointed out that Seibert had, in the previous five years, turned down "liberal offers" from at least five prospective buyers—any one of whom would have done a better job of managing the resource and the legitimate interests of people working for him.

Seibert, Howse wrote in his long memorandum to the government on June 8, "has taken advantage of the economic condition of the people knowing that they could not get dole while he offered them work, no matter at how small a pittance."

Summing up, he assured his superiors in St. John's that he was not overstating the crisis: "This is not a melodramatic picture of the situation in St. Lawrence. These are cold hard facts which have to be faced. To deal with them is the problem and the duty of the commission of government."

Howse then listed his recommendations: pay should immediately rise to twenty-five cents per hour; miners should be paid regularly and in cash; Kelleher should be removed. "My personal regard for Mr. Kelleher as a man," he wrote in reference to his final recommendation, "cannot affect my opinion that a man with his weakness for alcohol is not fit to have the lives and safety of other men entrusted to him."

Howse urged that it be made bluntly clear to Seibert that the government was on to him, and mightily unhappy. It was a draft ultimatum to Seibert to clean up his act.

If the Howse memorandum of June 8 wasn't enough to persuade his bosses in St. John's that there was a problem brewing in the Seibert operation, the plight of the local merchants and miners was underlined dramatically the next day by a St. Lawrence merchant, L.J. Saint, in a letter to his creditors in the city—a letter that found its way to the desk of the new commissioner of natural resources, Sir Robert Ewbank.

Hungry miners, Saint reported, were being turned down when they applied for dole—technically they had jobs, even if they weren't getting paid—"and then had to mortgage their sheep or cow to get necessary food . . . [T]he people are being treated like a bunch of coolies and have to accept it owing to the depression and nothing else to earn."[7]

EVEN given the times and the normal attitude of deference by politicians and bureaucrats towards businessmen like Walter Seibert, the Howse memorandum might have sparked outrage among responsible people, perhaps a political awakening of sorts.

It didn't, really. The response and subsequent developments

were cautious and slow in coming. It would be three more years before the miners' pay reached twenty-five cents an hour—and then only after they had formed a union.

The commission government drafted a letter to Walter Seibert after the Howse wake-up call. It essentially boiled down to a significantly less passionate summary of the geologist's suggestions—that Seibert pay his miners a living wage on the appointed paydays, that he fire Kelleher and that he find ways to stabilize the company's finances. "I am to warn you," an unidentified secretary to the commission wrote in a draft letter, "that the government is concerned."[8] That pallid warning was about as threatening a tone as the commission government could muster.

Miners should be paid promptly and in cash "on a scale which would enable them to live without public assistance," the letter insisted. The government was concerned that "a valuable natural resource of this country is being exhausted in a manner which is considered wasteful and, in some cases, dangerous to those employed."

The file does not have Seibert's answer. But by the spring of 1938, it was obvious to everyone, including Cornelius Kelleher, that progress—slow and modest, to be sure—could no longer be delayed.

DONALD Poynter's time in the United States would have been frustrating, given what he undoubtedly knew of what was going on back in St. Lawrence. His reason for leaving Newfoundland was mostly personal. His wife's complex illness was unresponsive even to the world-class treatment available to her in New York. She wasn't getting better. He had an infant daughter, a reminder of more blissful times.

Poynter wouldn't have been getting much satisfaction from his work in the States—Seibert apparently kept him busy exploring other possibilities for fluorspar development.[9] But it was a far

cry from the challenge and innovation that had kept him ener-
gized in Newfoundland. And from what he could surmise, there
were serious problems brewing in St. Lawrence.

It should not have come as a surprise when, in 1937, the St.
Lawrence miners hired a lawyer to challenge that undefined "back
time" withheld from their wages. Under legal pressure, Seibert
promptly put a stop to the practice.[10]

Men whom Poynter respected for their forbearance—the
willingness to put up with harsh conditions in the workplace,
low wages, irregularity in paydays—now were growing confrontational. The new boss, Kelleher, clearly lacked the tactfulness of
Doc Smith, who had always seemed to calm them down. Sooner
or later, the consequences would show up in productivity. But
that was Seibert's problem. Poynter had enough to worry about
in his personal affairs.

Then came the uproar in June 1937. Claude Howse was a reasonable man. For him to blow his stack was persuasive evidence
that Kelleher was seriously screwing up. And Donald Poynter
would not have been surprised when, early in 1938, Seibert asked
him to pack his bags and return to Newfoundland. He would be,
at first, the assistant manager. But he could be reasonably confident that before long, he'd be running the whole show.

As of March, he was back living in St. Lawrence, at the
Giovannini boarding house. And one year later, in March 1939,
he was boss.[11]

IT WAS clearly an unexpected blow for Kelleher. A letter he
wrote to Tom Pike in August 1939 displays surprising wistfulness about a place and people who had come to see him as an
unreasonable bully.

Pike, the First World War veteran and former relieving officer, was now working for the corporation and had obviously

become Kelleher's friend—had even named a son Cornelius in 1938. Kelleher makes reference to this in his letter, and to a family in Lawn who also named a little boy Cornelius. And to Pat Tarrant in St. Lawrence, who named his daughter Fluorina when Kelleher, perhaps facetiously, suggested it.

There are also brief references, tinged with unsurprising bitterness, to Poynter, Doc Smith and, predictably, Claude Howse. But Kelleher sends warm greetings to Father Thorne and Adolph Giovannini and the nuns who ran the local school. "Give my regards to the folks there that you think I should like to greet."[12]

He commented on his warm feeling of satisfaction when a crowd gathered on the wharf when he was leaving and cheered lustily as he sailed away. It didn't occur to him that the cheer was, perhaps, from a feeling of relief to see him go.

The situation in the workplace would gradually improve. But the atmosphere of confrontation would never dissipate for long.

26.

B Y 1939, a new company—called ANF, for American Newfoundland Fluorspar—the brainchild of yet another American investor, had started sinking a new shaft for what would turn into a significant addition to the local mining scene. The Director mine would have a major impact on the region during its long and productive lifespan.

From day one, miners for ANF enjoyed working conditions that swiftly became the envy of men in the Seibert mines. They had up-to-date equipment. They wore protection for their skulls and feet. The company made underground rain gear available. The manager was someone everybody knew—Warren "Doc" Smith.

The new mine would set workplace standards, but it was circumstances in the wider world that brought dramatic improvements to the lives of workers in St. Lawrence.

In 1939, with war in Europe looming, the strategic significance of fluorspar was lost on nobody, least of all producers of steel and aluminum. In December 1939, the American proprietor of ANF sold out to the Aluminum Company of Canada, Alcan. The mining operation dropped the word "American" from its name. It would be known, throughout the coming years, as Newfluor, for Newfoundland Fluorspar Company, or just plain Alcan.

The Director mine had started out as an open pit, but by late 1939 it had underground workings from a shaft 150 feet deep.[13] That was only the beginning.

EVEN with the influence of the new mine and the example of how working conditions could and should be upgraded at the Seibert mines, improvements were slow in coming. Finally, in the late summer of 1939, miners from the Seibert and Alcan operations formed a union—the St. Lawrence Miners and Labourers Protective Union. It was, in the beginning, a low-key advocate for change. The first president had never been a miner. He was, in fact, a local businessman.

From the start, the union made reasonable demands in a reasonable tone of voice. Nevertheless, Donald Poynter made his disapproval clear almost from the outset. Maybe it was philosophical. Like so many in his generation, he was leery of labour unions and the potential they presented for conflict, disruption. Perhaps it was from a sense of what was coming.

Poynter would have understood and maybe even sympathized with the miners' motivation. But Seibert was the boss. Despite his early promises that Poynter and Doc Smith would become shareholding partners in the corporation, Walter Seibert was still the sole owner, accountable to no one. The influence of local managers like Poynter was limited.

Poynter's job was to run productive, profitable mines, which from his perspective would be good for everybody. His preference was to work out grievances man to man, to improve the workplace and the wages as circumstances allowed. He believed in firm, reasonable dialogue, one on one. But the balance of power, one on one, was always going to favour the boss. He knew as well as anyone that with Seibert, promises and handshakes were no longer good enough. But Donald Poynter, no matter what his private disposition, was Seibert's man in Newfoundland. He had a job to do.

The creation of the union was a signal, and Poynter got the message: times were changing. But if the company's affairs were now to be determined by an adversarial dynamic—well, he was once a football player. He could butt heads as well as any of the soccer-playing miners of St. Lawrence.

THE union demands were swift in coming. Formal recognition. Bargaining. Better wages, paid promptly, in cash. Health and sanitation. Drinking water was a problem. Years of poverty had left many miners suffering from malnutrition. The ferocious dust was unavoidable. Combined with unsanitary conditions in the workplace, these factors left St. Lawrence miners more vulnerable than others to the scourge that was then sweeping Newfoundland: tuberculosis. And the standard treatment for TB didn't seem to work for St. Lawrence miners. It was worrisome. The men were already complaining of difficulty breathing, loss of appetite, lack of energy. Chronic stomach ailments. Maybe through negotiation between equal parties, there could be a start in addressing these persistent problems.

Presented with specific demands, Poynter stalled and stonewalled. He could truthfully argue that he was making reasonable improvements if and when and as quickly as he could. But the changes weren't coming fast enough to mollify the workers. By April 1940, when negotiations with Seibert's outfit bogged down after months of talk, the corporation's miners replied collectively by walking off the job again.

The commission government in St. John's ordered a magisterial inquiry. There was now a war on. Fluorspar was vital to the war effort. It was critical for the production of aluminum and steel. The union wanted recognition and a contract. Neither should have been difficult. But the company position at the hearings was defensive. Contract or no contract, wages were improving, the workplace was improving.

On sanitation in the workplace, Donald Poynter was unable to resist an offensively sarcastic observation: "When St. Lawrence will take an interest in its own sanitation and drinking water and show evidence of this interest in their own homes, this company will gladly give them the equal in their working conditions."[14]

The remark was deeply insulting, and it wouldn't be the last time that Donald Poynter belittled people who complained about health hazards in the workplace. But his mood in 1940 should, perhaps, be judged in the light of pressures he was under in his private life as well as on the job. His wife, Urla, was by then slowly dying in a sanatorium in Wyckoff, New Jersey, from an illness she had probably contracted in Newfoundland.[15] Poynter was under constant criticism from his family and in-laws. Against their wishes, he'd taken his new bride to what they considered to be a perilous and backward wilderness. Now they were convinced that his recklessness had destroyed his family, and they didn't hesitate to remind him of their earlier misgivings.

Poynter bore his family's complaints in silence. And now he was diminishing the complaints of his employees, who were also his neighbours and, in many cases, friends.

The role of manager or boss in a small company town, where almost everyone is either related or at least acquainted, makes for complex challenges—constant tension between a human need to "fit in" and a political requirement to stand apart. Poynter walked a kind of tightrope in St. Lawrence, and the need for balance would only grow more acute as years went by.

THE magistrate's report, when it finally appeared later that year, was silent on many of the miners' main complaints and, in a startling expression of paternalism, advised them to be friendlier. "To succeed [the union] must be prepared to discard its warlike actions . . . [and] frame its demands in a reasonable and intelligent manner and be prepared to discuss them in friendly co-operation with the Corporation."[16]

If the miners needed a reminder that they were going to have to fight harder for improvements in the workplace—and in their still-precarious lives—this was it. They also might have been aware of a report, released that same year, by an English expert on labour relations, who had been commissioned by the Newfoundland government to assess the growing militancy among the island's workers.

T.K. Liddell was contemptuous of Newfoundland, its people and, particularly, its industrial workers. They were inefficient and undisciplined and "easily led into trouble," he declared. "The majority . . . have yet to learn what trade unionism is . . . its claims, its rights, its duties and its obligations."[17]

The effect of Liddell's bias was implicit in the official government response to the complaints of workers in St. Lawrence in 1940 and long afterwards—which was, for the most part, to ignore them. The noise of war had deafened government to all but the most basic issue bothering the miners: money.

The deafness would linger on, in varying degrees, for another quarter century

IN August 1940, Seibert's corporation finally signed a formal contract with the new union. The miners got less than they'd been looking for. Poynter gave up more than he'd intended. He might have thought that it was the end of acrimony, a return to cordiality and cooperation. He couldn't have been more mistaken.

Mechanization was coming, but it was slow. The obsolete dry "hammers" were still prevalent. The lack of health care in the area—doctors, nurses, hospitals—added to the urgency. With no access to treatment for injury and illness, there had to be a focus on prevention. Health and safety. Quality of life. But these were only concepts, abstract issues. The official attitude seemed to be that future perils are impossible to contemplate in the here and now.

In the St. Lawrence mines, however, where the men spent their days and nights, the here and now was full of concrete warnings about perils that, if ignored, would inevitably lead to pain and worse.

The miners now had some understanding of their potential as a group. But the larger factor giving them new clout would come from dramatic circumstances unfolding in the world around them.

27.

BY 1940, Newfoundland and Britain were at war with Nazi Germany and its allies. Canada was in it. Much of Europe was either on the other side or neutral, occupied by the enemy or about to be reduced to ruins. It was just a matter of time before the United States was drawn in to the affray.

Whether for the fighting overseas or production back at home, ordinary working people now had unprecedented value. Seemingly unlimited employment options were driven by wartime construction projects, including several important military bases that were soon to be established in Newfoundland by the Americans.

Newfoundland fluorspar was vital to the war effort. It was essential for the production of steel, aluminum and chemicals. Mining fluorspar was recognized as the equivalent of military service. In fact, St. Lawrence fluorspar had strategic uses so secret that only a few Newfoundlanders would ever hear about them.

The Americans informed the government of Newfoundland they might need as much as fifty thousand tons of fluorspar a year for the duration of the war, maybe longer. Traditional European suppliers were now out of bounds, and American steel companies turned to Newfoundland. The US government offered loans for modernization and expansion of production. Walter Seibert suddenly was flush with funds to build modern new facilities, to upgrade equipment, to phase out the old "dry" drills responsible for the lethal clouds of dust.

He could even afford to be sympathetic to concerns about health and safety, but he felt those were matters under the control of governments, dictated by laws and regulations. Which was true. But it was also true that Newfoundland had no government, in the normal democratic sense. And practically speaking, there were no laws relevant to the health and safety of miners, no useful regulations. There were only vague, outdated rules and little evidence of the ability or disposition to enforce them.

DONALD Poynter took a break early in 1941 to visit the head office and the family in New Jersey. Seibert was fretting. The once cooperative Newfoundlanders were becoming hostile. But Poynter's primary concern at this point was that his wife, Urla, was on her deathbed.

In his absence, and apparently without his knowledge, there was a quiet coup within the union in St. Lawrence. There had been growing opposition to the leadership of the local president, Patrick Aylward, a non-miner, too easygoing by far and much too polite in his dealings with Poynter. Leading the rebellion was the local's secretary treasurer, Aloysius Turpin—a miner and a carpenter, and in the view of management, a mouthy troublemaker. Aylward, in fact, had urged Poynter to get rid of Turpin. Do us both a favour: fire him. But Poynter had refused, saying there had to be a better reason for dismissing Al Turpin than the fact that he was stirring up his brothers in the union local. That better reason would soon arise.

While Poynter was away that January, in 1941, Turpin led a putsch that ended with the defeat of Patrick Aylward. Al became the new president and promptly dissolved the St. Lawrence Miners and Labourers Protective Union and replaced it with a new one: the St. Lawrence Workers' Protective Union. The name hadn't changed much, but the corporation was about to discover that there had been a dramatic change in attitude and tactics.

The new union formally came into existence on March 15. Two days later, Turpin signalled the beginning of a fractious new dynamic in relations between St. Lawrence miners and their managers.

28.

~~~

St. Lawrence, Newfoundland
Monday, March 17, 1941

ALOYSIUS Turpin must have been in a very good mood pulling on his socks that morning. He was a carpenter by trade. It was a Monday, a workday, but he'd not be showing up today. Instead, he'd don a clean shirt and Sunday trousers. It was St. Patrick's Day.

The feast day of the Irish patron saint was a day of celebration wherever there were Irish men and women. And there were Irishmen and Irishwomen everywhere, especially on St. Patrick's Day, and especially in a place like St. Lawrence, Newfoundland, where even people with names like Etchegary and Giovannini could truthfully claim an Irish heritage.

Invariably, March 17 fell in the middle of Lent. It was, traditionally, like Mardi Gras—a time to go a little wild, to leaven the long, grim period of sacrifice and penitence. It was therapeutic and it was tradition. But St. Patrick's Day was not a public holiday. It wasn't even a holy day of obligation in the liturgical calendar of the Roman Catholic Church. At best, in St. Lawrence, it had once been a "church day."

By tacit agreement, in the old days, the people, the Irish and the almost-Irish, treated St. Patrick's Day as if it were a Sunday. They didn't work because they weren't obliged to. As fishermen, they were essentially self-employed. So they took the day off and attended Mass. And then they let their hair down.

This changed when the mining started. Tradition be damned. March 17 was another workday—unless, of course, it fell on a Sunday. Which it didn't in 1941. And so, by the power vested in Al Turpin as president of the new St. Lawrence Workers' Protective Union, an old tradition was about to be restored. St. Patrick's Day was about to *become* a holiday again.

He was sure that over the weekend, the membership had all agreed. They would begin the day, as called for by tradition, in church. He looked out a window to check the weather. It was clear and chilly. There had been a fall of snow over the weekend, and across the harbour, near the corporation offices, he could see men . . . shovelling.[18]

Shovelling? Yes. Men shovelling snow. Union men . . . *working*.

Surely an oversight. But maybe not. Poynter must have got to them. Al Turpin donned boots and coat and headed out for

Mrs. Giovannini's boarding house, where Poynter lived. Mr. Poynter wasn't there. He must be at the office.

The men were shovelling the snow not far from Aubrey Farrell's store, on the St. Lawrence harbourfront. The corporation offices were below the store. Al stopped to talk to them. Hadn't everybody agreed to take the day off? Well, yes, but it seemed that everyone had suffered a memory lapse. The mill was working. The men at Iron Springs were underground. Same at the Director and Blue Beach and Black Duck. Nobody could explain. Maybe it was a relapse into the soggy thinking of the early days, when they imagined they were part of a cooperative venture rather than pawns in a classic case of capitalistic exploitation.

So were they union men or pussycats? Hadn't they agreed that it was time to exercise collective muscle to get improvements in their pay, health and safety, holidays? The men sheepishly put their shovels on their shoulders. And resolutely followed Al towards the refining mill, which was in the general direction of Iron Springs.

DONALD Poynter might have had a premonition on that chaotic morning, St. Patrick's Day 1941, that something fundamental had changed in labour–management relationships in St. Lawrence while he'd been dealing with his problems back in the States. He must have seen it coming. Maybe that's why he was hard to find that morning.

He'd returned to St. Lawrence in March 1938, as Seibert's troubleshooter, aware that much had changed in his absence of almost three years. Morale was worse than he could have imagined. The place was struggling. Productivity was sclerotic, and he had to admit that a large part of that problem was technological. It would not have helped that the men who had to use the obsolete equipment were feeling bullied, underpaid and generally exploited.

The second-hand equipment Walter Seibert started with in 1933 was worn out in 1938. The physical conditions in which miners worked were beginning to make people sick. Men were passing out underground because of bad ventilation. The dust and blasting smoke were worse than ever. Iron Springs mine had turned into a replay of Black Duck. Miners were missing time because of stomach ailments that were linked to pollution, which was a result of primitive or zero sanitation.

Nowhere in the workplace were there basic facilities to take a shit or piss, and the men were drinking the water as they found it, where they found it. Underground, water was never in short supply. But clean, drinkable water was another matter. You didn't have to be a scientist to connect the dots.

These were the immediate challenges Poynter saw before him, and soon after he became the boss, he started fixing them. But anyone familiar with political theory might have told him that it's when material circumstances are improving that the social order is most vulnerable to instability—including revolution.

THERE could be no turning back the St. Patrick's Day rebellion. The union men were on the march and word was spreading fast. People on the east side of town could see them cresting the horizon on their way to Iron Springs.[19] They didn't even have to slow down at the mill. Workers and truck drivers were all heading out to join them even before they got there. For mid-March, the walk over fields and marshland was surprisingly easy. The snow was hard as concrete, the ground beneath still frozen. It was a perfect day for a revolt.

Al Turpin might have suspected but could not have known that Poynter was already on the phone, alerting Iron Springs about the protesters' imminent arrival, warning the supervisor there not to let the men who were working underground know what was happening on the surface. The warning came too late. Fred Walsh was already in the cage, heading down the shaft at Iron Springs to spread the word.

Walsh was among the first to feel sufficiently alarmed about the dust at Iron Springs to make an issue of it.[20] Working as a driller there, he would complain of long nights spent coughing for up to eight hours at a stretch, and he might even have suspected he was marked for an early death because of what was keeping him awake. He was only thirty-two, already feeling old.

Fred got word to the men below, and as Turpin's little army passed the headframe at Iron Springs, the miners were already straggling out to join their union brothers. What a day it was. On to the Director.

THE people of St. Lawrence had a history of solid, stolid patience in the face of hardship. As a fishing community for generations, they were familiar with the perils of an unforgiving workplace, the unpredictability of institutions and authorities whose imperatives and whims controlled the way they lived, how well they lived. And they had the recent memory of November 1929 to remind them just how limited was the attention span of governments in times of difficulty.

They'd been manipulated and exploited by outsiders since the area was first "discovered" by stranded English sailors in 1583. The ability to endure hardship without complaint was a mark of fortitude and a source of pride. For the previous ten years, the American accountant Walter Seibert had been building on this admirable virtue.

St. Patrick's Day 1941 would mark a dramatic turning point in their history. The walkout that day was four years in the making. The impact would reverberate much longer.

Doc Smith, now the manager at the Director mine, would certainly have seen them coming. Even if he didn't see them, it's hard to believe that someone—Donald Poynter, maybe—didn't call to give him a heads-up. But when Al Turpin tramped into the Newfluor office that morning, Smith was calmly waiting, a study in unsuspecting nonchalance. What was going on?

Al Turpin was momentarily confused. No way Doc didn't know what was going down, but Al explained the situation anyway. It was tradition. St. Patrick's Day. A time for prayer and celebration.

Doc Smith was listening, nodding sympathetically.

Well, Turpin, why didn't you tell me sooner? he asked. He seemed genuine. Had he known, he'd have given his people the day off—with pay. And he promptly instructed a supervisor to go below and release the men.[21]

And then, with the Director crew in tow, it was off to Number Three Shaft at Blue Beach, another corporation mine, where they found the men already streaming out to join the march. And then it was Black Duck.

All mining operations in the area were now idle—miners, mill workers, labourers, truck drivers all assembled on the shore at Herring Cove, where they lit a bonfire. Al had brought along old files, documents creating the union local he had just dissolved. The men cheered as he tossed the papers on the bonfire.

It was the beginning of a new era.

On March 18, the Director mine was back in operation. It was a different scene at the corporation mines, however. When the workers showed up two days after their St. Patrick's celebration, Poynter sent them home again, suspended without pay for three more days.

He then fired Aloysius Turpin.

29.

W HEN it came to confrontation, Al Turpin was fearless—with one exception: Father Augustine Thorne, the unofficial governor of St. Lawrence.

The disintegration of the harmonious, if less than productive, relationship between the union and the corporation since Al Turpin rose to power was troubling to the parish priest. St. Lawrence was a small town, a tight community. The last thing the people needed was a civil war.

The priest knew enough about Seibert's style to understand that the friction wasn't all Turpin's fault. Father Thorne was sick and tired of Seibert and his high-handed manner, especially regarding money. But for the most part, he'd been on friendly terms with Donald Poynter since the American had first arrived in town in September 1933.

Thorne was intimate with the human undercurrents causing unprecedented tensions in his town. Turpin was volatile, crude in many ways and inarticulate. He was the sort of individual Seibert would look down his nose at. Poynter was a realist. He was an American, an outsider, but he seemed to have a deeper understanding of the place than people who had been there for generations. He had been around long enough not to make the mistake of underestimating Aloysius Turpin.

Al Turpin had guts and he had a just cause: the well-being of his people. A parish priest could relate to that, even if he didn't sympathize with Turpin's tactics. Father Thorne could easily have given the union man the benefit of the doubt. And he'd also have understood Poynter's apparent intransigence as due, at least in part, to personal challenges—the dying wife, the domineering distant boss.

St. Patrick's Day had almost been entertaining. But it was a troubling indication that the miners had exhausted their reserves of patience with the Seibert "empire"—and specifically, with Walter Seibert. The priest was probably aware that the impromptu St. Patrick's Day parade was only the opening skirmish in what, by summer, would be war.

April 7, there would be a walkout for the dubious reason that someone from Lawn was given work that Turpin thought should have gone to someone from St. Lawrence. June 5, another walkout, this time over wages. Continual bickering.

It seemed as though every time the priest looked out his window, there were clusters of men milling around the union office. Parishioners were quietly complaining about the tensions in the town. The Farrells, who were close to Poynter, were confiding in the parish priest about the manager's frustrations.

It was no secret that Father Thorne had a pipeline to the corporation—his cousin was married to Aubrey Farrell's brother Howard, who was working for Poynter as a senior supervisor. Louis Etchegary was also on the Poynter team, another boss. His late wife's brother, Rennie Slaney, was a shift boss at Iron Springs. And there was persistent gossip in the town about Poynter and Florence Etchegary, Louis's lovely daughter. There was something going on there. Nobody knew exactly what, but she and Don were spending a lot of time together. And the Giovanninis, too, now had family working under Poynter. Even Aubrey Farrell was on the Seibert payroll.

Father Thorne could almost sympathize with Turpin and what he was up against. In a few short years, Poynter had managed to make strong connections with almost everyone who mattered in St. Lawrence. Tangling with Donald Poynter was taking on a lot of influential people.

~~~

THE friction and frequent work stoppages had reached a point where Walter Seibert felt obliged to come to town in early July 1941. He and Poynter were refusing to recognize the new union. On July 8, he telephoned Turpin and asked if he'd drop by the corporation office for a chat.[22]

Al said no. If Seibert wanted a conversation, he could come by the union office. Take a number. Al Turpin was a busy guy. It was like that. Kind of juvenile. Of course Father Thorne heard about it. He would hear about everything that mattered.

Two days after he'd arrived in town, Seibert met with the miners somewhere in between the two offices. There was some progress and there would be a bit more money in the pay packet afterwards. But still no recognition or prospect of a contract.

The overriding issue now became a union demand that the government in St. John's send in a third-party panel made up of independent outsiders to look into all the issues that were getting in the way of long-term peace and productivity in St. Lawrence. It was a reasonable request, but Seibert scuttled the proposal. The commissioners in St. John's, it seemed, were taking their instructions from New York.

Then someone in St. John's came up with the idea that Seibert might go along with an inquiry if Father Thorne could serve as chairman. But before Thorne had a chance to make up his mind, Al Turpin vetoed that idea. Shot it down in flames. Basically, he didn't trust the priest. And given all the priest's local entanglements, who could blame him?

In a rare gesture of conciliation, Poynter suggested that he and Turpin get together and try to agree on terms of reference that might lead to the creation of the outside mediation panel that the union wanted. Turpin seemed okay with that, until Poynter suggested that Father Thorne should sit in on their discussion, presumably to help. Turpin once again refused to approve the priest's involvement.

Word, of course, got back to the priest.

Then Turpin's mouth got the better of his brain. He met Howard Farrell on the street one day, and in a flash, years of festering animosity between Turpin and the Farrells spilled out in a tirade that included some ill-advised slanders against the parish priest, who was Howard Farrell's relative by marriage.

Father Thorne was obviously fuming when he heard, which he inevitably did. He was ready for a reckoning, and it wasn't long in coming.

The corporation workers had just staged one of their frequent work stoppages that summer. Thorne summoned Al Turpin to the rectory. There was no formal record of the encounter. Neither party would be eager for the townsfolk to hear precisely, or even anecdotally, what went on. There would have been an irresistible temptation to magnify the episode into drama—or worse, amusement, which would have caused a loss of face for both belligerents.

Al's eventual account was cryptic. Years later, at a time when he was obviously still feeling the sting of the priest's fury, he'd acknowledge only that "he [Father Thorne] gave me particular hell." And he apparently also gave Al particular instructions: to shut his mouth henceforth, and by the way, get the men back to work. Immediately.

"He was mad about it. So, I went around the harbour . . . and told the men, for Christssake, git back to work, boys. So, they went back to work."[23]

It was just a temporary lull. By mid–October, after yet another refusal by the government in St. John's to send in an independent panel to sort out the conflict, Turpin pulled his men out on strike again. And this time, there would be no backing down. God herself could intervene, but Al Turpin was dug in. Poynter dug in. The governing commissioners in St John's dug in.

Then Turpin raised the stakes. Ever since St. Patrick's Day, the Seibert mines had been plagued by work stoppages. But the Newfluor mine had continued working. Now Turpin pulled the Alcan miners out in sympathy with the corporation men.

The Dosco steel plant in Cape Breton, which depended entirely on St. Lawrence for its fluorspar, was already hurting and complaining to Ottawa. Ottawa had, for some time, been complaining to St. John's. Presumably, the US State Department was now complaining too. Alcan Aluminum was complaining to everybody. And with production of aluminum and steel imperilled in the middle of a war, everyone was listening. Finally.

30.

ON August 10, 1941, while Donald Poynter, Father Thorne and Al Turpin were playing mind games in St. Lawrence, two of the most powerful politicians on the planet were a hundred miles away discussing how, together, they could save the world. It was that kind of a summer in Newfoundland.

From an American perspective, the island was no longer at the edge of nowhere, but in the middle of the North Atlantic war zone and about to become a major base of military operations for the United States and Canada—a development that would create an economic boom in Newfoundland. The strategic value of the location was one of the reasons it had been approved by the US president, Franklin Roosevelt, for his summit meeting with the prime minister of the United Kingdom, Sir Winston Churchill.[24] It was also logistically convenient—approximately halfway between Washington and London. By August 10, the talks were under way, security and privacy assured by a flotilla of twenty-four American and British military ships.

Roosevelt had fond memories of Newfoundland and salmon fishing there in his younger days. He thought highly
of the place and the Newfoundlanders he'd met.[25] Churchill
might have had a different impression. For at least ten years,
Newfoundland had been a fiscal nuisance for the British government, the Dominions Office practically managing the place,
picking up the tab for interest on shocking debt and wasteful
social programs like the dole.

Beyond that, Churchill, according to those who knew him,
seemed to have a soft spot for the island and "always favoured
generosity" when dealing with the Newfoundlanders.[26] The
local hospitality during his visit in August 1941 could only have
enhanced his feelings for the place. A casual reference to fresh salmon over lunch with the Newfoundland governor, Sir Humphrey
Walwyn, swiftly yielded six fifteen-pound salmon packed in ice
and delivered the next day to Churchill from St. John's by private
railway car.[27]

The two world leaders spent four days moored just up the
shore from the town of Argentia, where construction had begun
on a major American naval air station. Their ideas, fanned by
summer breezes on Placentia Bay, became what history would
call the Atlantic Charter and would inform the creation of the
United Nations in 1945.

The island, in addition to location, had strategically important mineral resources: iron ore, copper, fluorspar—another factor
in the pressures being felt in St. John's and St. Lawrence to find
solutions for the grievances the miners there were raising with
their bosses. The mines in St. Lawrence were of particular strategic importance to Washington.

Whether or not fluorspar was specifically discussed during that
meeting on Placentia Bay, it was just two months later that the
leaders signed an agreement to cooperate on a highly secret scientific project: the production of a bomb that would potentially

have unprecedented destructive power. Newfoundland would make a vitally important contribution to the project: fluorspar of extraordinary quality. St. Lawrence fluorspar helped make the enterprise that history would remember as the Manhattan Project a frightening reality.

For explosive power, the atomic bomb would require uranium-235, which makes up less than 1 percent of natural uranium. St. Lawrence fluorspar became essential to the refining process that would provide U-235 in sufficient quantities to produce the bombs that would effectively end the Second World War—by devastating Hiroshima and Nagasaki in August 1945, immediately killing 120,000 people and dooming tens of thousands more to a slow death from radiation exposure.

Despite the carnage, the end of the war was good news for the winners, and amid the victory celebrations there was, in Washington in the spring of 1946, a small social gathering of scientists and government officials who had played central roles in developing the atomic bomb. One of the invitees was Claude Howse, by then Newfoundland's chief geologist.

Howse knew the Americans had a strategic interest in fluorspar and were, through Walter Seibert, diverting tons of it for special military purposes. Exactly what purposes, he didn't know. And then he received an unexpected invitation to that private luncheon in Washington.

The get-together was unpublicized and, at least in Canada and Newfoundland, remained unknown other than to a tiny circle of insiders until Howse, near the end of his career, produced a modest family history. The book has never been published and is basically a family tree and a dry account of his career trajectory—but for one intriguing reference to that quiet lunchtime gathering in Washington.

"I remember the catfish and the veal cutlets," Howse remarked. Then he wrote:

After the meal, the host, Assistant Secretary [for defense production] Mr. Lautenberg, the man who had invited me, gave a nice speech, thanking us one and all for our efforts, which had combined to make a most vital and necessary contribution to the victory of the United States and its allies.

Then, with a smile on his face, he told us something that had been known to the half of the group I hadn't recognized, but not known to the other half, of which I was one.

From the beginning of the fluorspar operation we had been told, as a matter of top secrecy, that the fluorspar was being used in the processing of high octane gasoline. He apologised for hoodwinking us in the interests of the war effort and then explained that the fluorspar had been the critical chemical in the separation of the U235 isotope from the predominant U238 in uranium ores.

Fluorspar had made possible the processing of uranium hexafluoride, and from this the deadly U235 used in the atomic bomb was extracted.[28]

It was, and is, no secret that Walter Seibert had a special relationship with Washington, and that his mining enterprise enjoyed its most lucrative years because of sales to the US government. It is also possible that he was involved in a second assignment related to the Manhattan Project. In the summer of 1942, he dispatched a team of Newfoundland miners to a remote section of Labrador, in the Torngat Mountains, to dig up and ship high-grade graphite to a secret American destination. It was at a time when scientists involved with developing the atomic bomb were having difficulty finding graphite of sufficient quality for the production of plutonium, which was potentially, like U-235, a weapons-grade explosive. U-235 and plutonium were the lethal elements in the bombs that destroyed Hiroshima and Nagasaki in August 1945.

Gus Etchegary, then a teenager in St. Lawrence, was part of the Seibert expedition to Labrador. He clearly remembered the four-month adventure in the wilderness and recalled that even at the time, he was aware of being a small cog in a much larger set of wheels. Later, he became convinced that the Labrador graphite was bound for a laboratory in Oak Ridge, Tennessee, where engineers and scientists were building one of the world's first nuclear reactors, a crucial part of the Manhattan Project.

WITHIN a few months of the Roosevelt–Churchill summit on Placentia Bay, America would be propelled into the war by the bombing of Pearl Harbor, and Newfoundland would become a vital base for American military operations in the North Atlantic and Europe. The little country would soon be a temporary home for ten thousand US servicemen.

One of the happy consequences of turning all those Americans loose in Newfoundland was a much-needed boost for the economy, which would hopefully reduce dependence on the mother country. A secondary, but more enduring, consequence of the American invasion was an unprecedented focus on what was perhaps the most pressing problem on the island at the time—the health of Newfoundlanders. The Americans' strategic interest in Newfoundland would lead to an assessment of the health risks their soldiers and sailors faced in the remote and isolated place.

Of course, they were concerned, as always, with venereal disease. (It would turn out that Newfoundlanders had more to worry about than the Americans—syphilis and other sexually transmitted diseases would spike *after* the Americans arrived.) But the Americans would discover a more surprising problem: the mortality rate for tuberculosis in Newfoundland was nearly 200 per 100,000 population, which was significantly higher than that in "any other portion of the British Empire inhabited by white people," according to a US report from the time. "The mortality rate compares with a rate of 70 in England, Scotland and Wales, and a rate of approximately 40 in the white population of the United States."[29]

On top of VD and tuberculosis, the Americans were also worried about the perils of diphtheria, dysentery, meningitis, scarlet fever and typhoid fever. And they were especially shocked by the poverty of health care—the scarcity of doctors and hospitals. These were just some of the issues "considered of actual or potential importance in the maintenance of health of armed forces in Newfoundland."

They sent their soldiers anyway, and most managed to survive the hostile germs and viruses. Some stayed and assimilated. Many went back home again to begin families with brides from Newfoundland.

But the presence of the Americans, by providing a major boost to the economy, would in turn empower working people who had, for generations, accepted hardship and danger as normal in a perilous and often brief existence. And that, in turn, would inflame demands for an end to medieval social circumstances— especially a crushing vulnerability to disease, especially in the town of St. Lawrence.

31.

THE government in St. John's, in late November 1941, finally announced the inquiry the St. Lawrence union had been demanding for about six months. There would be hearings by a three-member trade dispute board to investigate and find solutions for the labour troubles in St. Lawrence.

Workers at both the Seibert mines and the Alcan operation had been on strike since mid-November to enforce demands for outside mediation. Everyone was back at work by December 5. The panel—made up of an academic, a businessman and a retired bureaucrat—scheduled hearings to begin in January 1942.

For the miners, money was a major issue, and the board members would listen sympathetically. But the hearings also gave the workers in St. Lawrence a rare opportunity to talk about problems that, in the ten years since Walter Seibert set up shop in Newfoundland, had become more troubling than the paltry wages they were paid.

The workplace was making people sick. Turpin and individual miners complained about the dust and flooding in the corporation mines. The broken-down equipment. The lack of sanitation. And above all, the absence of health care—doctors, nurses, hospital facilities.

While the board members supported wage increases for the miners, they were deaf, or at least indifferent, to most other issues. In their final report, the commissioners declared themselves "genuinely impressed by what the Corporation has been able to achieve in a few short years."[30] They found the manager, Donald Poynter, admirably flexible, professional.

Echoing the observations of the English labour expert T.K. Liddell, the board members rejected a union demand for a closed shop, claiming that leadership seemed to have little control over an unruly and largely unprofessional workforce. The miners were, nevertheless, being underpaid, they acknowledged, and this should be corrected right away. The panel members were assured by Donald Poynter that past delays in payment were part of the growing pains associated with a new mining venture starting out in unusual circumstances.

On issues of health and safety, the commissioners were unmoved even when Fred Walsh, the driller from Iron Springs, described the dust in vivid terms, along with his sleepless nights, struggling to get his breath. His brother Alonzo, another driller, also spoke of working in the choking dust and smoke from blasting. Donald Poynter, when asked about the dust, wouldn't disagree: "He would not say [it was] innocuous, but claimed [he] had no knowledge of any ill effects."[31]

The St. Lawrence union brief complained that the absence of medical services near a workplace where conditions were routinely and officially described as "primitive" was inexcusable. Nobody—miners, managers or panel members—disagreed. But the panel was unwilling or unable to suggest a practical solution, other than to lobby health officials in St. John's.

The union had made one specific—and ultimately critical—request: that the company and the government arrange for regular x-rays for the miners. The board was again noncommittal. "We are not competent to pronounce as to the necessity for such an examination but we desire to place the union's wishes on record, as they were expressed very strongly."

A time would come when chest x-rays were a terrifying part of a frequent diagnostic routine. But that was far off in the future.

THE hearings in 1942—a grudging response to the union agitation that began on St. Patrick's Day 1941—were followed by years of relative harmony in labour–management relations and improvements in technology and productivity. But concerns about the "secondary" issues—health, safety and quality of life—would continue to be talking points for years to come. They would become priorities only after what, years later, was described officially as a "ghastly" consequence of at first indifference and then denial.

During the coming decade, doctors and nurses would arrive periodically in St. Lawrence, stay briefly and then leave. The hospital everyone agreed was a priority was also in the distant future. And when it finally arrived, more than a decade later, it was only after years of stonewalling by bureaucrats and politicians in St. John's.

That there would one day be a hospital at all was a response by American politicians to acts of heroism by the men and women of St. Lawrence.

The impetus and the money for a hospital would come not from Newfoundland or Canada, but from the government in Washington, at the insistence of the US Congress.

Conversations with the Dead II

v.

It floats in the memory without a specific time reference. My father being home for a while and using the time to wire the house for electricity.

Miners are multi-skilled. Jacks of all trades. They are plumbers because air and water are delivered underground through pipes. A lot of the mine machinery is air-driven. The water flows through drills to suppress the dust, at least a little bit. And because the underground environment is always changing, pipes are always being moved.

Of course, you learned about explosives, how to achieve a particular kinetic outcome in a wall of rock by drilling holes and stuffing them with dynamite.

You learned about electricity. Machinery of all kinds. Electric motors. Gasoline-driven pumps. Diesel-driven air compressors. You had to learn how to respond when one of these machines broke down.

There were, obviously, electricians and mechanics in the mine, but there wasn't always time to wait for them to come and solve a problem. Especially if it was a little problem.

You learned the basic principles of mechanics, engineering, geology and science.

My father was comfortable in all aspects of those occupations, even though he had no formal education. Not a single day in a school of any kind, other than what he loved referring to as the school of hard knocks.

I remember him crawling around the attic in our Cape Breton house with elementary tools and a lantern for light. Hammer, pliers, screw-driver, wire cutter, auger. Doing the wiring so all that was left for the professionals was the outside hookup.

The point of the memory is that the wiring project obliged me to stick my head up into the attic while he was there to find out what was going on. I remember being told to leave before I got in the way or smothered, but before I did, I noted that there were interesting boxes and old suitcases up there, along with other fascinating artifacts.

And when the coast was clear, I ventured up with a flashlight to explore the mysteries in the boxes.

There were embarrassing letters back and forth between my parents. One of the boxes yielded a document that shocked me at the time: a small blue card with my name printed on it and a heavy bold-faced stamp that screamed "Landed Immigrant." Huh?

Later, my mother, who was a teacher, assured me that I was not adopted, and not a DP. Neither a displaced nor misplaced person. I was not a foreigner in the literal sense, though I was, in fact, born in a foreign country. Newfoundland.

I had assumed that Newfoundland was always a part of Canada.

—No, she told me. Not before 1949, which was when Newfoundlanders joined Confederation.

—And what was it before that?

—Well, for many years it was a colony of Britain. And then it became a dominion, a sort of independent country with ties to the British Commonwealth. But that all failed for complicated and controversial reasons. And for another spell, it was like a colony again, ruled by unelected big shots.

So that's why I was technically an immigrant. I was born there but moved to Canada while Newfoundland was still a responsibility of Britain. But when it became part of Canada, in 1949, I became as Canadian as everybody else.

I recall a feeling of disappointment, of having lost the brief cachet of being, somehow, exotic and mysterious. That I had somehow lost a *desirable identity. A feeling that was and still is, in many quarters, not uncommon throughout Newfoundland.*

vi.

~~~

</div>

—*Summer 1942. You saw St. Lawrence for the first time. Arrived on a boat. What was the boat?*

    —*It was called the* Home.

    —*And maybe only about ten months later, you arrived for the second time. Same boat, but with someone else.*

    —*Yes. You. Coming from the Burin Cottage Hospital.*

    —*What was my first impression of the place?*

    —*A high, round knobby hill on the left. Cape Chapeau Rouge. Shingle Point jutting out. Houses clustered around the harbour. Big church on the right, on the hillside. It was early June. Nice weather. The week before, your father and Jack MacIsaac had walked all the way to Burin on the old Corbin Road, just to look at you.*

    —*That would have been a long walk. It was a happy time of your lives, I think.*

    —*I suppose so.*

    —*Lots of friends. Socializing. You were. Fond of. Each . . . other?*

    —*When you're young, everything is possible. Happy? Maybe.*

    —*I got that impression from the sappy letters you wrote to each other any time you were apart.*

    —*You shouldn't . . .*

    —*How long did it last?*

    —*What?*

    —*The happy.*

    —*Who knows? Who knows about the happy? Ever.*

<div align="center">

~~~

—*I used to think that I existed because of an earthquake. Part of the fallout from 1929. The tsunami. Hardship exacerbated by the collapse of the fishery. Walter Seibert gets his mining industry thanks to local desperation. The mining industry eventually brings in outside workers. Your boyfriend from back home is one of them. He's impressed by the place. Sees potential for a family. Marries you and starts one.*

—*And you don't think that now?*

—*It was exciting to think that the cause of my existence was so dramatic. Earthquake and tsunami, et cetera. But maybe it was more mundane than that. A government report. A trade dispute investigation. Boring politics.*

—*Not sure that I know about that.*

—*There was an inquiry in 1942 because of serious labour problems in St. Lawrence. Miners all riled up. Among the less talked about observations of the trade dispute settlement was that maybe St. Lawrence needed miners with outside experience. So the inquiry people said perhaps it was time to send some of the local miners away to work with more experienced people. Or to bring in some experienced outsiders. That's how we got there. Your future husband came, looked around, said to himself, Hey, this is a big improvement over where I've been before . . . in the wilderness. Here there's a town. Families. Church. Schools. A fellow could have a life here.*

—*And?*

—*And that was where he decided to start a family.*

—*I guess that was it, essentially. Poynter promised to build a house for us, out by the Iron Springs mine. It took quite a while, but he eventually came through.*

—*And you remember Poynter?*

—*Of course.*

—*And what was Poynter like?*

—*Smart. Blunt. Sarcastic. Loved to socialize. Dinners. He'd have what he'd call cocktail parties. Just drinks, basically, celebrating little things. Even small improvements. He had a lot of enthusiasm.*

—*Sarcastic?*

—*He gave me a Christmas gift one year. A box of fancy hankies. Next time I saw him, I thanked him. Said I hadn't expected a Christmas gift, but thanks anyway. So Poynter says, Don't mention it. The handkerchiefs will save your sleeve. He was quick like that.*

—*Did it bother you that there was no hospital in St. Lawrence?*

—*That was normal for us. Where we came from, in Cape Breton, hospitals were few and far between. But there was no doctor there. That was a problem.*

—*But there were lots of midwives.*

—*Yes. There was a midwife for your sister. But there was lots of sickness on the go.*

—*Is that the reason we moved away eventually?*

—*Part of it.*

—*What about the miners' sickness?*

—*That came later.*

SIX

The Rescue

32.

THE men of the day shift were killing time around the head-frame at Iron Springs, lingering over cigarettes, complaining about the weather and the day ahead. It was Ash Wednesday morning, the first day of Lent, the start of six bleak weeks of self-denial—the booze, the sweets and the music—all luxury suppressed in the cause of spiritual improvement. Nothing but prayer and penitence and aggravation. A grim day all around.

There had been a terrific storm all night, with high winds and heavy drifting snow. The snow had stopped and the winds had fallen off, but the men could tell that it was just a lull in what was going to be a stormy day, a good day to be underground.

They were in no great hurry to enter the open cage—to be lowered down the shaft to the drifts, stopes, raises, piles of broken rock drilled and blasted by the night shift. The mine was waiting to be mucked out, to start the cycle once again. Muck. Drill. Blast. Repeat.

So let it wait a few more minutes.

The holdup was the daily consultation between Louis Etchegary, the mill manager, and Rennie Slaney, senior supervisor underground that day.[1] The atmosphere was relaxed. Poynter was away in the States. His wife was dying, it was said. Or had already died—Donald Poynter wasn't much for personal disclosures. But everybody knew about this burden, this private tragedy. She was a very nice lady, Mrs. Poynter, in the time she was around, living in the Giovannini boarding house. A shame she had to go away. But there was no doctor in St. Lawrence. No hospital. To get seriously sick or injured here is probably to die here. Poynter didn't have much choice but to take her home to New Jersey, where she might have had a fighting chance.

Maybe someday there would be such a blessing in St. Lawrence. A hospital. There was agitation for it. And there was sympathy. Just the month before, in January, the members of the dispute panel sent in by the government in St. John's all agreed. It was shocking: no clinic, no doctor in a mining town.

However, all sympathy aside, *there was a war on*—the response to everything, it seemed. Buckle down. Suck it up. Sacrifice for a greater cause. Men and women overseas, risking lives for liberty. Folks at home should count their blessings. Et cetera.

There was a high arctic wind picking up again. The snow was drifting. The darkness was withdrawing. Mike Turpin was the first to see the apparition in the milky morning light.

A stranger, coming out of nowhere.

HIS name was Edward Bergeron. He was an American sailor. He was eighteen years old. He was wet, exhausted, freezing. He forced his body to keep moving.

From a distance he had seen the twinkle, a faint glimmer often lost behind the veils of snow drifting on the lifeless landscape. It might have been a star, this tiny evanescent flicker, but for Bergeron it was a beacon, a sign of hope for him and several hundred of his shipmates, now stranded on the rocky southern coast of Newfoundland.[2]

And then, the light appeared to be on top of an unfamiliar structure. Tall, skeletal, roughly A-shaped. It was like a star atop a Christmas tree. And below it, potentially the gift of life. Industrial buildings and, through open doorways, the shapes of people. And more small twinkling lights. And then, men staring at him. Hands paused in mid-air, cigarettes and conversations momentarily suspended.

He might have known that they were miners. Perhaps not. He was barely out of boyhood. Maybe he'd seen pictures, but it didn't matter who or what they were. They personified survival.

The miners, dressed for underground in hard hats, oil pants and jackets, headlamps dangling casually around their necks, gathered around him. He was barely coherent. His clothes were frozen and he reeked of diesel fuel. He was, they quickly figured out, from a US Navy vessel that was hard aground and breaking up nearby. The Americans needed help. The situation was desperate.

His ship was a naval destroyer, the USS *Truxtun*, named after the founder of the navy—and a name that would, for all future time, be intimately tied to St. Lawrence and her people. The *Truxtun* had a crew of 156 sailors, and many were already dead even before Bergeron had clawed his way ashore and up a hundred feet of an icy embankment in a place that was almost inaccessible—Chamber Cove, a mile to the west of the mine site.

In Donald Poynter's absence, Howard Farrell was acting manager. Louis Etchegary got him on the phone, explained the situation, told him he and Rennie Slaney had decided the mine should immediately suspend production for the day. Farrell agreed. There was more important work to do in Chamber Cove.

Farrell then called Doc Smith at the Director mine. In an instant, Smith had ordered all the men working underground to report to the surface.

IN recent months, there had been improvements at Iron Springs, and one of the new facilities at the workplace was a "dry," a kind of locker room where miners changed into their invariably filthy work clothes before heading underground, or out of them before heading for their homes. There was also a new "mess house" or lunchroom, and this too became a rescue centre and a place of triage.

Runners were dispatched to town to bring back men from the night shift and every woman available for what was soon to be a desperate situation at the mine. Loretta Walsh, Julia Skinner, Theresa Saint, Ethel Giovannini, Doris Turpin—all dropped whatever they were doing and were among the first to head for Iron Springs.[3]

Lillian Loder's husband, Leo, a miner, was already on his way to Chamber Cove when she decided she just had to be at Iron Springs with the other women. She was needed. She was seven months pregnant with her fifth child, but she set out anyway, on foot.[4]

Nobody at the mine or in the town—not Lillian or Howard Farrell or even Edward Bergeron—could have known the extent of the challenges facing the people of St. Lawrence on that day. Just about a mile west of Chamber Cove, at Lawn Point, a larger US Navy vessel, a supply ship, was aground and it, too, was breaking up. On board the USS *Pollux* were 233 men and tons of military hardware, including bombs.

A crew of miners began assembling what they were sure they'd need for the still-unimaginable task ahead of them. They knew Chamber Cove, with its towering cliffs, reaching nearly three hundred feet at Pinnacle Point, and they knew that they'd need rope. Lots of it. Kevin Pike, who was only eleven years old but working as an office boy, was assigned by his father, Tom Pike, the warehouse manager, to drag out every bit of rope that he could find and get it ready to be shipped to Iron Springs.[5]

Mike Turpin, Celestine Edwards, Tom Beck and Fred Walsh, with young Bergeron leading the way, headed off towards the cove immediately. Rennie Slaney and Robert Turpin were close behind.

Slaney would never forget a young sailor staggering towards them through the snow in bare feet. When Turpin removed his own socks to give to him, the sailor protested that "his buddies on the ship would need them worse before the day was gone." It could not have occurred to the Newfoundlanders in those early moments that the arrival of these strangers from another country would fuse the issues foremost in their lives—war, industrial production, health, safety and survival.

ED Bergeron had been among the first dozen sailors from the *Truxtun* to make it to the shore, a tiny strand of gravel beach at the foot of daunting cliffs.

The vertical black walls were unapproachable. But there was one section to the east that was lower. You could see the top. Bergeron and another sailor, Edward Petterson, volunteered to attempt the climb after noticing what seemed to be a fence above them. Perhaps there was a farm nearby.

Using knives to carve notches in the ice on the steep slope, they inched upwards, but when they finally reached the top, they found only a small shack nestled in a gully. They rested there. Petterson was exhausted. Bergeron felt fit enough to follow the fenceline to see where it would lead him. After what seemed like an endless struggle through the snow, he saw the light flickering atop the Iron Springs headframe.

Back at the cove, there were by then nearly thirty men on the shore, but more than a hundred of his shipmates still clung to the crippled warship. The land was so close, and yet the wind and the crashing waves and the fuel oil now floating on the sea made it seem a world away.

Fireman Ed McInerney, now stranded on the narrow beach,

might have wondered if he was really better off than the men still back on board the *Truxtun*, bucking on the waves as the shattered warship slowly filled with water, pounded on the rocks. Behind him, the towering pinnacle, the black walls of the impossible cliffs.

Along the shore, to where Chief Fireman Petterson had started climbing with their shipmate, young Seaman Bergeron, seemed an impossible distance to cover, and yet his only hope for survival. Already, the hands and feet that he would need for getting through this awful day were almost without feeling. He forced himself to move.

Onboard the ship, Ensign James Seamans, twenty-three, from Salem, Massachusetts, and his fellow officers were attempting to untangle the lifeline that had enabled the first group of sailors to get off safely. They'd already watched helplessly, when the lifeline failed, as young shipmates, desperately attempting to swim the short distance to land, had either drowned in the sludge of sea water and heavy fuel oil or been hurled against the rocks by the rising wind and waves.

And now the lifeline was disabled, the wind howling once again and shifting south and west, to more directly pound the ship. Now it was every man for himself.

THE wind was at gale force by the time Turpin, Edwards, Beck and Walsh arrived at Chamber Cove near mid-morning. The sailors who were still aboard the *Truxtun*, their numbers now conspicuously diminished, were being battered. The ship was obviously breaking up. Her stern was nearly gone. The miners calculated there were about a hundred men clinging to rails on the side of the listing, thrashing ship. Others were flailing in the water, which was now almost impossible to swim through.

Bergeron and Petterson had dragged a long rope to the top of the cliff. Turpin found it. Walsh, Beck and Edwards quickly rappelled down and into the pounding surf to begin dragging men, dead and alive, onto the narrow beach.

The manager at Alcan's Director mine, Doc Smith, had by then joined the rescuers and would, four days later, describe the scene that they'd encountered at the *Truxtun*: "The aft end sunk immediately and the forward end was awash. A hundred men were clinging to the greasy overturned hulk, but they had no lifeline around them and the seas were breaking over the ship in heavy solid waves. This group of clinging doomed men was the most awful spectacle of that day of tragedy."[6]

Eventually, Smith wrote, "a huge wave breaking across washed half the men away in one surge . . . toward the Pinnacle cliffs. Almost none of those swimming men reached safety and no help for them from the shore was possible . . . By one o'clock only a dozen men were alive on the hulk and almost none of the men in the water had any life left, though workers [from the mine] were still bringing them to the cliffs."

Gus Etchegary, who was then nineteen, arrived at the scene with his older brother, Theo, and his father, Louis. Soon they, too, were on the beach, Louis and Theo wading out towards the struggling sailors. Louis instructed Gus to stay ashore, stay dry and light a fire. A sailor from the *Truxtun* helped him. His name was William Butterworth and he was in a desperate condition. Gus forced him to his feet, made him walk around the fire. Keep moving. But it was all too late for the young American, who slipped away as Gus implored him to hang on.[7]

A young signalman, Clifford Parkerson, refused to leave the beach as long as he could communicate, using flags, with the men still on board the *Truxtun*. Even after the signals from on board the ship had stopped, Parkerson refused to leave. He walked in circles around the fire until he collapsed and started shaking violently.

Gus Etchegary and the others attempted to revive him, but he died after uttering a single word: "Mother."[8]

~~~~

ENSIGN Seamans saw the fire. He hesitated. He had watched many of his shipmates vanish as they struggled through the sludge of heavy oil and sea water. And then he was among them—a wave crashing over the ship snatched him from the rail he'd been desperately clinging to. Now he had no choice—swim or sink.

Sick from swallowing oil-fouled water, desperately tired, hopelessly disoriented, he swam slowly, deliberately, trying to preserve his strength. Then he was picked up by another surge and could suddenly feel his feet touch bottom—but almost simultaneously, the relentless pull of the undertow dragged him back. And then, miraculous, unexpected help—strong hands grasping, one of the St. Lawrence rescuers had him, held him, hauled him up onto the little gravel beach, where others wrapped rope around him and yet others, unseen, far above him, began to hoist him upwards.[9]

THE miners from St. Lawrence were now hauling nearly helpless survivors up from the shore on ropes; if a sailor was too weak to help himself, his rescuer would strap the man to his back for the painful journey to the top. The miners would carry the rescued sailors to the abandoned shack, first discovered by Bergeron and Petterson, to be revived, and then load them onto horse-drawn sleds for a rough ride through the snow to the triage station at the mine.

Ensign James Otis Seamans, a Harvard graduate just a few months out of the US Naval Academy, was one of only three of the *Truxtun*'s eleven officers who would survive that day. There were persistent rumours afterwards that the senior officer on board, Lieutenant Commander Ralph Hickox, shot himself when he realized that his ship was lost.[10]

~~~~

THE women of St. Lawrence were waiting for the rescued sailors, cleaning and clothing and restoring the injured and the frozen with soup and tea and coffee before they could be transferred to town and hot baths and beds warmed by heated stones in the homes of the same people who had saved them from the sea.

The entire town became an extended rescue station, and one of the survivors, an African American named Lanier Phillips, from Georgia—who said that he had never before in his life experienced an act of kindness from a white person—would later declare that the generosity of the people in St. Lawrence permanently transformed his feelings for mankind and for himself. "We are creatures of what we're taught and the people of St. Lawrence, Newfoundland, taught me that I was a human being," he later told an interviewer.[11]

Mid-afternoon, the St. Lawrence men lowered a dory down to the shore from Pinnacle Point. Five rescuers went down with the dory, and after a struggle to save the last twelve sailors clinging to the *Truxtun*, they managed to get only two of them ashore before their own boat was smashed to pieces against the rocks. These were the last two survivors of the *Truxtun* crew, and it took two hours to get them and their five rescuers up the cliffs to safety.

Of the 156 seamen on board the *Truxtun*, only 46 survived.

LIONEL Saint, one of the first of the rescuers at Chamber Cove, had seen what seemed to be a heavy oil slick coming from the west. He realized it couldn't have been from the *Truxtun*—its leaking fuel was moving east away from the wreck, towards the shore. He guessed that there must be another wreck, and that it wasn't far away. His guessing was more prescient than he realized.

The *Truxtun* had been one of two destroyers escorting the supply ship USS *Pollux* from Maine to the new American naval base in Argentia, Newfoundland. All three ships had run aground along a two-mile stretch of reef-studded coastline between the communities of Lawn and St. Lawrence because of a navigation error and the storm. The second destroyer, the USS *Wilkes*, had jettisoned fuel and, after hours of manoeuvring, had freed herself with minor damage to her hull. She was now lurking near the *Pollux*, but unable to get close enough to help.

Lionel Saint pursued his hunch by walking west along the cliffs, and it was near noon when he came across a group of survivors from the *Pollux* at Lawn Point, just above where their ship was wedged between two massive rocks. The *Pollux* broke in two at midships just before noon, and even from the clifftops, it was clear that there was pandemonium on board.

Fearing that the ship was going to sink, about sixty sailors leapt into the sea. Almost all were instantly lost.

One of the men in the small group of sailors that Lionel Saint had encountered at the top of the cliff, William Derosa, was near death. The options available to the other men were grim—stay and die alongside Derosa or try to make it to Iron Springs.

As Lionel Saint and the Americans were making their life-and-death decision, word had just reached the community of Lawn, a few miles to the west, that there was a ship in trouble on the shore. It was a nearly impossible journey, but eight men from Lawn decided they had no choice but to make the effort.

BY the time the Lawn men reached the *Pollux*, more than a hundred sailors had come ashore, thanks to a lifeline and one surviving lifeboat. Officers on the USS *Wilkes*, which was still hovering nearby, could now see people moving at the base of the cliffs and, according to a detailed record kept by a crewman, decided there was nothing to be achieved by waiting there. They left for Argentia at 3:40 that afternoon.

They had no idea what they were leaving behind.

One of the *Pollux* crewmen, Henry Strauss, would later describe what he had been certain were the final moments of his life, standing on a slippery ledge just above the thrashing sea, at the bottom of an almost vertical precipice: "The tide was coming in. Guys started getting picked off one by one." It was late afternoon and the sun was going down rapidly. "All of a sudden, out of the blackness, we heard a voice saying, 'Is anybody there?' The next thing I knew these guys were being hauled up the cliff."[12]

The rescuers from Lawn had arrived and set to work. By eight that evening, they'd been joined by another crew from St. Lawrence and by navy personnel from Argentia, who had arrived in St. Lawrence by floatplane that afternoon.

The rescue of the sailors and the struggle to keep them from dying of shock and exposure would last all night. Near midnight, the last man came up the rope—the *Pollux* captain, Commander Hugh W. Turney.

THE scene at Iron Springs mine, as the survivors from the *Truxtun* and the *Pollux* arrived throughout the day and all that night, was vividly described in Doc Smith's unpublished account of the rescue operation. He praised the local women for bringing half-dead sailors back to life. "Many were in bad shape from frostbite; all were famished; all were soaking wet and smeared with filthy crude oil," he wrote. "Soup was heated and coffee was made by the bucketfuls. Blankets were found both from the ships and from the homes in St. Lawrence and all private homes were stripped of clothing. Hot water brought the frost from the men's feet but with painful results."[13]

A total of 203 American sailors perished in the course of that long and bitter day. But 186 survived, by the strength of their own stamina, an inexhaustible will to live—and the heroic generosity of strangers.

33.

THE surviving sailors would be gone from St. Lawrence by the next night, Thursday, February 19, but they'd not soon forget the place, nor would they be forgotten. A crisis generates a peculiar human chemistry, and it was clearly active at Iron Springs and in the town on that day in 1942. In just a few hours, bonds were formed to last a lifetime. Ensign Seamans and the Loder family; Ed McInerney and the Tobins; Lanier Phillips and everybody in the place.

Lillian Loder met James Seamans at the mine site and was appalled at his condition. She helped stabilize him and then had him transported to her home, where she nursed him through the night. She was convinced that he'd never live to see another dawn. But he did. And when it was time to deliver him to the ship that would remove him and the other survivors to a hospital in Argentia, Lillian argued with the navy medics: the sailor wasn't fit to leave her house. They insisted and placed him on a stretcher. Lillian Loder, seven months pregnant, put her coat and boots back on and walked beside the stretcher as they carried Seamans to the dock.

McInerney's feet were frozen, and Theresa and Robert Tobin spent the night reviving him, dealing with the excruciating pain as his body thawed. When he could move, they loaded him into a huge washtub to let him soak away the chills and aches and pains. Then they put him in a warm bed vacated by their children. He would leave the next day, but in those few hours, McInerney had become a member of the Tobin clan.[14]

Lanier Phillips, the son of Georgia sharecroppers, had regained consciousness, naked, on a table in Violet Pike's kitchen, being scrubbed by women who were white. His first thoughts were of lynching, or at least a whipping. Naked black man. Vulnerable white women. This was a horror story he'd seen and heard too many times before. He feigned unconsciousness until he realized the words that he was hearing were expressions of compassion mixed with curiosity. He was the first black human being these women had ever seen.[15]

Before that day, life for Phillips was typical for an African American in the southern states. He'd learned early on to avoid white women, avert his eyes from the gaze of a white man and keep his mouth shut, even when the Ku Klux Klan burned down his school. Even the navy was segregated, and on board the *Truxtun*, where he was a mess attendant, he'd not been allowed to eat with his white shipmates. He took most meals standing up in the galley.

He vowed that day to leave that life behind and soon applied, successfully, to become the US Navy's first African American sonar technician. The navy had discouraged him from applying for the all-white trade, but he persisted. He would, in 1965, march with Martin Luther King Jr. in the campaign for equal voting rights. And he would become a frequent visitor to Newfoundland, where the people of St. Lawrence continue to commemorate the tragedy that touched both rescuer and survivor indelibly.[16]

Doc Smith, in his private memoir, and with characteristic understatement, recalled the parting on the evening of February 19: "The men had quickly endeared themselves, and, particularly the injured, left heartbroken homes when they had to be moved."[17]

ON Friday, February 20, the recovery of bodies began; it would continue through the weekend. Almost every man in the place turned out to help. Thus began an almost daily procession to the St. Lawrence cemetery, not far from the original Black Duck mine site. The townspeople temporarily buried ninety victims there, until they could be returned in springtime to their home communities. Another forty-eight were taken to Argentia for burial.[18] More than sixty of the victims of the *Truxtun* and *Pollux* tragedy had disappeared forever, like countless Newfoundlanders, into the vast Atlantic Ocean grave.

IF THE survivors on USS *Wilkes* had been expecting sympathy and comfort when their ship limped into Argentia on the morning of February 19, they were in for disappointment. They tied up just after 4:00 a.m. The flag officer, Rear Admiral Arthur L. Bristol Jr., support force commander for the US Atlantic fleet, ordered the two senior officers on the *Wilkes* to have their reports on his desk by eight that morning. It was fairly obvious where this was heading.

There would be a court of inquiry during the following weeks in Argentia. Seven officers from the *Wilkes* and the *Pollux* would face a court martial. The evidence would reveal lapses in competence, communication and decision-making.

Neither the *Pollux* nor the *Truxtun* had radar, and the system on the *Wilkes* was obsolete and originally designed for navigation in the air, not at sea. This important detail—clearly a factor in the causes of the disaster—would not come up in the subsequent process of accountability.

The court of inquiry heard that there had been a crucial moment, just after midnight on the eighteenth, when the navigator on the *Pollux*, Lieutenant William Grindley, urged his superior officer, Commander Turney, to change course. Grindley knew that the wind and unexpectedly strong currents had knocked them off course and they needed to adjust. Turney vetoed the idea. Their course had been established by navigation officers on the *Wilkes*, the leader in the little convoy, and there could be no change without permission from them. And given the storm outside and the inadequacy of their communications, permission wasn't going to happen.[19]

The later court martial would never hear of this exchange, and Grindley, in the final reckoning, faced the severest penalty of them all—discharge from the navy.

Of the seven men charged, the five most senior officers, including Turney, faced disciplinary action, but it was all on paper, and given the men's importance to the war effort, the tragedy made little or no difference to the trajectory of their careers.

Grindley finished out the war as master in the merchant navy, a non-military shipping service that heroically maintained supply lines to Europe throughout the war. Lieutenant William Smyth, deck officer on the *Wilkes* on the morning of the eighteenth—and the man whose job it was to plot the course—was charged, but the charges, in civilian terms, were stayed. It soon became clear, however, that Smyth had been blackballed by the navy anyway. Although he retired in 1951 with the rank of commander, his work, after February 1942, had been buffeted by the disdain and disrespect of fellow officers. Nevertheless, in spite of obvious obstruction, he had a distinguished record before and after the disaster. A witness at the board of inquiry had, without prompting, praised Smyth as an exemplary officer. "I have never in my cruise since I left the academy seen him sit down on watch," declared Ensign Henry Quekemeyer, "that is, in the chair that is provided for him while he was the officer of the deck."

It didn't matter. Smyth would have been a natural for promotion to captain. But every effort, from that day forth, was blocked in Washington.

In 1977, interviewed by the journalist and author Cassie Brown, Smyth speculated that he and Grindley were made scapegoats by a navy cabal known as the Green Bowlers—senior officers who had been classmates in the US Naval Academy and members of a secret society dedicated to looking out for one another as their careers advanced. The name Green Bowlers came, he said, from an initiation rite that involved drinking "a potion" from a green bowl.[20]

~~~

IN time, the survivors who stayed in touch with the people of St. Lawrence would understand that almost everyone who turned out that day had a deep personal memory of disaster—of an undersea earthquake and a tsunami only thirteen years before; of lost relatives and friends; of a lost livelihood; and of a strange series of events leading to a mining operation and that providential light at Iron Springs.

The survivors would, in time, get to know the community, the people, the history—and they would be astounded to discover that this little town, economically dependent on an industry that was dangerous and risky to the health of workers, didn't even have a doctor, didn't have a hospital; that the quality of public service on the south end of the Burin Peninsula hadn't changed in the thirteen years since that same angry sea attacked the people living in forty Newfoundland communities, including St. Lawrence and Lawn.

They would have been amazed to learn that the mine at Iron Springs was there because of an American financier with an over-large ambition to become a wealthy mining magnate. That the financier was, like so many of them, from near New York. And that these same Newfoundlanders, in an astonishing gesture of faith in human nature, had helped to make it happen for him. And yet, little of the benefits came back to them.

They would learn of Newfoundland's long history of illness caused by isolation, poverty, harsh weather and a livelihood that, while strenuous and perilous, offered little more than a subsistence existence. That while the island was, in 1942, enjoying a period of war-related prosperity, it still lagged far behind the rest of North America in the availability and quality of essential services—like health care.

They would conclude, collectively, that they could and should do something to correct at least that one shortcoming.

~~~~

DETAILS about the efforts of the people of St. Lawrence and Lawn passed up through the chain of military and political command with unusual swiftness. On February 24, six days after the shipwrecks, President Roosevelt drafted a personal telegram to "the people of St. Lawrence," thanking them for their "courageous and magnificent work" and "the sacrifices you made in rescuing and caring for" the survivors of the disaster. The heroic action was "typical of the history of your proud seafaring community," Roosevelt declared.[21]

On February 26, Admiral Bristol, the senior naval officer in Newfoundland, wrote a detailed memorandum for the US secretary of the navy, Frank Knox, in which he profusely praised the Newfoundlanders, declaring that "without the prompt, efficient and tireless effort of these people, only a handful of our men would have been saved."

He continued: "Furthermore, of the number rescued, few would have recovered from the effects of the immersion and cold had it not been for the manner in which these people gave further assistance.

"They took off their own clothes on the spot in order to clothe our men, and in addition brought from their houses all the articles of clothing which they could gather."

The rescuers, Bristol wrote, "had worked in some of the worst terrain that I have ever encountered."[22]

To make his point, he sent a map to the secretary—who might have already been familiar with the region. Frank Knox's mother was from Charlottetown, PEI, and his father was born and raised, to age nine, in New Brunswick.

"You will note that this is an isolated series of small communities connected by a single road. Their only communications with the rest of Newfoundland is by water. The people are a hardy race of English and Irish descent, quiet, dignified and reserved; also, hard to know and very sensitive. Almost without exception they are poor and with few possessions."

Admiral Bristol argued—hoping, he added, "that I am not being too sentimental"—for some lasting expression of gratitude from the United States. He was sure that there would, one day, be a memorial of some kind. But, he wrote, "I can't help thinking how much better it would be if anything, which might eventually be done . . . took the form of something practical in the town of St. Lawrence." He suggested a small, fully equipped hospital, in memory of the officers and men of the *Pollux* and the *Truxtun*.

There is no available record of the response by the secretary of the navy. Admiral Bristol, who was only fifty-five years old, died suddenly of a heart attack on his flagship, the USS *Prairie*, in Argentia two months and one day after he wrote his memorandum. His generous proposal, however, would survive.

MEN returning to their homes from Iron Springs, Chamber Cove or Lawn Point on February 19, hoping for a rest or at least a change of clothing, would have been surprised to find strangers in their beds, their meagre wardrobes and dressers emptied out, their wives sheepishly explaining that they'd given all their spare clothes away to the Americans who now had nothing.

The miners understood. The men retrieved what their wives had overlooked—and some would one day admit that they had even borrowed underwear from the womenfolk until they were able to replace their own.

For many years after February 1942, when families in St. Lawrence were facing poverty because of yet another tragedy, one yet to manifest itself, there would be annual deliveries of clothing, new and second-hand, from the survivors of the shipwreck.

Leo and Lillian Loder named one of their thirteen children after Ensign James Seamans, who would, over the following years, send "barrels" of clothing to keep the family going in times of hardship. Leo Loder became ill and died at the age of fifty-four in

1958.[23] His youngest son and namesake, Leo Loder Jr., was born three weeks after his father's death.

Ensign Seamans outlived his rescuer by forty years. He would visit St. Lawrence periodically, and he made a special trip in 1988 for a commemorative service at the local Catholic church.[24] Lillian, by then, could walk only with difficulty. As they arrived at the church that day, she was in a wheelchair. Seamans was behind her, gently guiding the wheelchair through the crowd— reminding onlookers of an evening many years before when Lillian had walked beside him as he was carried on a stretcher to a waiting ship.[25]

IN retrospect, 1942 was another major turning point for the community of St. Lawrence. It was a year in which the people would encounter many strangers in their town. It was a year in which the insemination of an idea would lead to a transformation in the quality of life there.

Possibly in response to the suggestion by members of the trade dispute panel—that for all the resourcefulness and dedication of the existing workers, there was a need for outside mining expertise—the St. Lawrence mining operators now began to look outside for people with a broader, deeper background in the business. And so, in the spring of 1942, the corporation and Newfluor began recruiting hard-rock miners from Nova Scotia, men with experience in mines in other parts of Canada, to provide new leadership underground.

It was certainly a year of transformation for Donald Poynter. The bride who had eagerly accompanied him to St. Lawrence in 1933 died after her long debilitating illness, in a sanatorium in New Jersey. He would, in time, begin another family, this time with a woman who had deep roots in the community.

In 1947, he married Louis Etchegary's daughter Florence.

34.

Aᴄᴛᴇʀ the adventures of February 1942, life quickly returned to "normal" in St. Lawrence. Rennie Slaney would remember August 19 as a bad day. It was the day he had to gather up what was left of Gus Haskell, transport his broken body to the surface at Iron Springs mine and lay out the remains on a table in the miners' lunchroom.[26]

There was nowhere else that was appropriate. There was no clinic or hospital. There was no doctor to certify that Gus was dead. There was a company nurse, but she was home sick that day.

Of course, it was obvious to anybody who was there that the man was dead. But in most circumstances, the opinions of lay observers are insufficient. Death is a formality with legal protocols.

For Rennie Slaney, this situation would have been a bit much—more than a little sickening. Same thing when Ed Stapleton was caught in an explosion at Black Duck in 1936. And when Peter Spearns was caught under a slab of loose rock in 1939. With Gus, it was doubtful that a doctor would have made much difference. But it would have been helpful if there had been a medical professional to take charge of the messy aftermath, or a more appropriate place to take a body.

Aᴜɢᴜsᴛᴜs Haskell and Amos Beck had been working on a platform in the shaft—a kind of hatch that could be raised and lowered for the protection of men who were working farther down. A hinge was broken. The hatch was secured, during the repairs, by a cable attached to a skip—a large bucket that was used for hoisting ore to surface. The two men were kneeling on the hatch to fix the broken hinge when the skip jerked upwards. Amos Beck tumbled into the timbers and snagged there. But

Haskell plunged to the bottom of the shaft, a distance of more than a hundred feet.[27]

It was never determined why the bucket moved. The hoist-man, in his control room on the surface, swore he'd heard a signal instructing him to lift the skip. Several men who were present when the accident occurred testified in the subsequent inquiry that nobody gave a signal, which would have involved a brief tug on a cord hanging near where the men were working. And in any case, nobody was close enough to the signal cord to be able to reach and yank it before the bucket suddenly and disastrously moved upwards.

The investigating ranger, part of a law enforcement system created by the commission of government for small places like St. Lawrence, concluded that it would be impossible to establish with any certainty what had caused the accident. The hoistman, if he was to blame, was already devastated and would spend the rest of his days silently punishing himself for the needless death of a colleague. There was no need for pointing fingers.

What was called for, however, was some direct commentary on a related issue.

The investigating ranger noted, angrily, that when the senior underground supervisor that day, Rennie Slaney, brought the dead man to the surface, there was no ambulance. There was no first aid facility. There was no doctor. There was no hospital. There was a company nurse, but even if she had been present in the lunchroom, she would not have been qualified to record an official cause of death.

Between 1933 and 1941, as the mining industry was beginning, there had been no doctor at all. In 1941, a doctor showed up and stayed for nine months. The next doctor arrived in 1943 and stayed a year. There was no ongoing presence until 1949.

For all the deficiencies in the St. Lawrence mines, all the illnesses and injuries, fatalities were uncommon. There would have been a feeling of utter shock and impotence as the men of Iron Springs stood quietly around that table, staring at the corpse of someone they knew, someone they had grown up with, joked with just hours earlier as they crowded into the cage that lowered them down the shaft to begin the workday.

It was probably merciful that Gus Haskell had died quickly. But even if he'd had a chance, there would have been no hope of saving him or easing his suffering. The ranger's report on the fatality spoke for all of them. "When an operation of the nature and scale of the one now being carried on here, is going on," he wrote, "it is, in my opinion, nothing less than criminal to be without competent medical aid."[28]

He was backed in that view by the district magistrate, H.W. Quinton, who said: "[S]uch a situation, wherein several hundreds of workmen who are engaged in dangerous occupations are without a resident doctor's services, is probably without parallel in the whole of the British Commonwealth of nations."

There would be no response from St. John's. But the officials in St. Lawrence might have been encouraged had they known that a solution to the problem was slowly gaining traction—in Washington.

JUST months before the accident at Iron Springs, Rear Admiral Arthur Bristol had written his memorandum to the naval secretary, and his comments, in tone and substance, were identical to those of the ranger and the magistrate who investigated Gus Haskell's death. Bristol had also discussed his proposal for a small but well-equipped hospital for this remote place—a mining town that, unfathomably, didn't even have a doctor—with Captain Gail Morgan, one of his senior officers in Argentia. When Admiral Bristol died suddenly, just two months after writing to the secretary of the navy, Morgan tried to keep the dream alive. He embraced the idea and began lobbying senior military officials in Washington.

It was an impressive tale—the loss of 203 sailors in a shipwreck, the dramatic rescue of 186 survivors. But in the middle of a war, it was easily lost in the larger global drama. For one American, however, the story of what had happened to the USS *Truxtun* was the memory that would define much of his long, productive life.[29]

Ensign James Seamans couldn't stop thinking about his brush with death on February 18, 1942. How, but for the meaty hand of a St. Lawrence miner, he'd probably have been hauled back out to sea by the wave that had tossed him onto a beach in Chamber Cove and drowned with so many of his shipmates. How they'd trussed him like a side of beef and hauled him on a rope to safety. How this merciful family, the Loders, and this extraordinary mother, Lillian, had nursed him, cared for him. Seemed to *love* him, a total stranger.

Among those he told about it was his father, Richard Seamans, a prominent Republican and a friend of the local congressman, George Bates, who also lived in Salem, Massachusetts. Seamans and Bates were, like the ranger and the magistrate, indignant that a mining town would have no doctor, no hospital. And that the survival of 186 Americans was only by the grace of God and the courage of civilians who, for all their kindness, could possibly have helped save even more lives that day if there had been a hospital.

Before the year was out, Bates formally proposed that the United States allocate $50,000 to help start a hospital in St. Lawrence, Newfoundland. The proposal was well received but went nowhere. Bates, however, was persistent, and for the next seven years, he continued, with the encouragement of Richard Seamans, to pursue his goal—a suitable demonstration of American appreciation.

~~~

CONGRESSMAN Bates was a frequent passenger on the Eastern Airlines shuttle from New York's LaGuardia Airport to Washington, DC. He was one of fifty-five passengers and crew on board the shuttle as it approached Washington National Airport, as it was then known, just before noon on November 1, 1949.

He would not have known that a new American-built P-38 fighter jet was nearby, being tested before delivery to the Bolivian air force. And he could not have known that the warplane had just taken a wrong turn half a mile southwest of Runway 3, the destination of the Eastern shuttle. It's doubtful if Bates even saw the P-38 before it slammed into the shuttle mid-fuselage, cutting it in two. Nobody would ever know what, if anything, the unsuspecting passengers were aware of. The pilot on the P-38 jet fighter survived. There were no survivors on the shuttle.[30]

Among the many legislative projects left unfinished on Congressman Bates's desk was a proposal for funding a hospital in a place that would have meant little to him—Newfoundland, a former British colony that had recently become a province of Canada. The item had been on his desk for a long time—since late 1942.

IT WAS a freak accident. The test pilot at the controls of the military plane was having engine trouble, asked for clearance to land, was told to come down behind the Eastern shuttle on the same runway—misunderstood, thought he was to go ahead.

It might have been the end of an idea that had promised to profoundly alter the quality of life in St. Lawrence, Newfoundland. The congressman's project, however, didn't die that day. In fact, it got new life and impetus. Congressman Bates had been immensely popular in Washington, and some of his colleagues remembered this passion of his, this dream of helping to build a little hospital somewhere in the middle of nowhere, a place where there lived simple people who were unusual for their generosity.

And so it happened—the eighty-first sitting of the US Congress, in 1949, finally approved an appropriation of $375,000 to build a hospital in St. Lawrence. There were no votes there for American politicians. There were no lobbyists, other than a grateful dad. There were no influential "interests," except perhaps the US Navy, which, for all its lack of action, still seemed interested.

By April 1950, navy officials from Argentia were sitting down with members of the new provincial government of Newfoundland, Canada, and local officials from the Burin district, drawing up a plan. Construction started in 1951. By then, the estimated cost had risen to $400,000 and so Congress amended the appropriation to add another $25,000.[31]

On June 6, 1954, at an official ceremony that drew, as reports would state, "Americans and Canadians from all walks of life," including the premier of Newfoundland, Joseph R. Smallwood, and the US ambassador to Canada, Robert Douglas Stuart, the new facility officially became a part of Newfoundland's system of "cottage" hospitals.

It had taken twelve years to evolve from a vague idea in the mind of Rear Admiral Arthur Leroy Bristol Jr. to this reality. But, finally, St. Lawrence and the nearby communities had a small but modern, fully equipped hospital, an incentive for doctors and nurses to come to town and stay for more than a month at a time.

It had been twelve years of political and bureaucratic paper shuffling, mostly in Newfoundland, and responses to many practical questions. What if the $400,000 isn't enough? What about resentment in other places? So the rich Americans will pay to build it, but who will pay to run it?

US naval officials had suggested that because there were already two cottage hospitals in the Burin region, the money should be spent on a facility especially for the treatment of tuberculosis. The practical merit in that idea was that Ottawa would pay to run a regional TB hospital, while the financially strapped Newfoundland government would have to fund a new facility in the cottage system by itself.

One senior provincial official, the deputy minister of health, Leonard Miller, strongly opposed the project and suggested that they take the money from the Americans, thank them, then spend it somewhere else, where the need was greater than in St. Lawrence. Joey Smallwood vetoed both ideas, to the warm approval of the people of Lawn and St. Lawrence, who were insisting on a "general" hospital, with perhaps a special wing for the treatment of tuberculosis.[32]

And so, in mid-1954, the place was finally opened with great fanfare. They called it the US Memorial Hospital. There was a plaque with an inscription: "Presented by the President of the United States . . . in gratitude." There had in fact been three US presidents since the idea first arose—Roosevelt, Truman, Eisenhower. From a political perspective, the old cliché "better late than never" justified forgiving any tardiness in the long, long journey from idea to reality. But from the practical point of view of many families in the area, "late" was just another word for never.

Conversations with the Dead III

vii.

~~~

I turned nineteen on the 450-foot level in Tilt Cove on the northeast coast of Newfoundland. Notre Dame Bay. I felt dramatic, turning nineteen underground. Manly. There was nobody with me in the drift, or even on the level. I was on maintenance that night and bored. Working alone, I had a lot of time to think.

A miner was killed that summer when he fell into the crusher. I was working night shift that week too. Perhaps it was the same night, the night when, at midnight, I realized: Hell, I've just turned nineteen.

I sat down on a large rock. I reached up to my headlamp, found the little knob and switched it off. It was absolute, the darkness. The only absolute that I will know until I die. And then, of course, I won't know anything. A wasted experience, death. A chance to know an absolute, but no opportunity to think about it, talk about it.

Then again, what's to think about? And why talk? Sooner or later, everyone will get an opportunity to know it for themselves.

I could hear water trickling. There were rumbles in the rock around me from drills on other levels.

~~~

The man was killed in the early evening. Around five. They blew a whistle, shutting down briefly. I was on my way to the cookhouse. Early supper. Pick up the lunch can. By seven thirty I was in the dry, putting on my work clothes. There was a first aid room in the dry, and that was where they'd put the dead man.

There was a company doctor. He'd come and gone from the first aid room. The man was dead, officially. Certified. It was the same doctor who had examined me when I'd arrived. A stethoscope to my chest. Breathe deeply. In. Out. Say, Ahhhh.

—You'll do. How old are you?

—Eighteen.

—You're supposed to be nineteen.

—I will be, soon.

—I'm sure you will.

My father asked, How was the physical?

I laughed.

—Was that the physical? It was harder getting into Sea Cadets.

The dead miner was on a metal table in the first aid room. Naked. There was a small towel over his privates. There was a fifty-cent coin in each eye socket.

We stood around and stared. Nobody spoke. Charlie Angus MacLeod was silent, the only time I'd ever seen him speechless. An older miner named Philip MacPhail, who was a war vet, touched the dead man's chest. It moved like jelly. One by one the living miners sighed, shrugged and left the room.

It felt odd, sitting in the absolute absence of light, hearing the drip of water, the buzz and rattle in the rock around me.

When I was getting off the cage at the 450, someone asked if I was working there alone. I nodded. Someone else said that in places, it was illegal to work alone like that. A third person chuckled.

214

—*In Newfoundland, nothing is illegal.*

—*Not without a union, a voice said.*

And someone else scoffed,

—*Unions. Hah.*

I turned the lamp back on. After the absolute darkness, the light seemed to be coppery. The walls glistened with the seeping water. In places there were little rivulets. And the rock around me buzzed and rattled.

I stood, picked up my shovel. I felt chilled. There was a slight ache in my joints from sitting down.

Nineteen, I thought. Getting older. Getting up there.

My father woke me up that morning. I was confused at first. Then he threw two packages of Export A on the bed.

—*Happy birthday*, he said. Then sat down on the other bed.

—*How goes it?*

—*Good.*

—*Nineteen, eh?*

—*Getting on.*

I opened one of the packages. We lit up.

—*So, you'll be going back soon.*

—*Back where?*

—*You know where. Back to the books.*

—*I'm not so sure about that.*

—*Why not?*

—*Just not.*

—*You get the marks?*

—*I got the marks.*

—*And how were the marks?*

—*So-so.*

—*They haven't kicked you out?*

—*Not yet.*

—Then you're going back.

He stood.

—You're just passing through here.

—Maybe not.

—No maybe about it.

He poked the half-smoked cigarette into an empty Coke bottle. The smoke curled and expanded in the bottle, looking for a way out.

—No maybe about it, he repeated. And left.

One of my father's close friends in Tilt Cove was another itinerant Cape Breton miner, Angus MacDonald. A very common name where we were from. Everybody knew him as Black Angus. He'd probably had very black hair once, but he was going grey.

They were old men, I thought, Black Angus and my father, in their early forties, more than twice as old as I was.

They preferred to converse in Gaelic, which seemed to make them even older, and I tended to be invisible when they were talking to each other. I wouldn't have expected Black Angus to recognize me if I was shouting at him. And then I found out. He'd recognize me anywhere.

My father went home to Cape Breton for a holiday and I was on my own. There was a beer hall not far from the bunkhouse. The proprietor was a mysterious individual whom everybody called Itchy. I think it was a corruption of a difficult European name. He didn't seem to mind.

The evening of the day my father went away for his holiday, I went to the beer hall for the first time. I was nineteen, still underage but I didn't think anyone would notice. I bought a beer and sat down, listening to all the exciting noise. Men over-talking one another. Everybody working hard at seeming hard.

Then Black Angus pulled up a chair and sat down. He stared at me for a while and then he stared down at the tabletop, at the beer bottle. And then back up at me. And gesturing towards the bottle, he said,

—I'm going to tell your father.

—Tell him what? I said.

—That you were in here.

—He won't mind.

At that, he looked away towards a noisy table full of younger hard guys, maybe in their early thirties. Going at each other. Test-driving masculinity.

He looked back at me, nodding. He sighed.

—He'll mind.

I took a defiant swig from the bottle.

—You're not the boss.

I smiled.

He stood and hitched his trousers.

—We'll see about that.

And he walked over to the bar and chatted for a little while with Itchy. I was reassured because neither of them looked in my direction.

But when I went over for my second beer, Itchy said,

—Sorry.

And he nodded towards where Black Angus was now sitting among the hard fellows.

—Not while he's here.

—What's he got to do with it?

I was suddenly feeling very cocky. A miner. Nineteen years old.

—He's supposed to be looking after you, said Itchy.

viii.

~~

My father told me an interesting story about St. Lawrence, from when he worked there, when he was just a little older than I was. Nothing instructive or significant. Just interesting. There were miners from St. Lawrence working in Tilt Cove.

He had two close friends in St. Lawrence when he worked there in *the forties, two other miners from Cape Breton. I have a vague impression he told me they had all worked together driving tunnels on the south side of St. John's Harbour in the early part of the war. The tunnels were for storing munitions. I later found a travel document from 1941. He was going to Newfoundland on behalf of the Department of Munitions and Supply, Dominion of Canada. Something about the secret nature of his work. Obviously, the tunnels.*

They got word near the end of that job that there was work down in St. Lawrence, down at the end of the Burin Peninsula. You had to get there by boat. They were looking for men with hard-rock experience. They were mining fluorspar. A strategic mineral. The war was raging overseas. Mining fluorspar, like driving tunnels for munitions, was considered military service. And maybe healthier than the battlefield.

The tunnel men had all worked in Northern Quebec before New-foundland. A group of them headed for St. Lawrence. Got on. My father and his buddies were supposed to raise the standards of professionalism in the local mines. My father was only twenty-three, going on twenty-four. He'd already been a miner for about seven years. They made him a shift captain. A boss of bosses underground.

Two of the friends were Jack MacIsaac and Joe MacNeil. They were from Inverness County, in Cape Breton, which is where my father and a lot of hard-rock miners came from. Jack and Joe were contract workers, sinking a shaft for one of the new mines in St. Lawrence.

The story started like this.

—Those skates you have at home?

—Yes.

—They belonged to Jack MacIsaac.

—And who was he?

—He was from home. Long Point. Brought up on the Chisholm Road.

—Right.

And one Christmas, my father and his friends were talking about the coming celebration. How nobody would be getting home because of the difficulty travelling, especially that time of year and the war and everything. And how the festive season was shaping up to be kind of grim. You couldn't buy liquor in St. Lawrence. But you could get it in Lawn, which was about eight miles away. Lawn was that much closer to St. Pierre. There were bootleggers in Lawn.

Jack and Joe volunteered to walk to Lawn to get the Christmas liquor. What was Christmas without a treat? And then, of course, New Year celebrations.

They all chipped in, and Jack and Joe set off on foot for Lawn one morning just before Christmas. It was a clear day, chilly but not too cold. But the weather turned.

By the time they were on the way back, it was a howling blizzard.

Father Thorne was on a sick call that evening with the horse and sleigh. He came across one of them half in, half out of a brook. He was already gone.

The second man was barely alive, a little farther on, trying to get a fire started by burning the alcohol. The priest got him on the sleigh, but he kept rolling off. And by the time they got to town, he was dead.

—So that's where your skates came from: Jack MacIsaac.

They all chipped in again and sent the boys back home for burial in their own Cape Breton parishes, Margaree and Judique. Alex MacDonnell from Mabou went along—making sure they made it home okay, to their waiting families. Looking after them. To the very end. The absolute end.

That was the story he told me. And I thought, Isn't it peculiar how conversations about the mining business always seem to end with someone being dead?

SEVEN

Mr. Isaac's (Extraordinary) Wake

35.

~~~

I N St. Lawrence, in early December 1952, Therese Slaney was
expecting her first baby, so to be on the safe side, she decided
to go to the little cottage hospital in Burin for the delivery. There
was talk about a new hospital for St. Lawrence, but it was still
almost two years off in the uncertain future.

It was a daunting prospect, having this first baby. Her family
had originally been from near Lord's Cove, but after losing all
they owned in the 1929 tsunami, they'd relocated to St. Pierre.
Therese was born and raised there, and was technically a citizen
of France. English was her second language.

Burin could be intimidating. But she was nervous about having
her first child at home. There was much that could go wrong. And
there was so much illness lurking, preying on the vulnerable, the
elderly and the newly born. Which reminded her: before setting
out for Burin, she should look in on her ailing neighbour, Isaac
Slaney, or Mr. Isaac, as he was known around the neighbourhood.

Isaac Slaney, a distant relative and close friend of her father-
in-law, Rennie Slaney, had been a miner and, like Rennie, had
started out at Black Duck back in the early thirties. Now he was
very sick, possibly dying from some mysterious disease.

He was weak when she dropped by and apologetic for the
fact that he probably wouldn't be alive when she returned—that

he wouldn't get a chance to meet and celebrate the new addition to the Slaney clan. It was just a feeling he had.

This premonition weighed upon his cheer, and Therese went out of her way to reassure him—of course he'd be there when she came back, and he should not lose hope. But deep inside she knew that his words were no appeal for encouragement or sympathy, and that they came from a profound subconscious knowledge of his fate.

She brushed aside the fatalism anyway, urged him to keep up the good fight for her sake and for the sake of the baby and the celebration that always accompanies new life. He smiled thinly and shook her hand, and she departed for Burin to begin the prenatal waiting.[1]

SHORTLY after her arrival at the hospital in Burin, Therese was surprised to see her husband, Herb Slaney, at her bedside. She hadn't been expecting a visit, at least not right away. But there he was, looking fidgety as would be expected. He also seemed to be in a hurry, and when she asked him why, he told her that he was actually in Burin on a secret mission and would explain everything in due course. But for now, he couldn't.

And by the way, he added, Mr. Isaac had passed away on December 4, shortly after her departure. Everyone back home was mourning. Mr. Isaac was a true gentleman, but his death was also merciful because he had suffered greatly, and all the doubts and questions about the mystery illness that was killing him had increased his agony.

Isaac Slaney was forty-six years old.

SUCH deaths were not yet especially remarkable, although St. Lawrence miners had been suffering from mysterious and usually fatal illnesses since about 1945. Isaac might even have considered himself fortunate. He'd have known Augustus Pike, who had also started work at Black Duck. Pike, when he was little more than a boy, started out picking spar—literally working at a sorting table in the mill. Like many of his generation, he then moved underground, where he continued working until his health gave out. He died in 1946, at the age of twenty-seven. He left a wife and four children, one of whom was suffering from polio.[2]

There is no official record of the cause of his death, but to his friends, neighbours and family, there was an unavoidable suspicion. His suffering and his symptoms were becoming familiar, even in the mid-forties. The dead and dying all had worked in Black Duck mine. It was becoming difficult to avoid the obvious conclusion: there was something sinister and deadly lurking underground.

Patrick Rennie, who'd lost his wife and three of his children in the tsunami of 1929, died in January 1951, after debilitating health problems. Patrick, like Isaac Slaney and Augustus Pike, had gone to work at Black Duck when it started up in 1933. A decade later, there was obviously something wrong with Patrick's health, and soon he couldn't work at all. He was forty-two and healthy when he started mining at Black Duck. He was sixty when he died.

Rennie Slaney, who had also gone to work at Black Duck at the beginning, suffered from chronic breathing problems and had his first heart attack when he was in his early forties. In early 1952, he had actually missed the marriage of Herb and Therese, his son and daughter-in-law, because of illness. He was very much aware of Mr. Isaac's decline, which had started in about 1946, and he was concerned about the health problems of many of their contemporaries, almost all of them miners or former miners at Black Duck and Iron Springs, even the relatively modern Director mine.

He was especially worried about his brother, Arcule, who

seemed to be aging before his eyes. Arcule was ten years older than Rennie, but he had always been a healthy six foot four. Now he was slowing down, almost withering. The consensus was tuberculosis. There was a lot of this in St. Lawrence—men breathing with difficulty after exertions that they once would hardly have registered. But it had to be more than tuberculosis. Miners with TB were dying. Other people with TB were being cured.

It bothered Richard Clarke to the extent that once the fishery had recovered in the forties, he'd spend as many months of every year as possible on the water—the physical effect of working underground was alarming to him, even when he was a young man. In 1997, he told his nephew, the historian Richard Rennie (Patrick Rennie's grandson) how much it had bothered him: "I knew that there was something down there because when I went in the mine after fishing all the summer up to November . . . after you'd get there for a couple of months you'd start losing your appetite and the strength would go, you'd start losing the strength in your legs, and you'd find it hard to breathe."[3]

Isaac Slaney, like Clarke and most underground mine workers, had experienced shortness of breath in the beginning and then symptoms that seemed to be from tuberculosis, which was raging across the island at the time. Herb Slaney had attended high school in St. John's and would frequently visit the TB sanatorium to comfort the men from St. Lawrence he'd routinely find there—up to twenty at a time. He would, much later, describe the hospital visits to Richard Rennie this way: "It became so common for miners to be admitted to the sanatorium that people began referring to their condition as 'miners' TB.'"

Herb's brother, Adrian, had a similar experience visiting the hospital, according to Richard Rennie, who became a meticulous chronicler of the mining history of his hometown. Richard Rennie wrote: "[T]here were 'all these men from St. Lawrence, and the ones who were there before had come home and died,

while men from other places treated for TB were recovering.'
One former tuberculosis patient . . . even went back to work at
the mine, and died two months later. As Adrian Slaney put it, it
was obvious by the early 1950s that St. Lawrence miners were
dying but 'we didn't know what they were dying from.' "[4]

Rennie Slaney, Adrian and Herb's father, would later write:
"[T]he men of St. Lawrence could not be cured. They received
the best of treatment. They were given all available drugs and
needles. They gained in weight and even looked healthy, but
their shortness of breath could not be improved. After being dis-
charged from the San, some lasted a very few months and others
somewhat longer. All are now deceased."[5]

JEROME Kelly suffered injuries to his chest and back working
underground when he was jammed between a tramcar and a chute
in 1951. He had five kids between five and twelve and had to struggle back to work. By February 1954, he had to stop again, this time
permanently, because of failing health. That month, he went to the
sanatorium in St. John's, where he was told that he had tuberculosis. He refused the standard treatment and told the doctors he just
wanted to go home to St. Lawrence and die there.

They sent him home, and on October 15 that year, he died.
He was thirty-five years old.[6]

His widow applied for workers' compensation—her husband
had been working around fluorspar for twenty years. It took her
fifteen years to get it. In the interim, she supported herself and her
family by collecting welfare of eighty-five dollars a month.

IT WAS ingrained in the character of people like the Rennies
and the Slaneys, the Pikes and the Kellys, to endure challenges and
hardships with minimal complaint. Their feelings, as they struggled

through unimaginable suffering, are difficult to grasp. Richard Rennie, Patrick's grandson, assembled an encyclopedic record of the St. Lawrence mining story for a doctoral thesis. But the story of his own family connection is absent from the narrative.

Self-effacement seems to run in the Rennie family. His grandfather, Richard recalled in correspondence, was "a bit of a private man." Paddy Rennie's sorrows after 1929 were private matters, not to become burdens for others who had troubles of their own. "No one knows or will ever know how his loss affected him," Richard Rennie explained. "My father [Albert Rennie] likewise did not speak much of him, except to relate things about particularly difficult or successful fishing seasons, etc. The history of the tidal wave and the death of my father's family . . . was a thing that was somehow always there but seldom spoken of."[7]

Even the specifics of their work-related illnesses were unspoken—until much later in their lives, or after death.

THEN, in the late forties, a potential explanation for the deadly mystery. A word. A word that only doctors used, but that would soon become part of the industrial vernacular in St. Lawrence: silicosis.

A crucial part of the health care system in Newfoundland in the late forties was a floating clinic, a boat called the *Christmas Seal*. The little ship had a daunting mission—providing care to more than twelve hundred small communities scattered along six thousand miles of coastline.

She visited St. Lawrence in 1947 and again in 1950. During the 1947 visit, three of the miners who showed up for x-rays were found to have "suspicions of silicosis."[8] Isaac Slaney was one of them. It was on the strength of that x-ray that a young doctor, John Pepper, who'd arrived from England in 1949 and settled in

St. Lawrence for a while, concluded that Mr. Isaac was suffering from a work-related illness.

Dr. Pepper's diagnosis, while clear to him, was inconclusive to almost everybody else. Silicosis, at least in the early stages, is hard to diagnose by x-ray. Dr. Pepper didn't dispute the fact that Isaac Slaney probably had tuberculosis, but it was his opinion that the TB was secondary—perhaps even caused by respiratory vulnerability resulting from pre-existing silicosis.

There was only one sure way to diagnose silicosis—studying the lung itself, before or after death. Before 1950, when silicosis was first recognized as a compensable disease in Newfoundland, there was little interest among the dead and dying and their grieving families to go through the discomfort, not to mention the medical and bureaucratic hassles, of a biopsy or an autopsy.

It has been around for a long time, this curse on the health of people who work in dusty subterranean caverns and tunnels. It was mentioned by Hippocrates two thousand years ago. In *De re metallica*, his 1556 German tome on mineralogy, Georgius Agricola observed that when "dust is corrosive, it ulcerates the lung and produces consumption."

It's an insidious disease. Besides being difficult to diagnose, silicosis is cumulative. As the time of exposure to fine rock dust particles goes on, it becomes more serious. It will continue to compromise the lungs years after exposure ends. Its symptoms—a nagging cough and shortness of breath—can continue to grow more debilitating even after a miner stops working underground. It will often lead to fatal stresses on the heart. It is, essentially, irreversible, incurable.

Dr. Pepper's conclusions about the real cause of Isaac Slaney's ailment should have explained why so many St. Lawrence miners diagnosed as having TB died after standard treatment for the disease, while men from other occupations, like fishing, were cured. But the doctor's link between silicosis and tuberculosis raised troubling legal questions about corporate and political accountability. Which meant Mr. Isaac's case was likely to be controversial. And so it was ignored.

A.V. CORLETT, a mining engineer from Queen's University in Kingston, Ontario, was familiar with the St. Lawrence mines. The commission government of Newfoundland and the new provincial administration, after 1949, had both retained Professor Corlett on several occasions to inspect mining operations in various parts of the island, including St. Lawrence—and to pay special attention to working conditions for the miners.

His main focus was on safety. But he commented on the need for improved ventilation underground at Iron Springs and had been advised in 1949 by an underground captain that the corporation was committed to driving new raises from underground to surface for ventilation and emergency escape. Corlett made subsequent visits in 1950 and 1951, but he found no evidence that the corporation had followed up on its assurances.

Newfoundland mines generally fared well, in terms of serious mining accidents. In St. Lawrence fatalities were rare, but there were too many lesser lost-time accidents at both fluorspar operations, Corlett found. The professor considered the Alcan mine in St. Lawrence to be "carefully run," while the St. Lawrence corporation had "grown up the hard way" and needed improvements. Corlett noted that even at the corporation mines, "the attitude of management towards the crew" mitigated risk in a work environment that might otherwise have been even more dangerous.[9]

Given his awareness of the ventilation problems in the corporation mines and his concern for the well-being of the miners, Professor Corlett's reaction to Isaac Slaney's medical file is puzzling.

He discovered Isaac Slaney's case in 1950, and it should have served to buttress arguments he was making for better ventilation underground. Mr. Isaac's medical file seemed to prove that there was a causal link between poor ventilation, dust, silicosis and TB. His ailment was interesting and perplexing, and the suggestion of silica-related tuberculosis was troubling. But after studying the Slaney case, Corlett concluded that Dr. Pepper was mistaken and became aggressive in his efforts to debunk the doctor's findings.[10]

It was "highly unlikely that a miner would contract silicosis in the extremely wet mines that prevail in St. Lawrence," Corlett insisted in his report to the government in 1950. He presumed that the notorious water problem in the mines there would have had the salutary effect of suppressing dust. That Isaac Slaney had worked in choking dust caused by the dry drills and jackhammers at Black Duck mine was irrelevant, in Corlett's view, as Black Duck had been an open-cut operation, where dust would have quickly dissipated in the fresh air.

The observations were surprising for their superficiality. Black Duck, after about two years, became an underground mine. The drifts were narrow, as they were in Iron Springs, and ventilation was mostly from the natural airflow through the main production shafts. Dust and smoke, from primitive equipment and blasting, were often overwhelming, especially when the mines worked on a three-shift rotation. Miners at Iron Springs, where water poured in constantly, frequently complained of gagging and vomiting, and they often passed out from dust and lack of oxygen.

Corlett, however, had referred his opinions for review and comment to medical specialists in St. John's and Ontario. Both specialists expressed ambivalence about the Slaney case and were unwilling to either confirm or challenge Dr. Pepper's diagnosis. Professor Corlett, however, cited these two non-opinions as proof that there was no scientific basis for claiming that Isaac Slaney had silicosis. In 1951, he noted that Isaac Slaney had, in fact, been released from the St. John's sanatorium and was back at home in St. Lawrence.

Then, in December 1952, Mr. Isaac died.

36.

~~~

THERESE Slaney arrived home in St. Lawrence from the hospital in Burin with her new baby girl, Christine (the first of ten children), and a throbbing curiosity: What was the "secret mission" that had led her husband to her bedside? Now that the mission had been accomplished, Herb was happy to explain.

After her departure, Dr. Pepper and Rennie Slaney had been in deep discussion about health matters in general and the death of Isaac Slaney in particular. The doctor then called on Rennie's son, Herb, with a proposition. Dr. Pepper knew that Therese was giving birth in the Burin cottage hospital and he asked if Herb would like a free trip to visit his wife. Herb was delighted to accept the offer, and the undertaking that accompanied it—that he pick up a package while there and bring it back to St. Lawrence. No questions to be asked or information to be disclosed about the real reason for his trip to Burin.

Mr. Isaac was being waked in the traditional manner, in his own home. His body would be available for visitation there, the family available for condolences. There would be long conversations about Isaac's virtues, his fortitude. There would be prayers and laughter. There would be food and, maybe, drink. But Mr. Isaac's wake would be unusual in one respect.

Before the public viewing, Rennie Slaney and Dr. Pepper removed a kitchen door from its hinges and placed it on the dining room table, near where Isaac Slaney's body had been laid out. A sheet was placed on the door, and Mr. Isaac's body was placed upon the sheet.[11] Herb Slaney was instructed to sit outside the room and prevent anyone from entering. Rennie Slaney agreed to witness the procedure that would follow. For Rennie, who was a management official at the corporation and not a member of the union, this was a dicey situation. He had a large family—eventually fourteen children—and he was the uncle of Donald Poynter's second wife. If Seibert ever found out what was going on there, Slaney could lose his job. But what he witnessed in that room would have greater consequences than dismissal—it would shockingly identify a time bomb that was ticking in the local mining industry.

Dr. Pepper opened Isaac Slaney's chest with the surgical instruments that were in the package Herb Slaney had picked up in Burin, and he carefully removed tissue samples from Mr. Isaac's lungs. Rennie described the condition of Isaac's lungs to his son, who later told his wife they were "coated, flat and black." The doctor shipped the lung tissue to a mainland laboratory for examination and a diagnosis of what really killed Isaac Slaney. He and Rennie then restored the body and the room. The wake began with nobody but Herb and his father, the doctor and Mary Slaney, Mr. Isaac's widow, aware of what had just transpired.

THE expert finding was unambiguous. Mr. Isaac Slaney had definitely been suffering from silicosis. The corporation had a problem. The new provincial government of Newfoundland had an even bigger problem.

37.

THE late forties and early fifties were an inconvenient time for controversy, for both the government of Newfoundland and the mining companies in St. Lawrence.

The Second World War had been a godsend for business and the chronically depressed economy of the island. The bad management of economic resources had resulted in a suspension of responsible government in Newfoundland between 1934 and 1949. But the war created a boom that, in a few years, changed everything—at least long enough to persuade the dominion authorities in London and St. John's that, maybe, Newfoundlanders could once again be trusted to run their own affairs.

And so, as of April 1, 1949, democracy was back, with a fledgling provincial government struggling to learn the ropes of statesmanship. It had been a bruising campaign, with Newfoundlanders forced to choose between independent nationhood, Confederation and even joining the United States. The population was roughly split between the townies in St. John's, who supported an independent nation, and the baymen in outports like St. Lawrence, who saw the practical advantages in being part of Canada.

Whatever the outcome, the hunger for democratic self-government had been sharpened by self-confidence that was nourished by prosperity. The arrival of ten thousand American service personnel and the construction of two large military bases early in the war had created such a demand for workers that the traditional occupations, like forestry, the fishery and mining, were suddenly competing for a resource that had long been taken for granted: labour, skilled and otherwise.

Wages in the woods and underground were suddenly increasing. Passive unions were becoming more aggressive. It was not coincidental that in early 1941, the St. Lawrence Workers' Protective Union started butting heads with bosses.

THE boom, of course, subsided, and by the late forties, Seibert's operation in St. Lawrence—now overly dependent on a shrinking US market—was struggling again. But after 1949, there was a "real" government in St. John's and a real political dynamic. Seibert wasted no time in cultivating cordial relations with the new premier of Newfoundland, Joseph R. Smallwood, who was obsessed with catching up—and quickly—with Canadian prosperity.

Joey Smallwood was born in a hurry. His parents married on December 21, 1900. Baby Joseph arrived three days later, on Christmas Eve. From early childhood, he aspired to journalism and politics, symbiotic occupations back in those free-wheeling days, and by the age of fourteen, he was a printer's apprentice at a newspaper in St. John's. By eighteen, he was (temporarily) writing editorials for the city's leading paper. Early in his journalistic career, he became a socialist through association with the prominent politician and union leader William Coaker, who also owned a newspaper and was, for a while, politically influential.[12] Coaker, who was an admirer of dictators like Benito Mussolini but had failed to find the equal of his Italian hero in Newfoundland, became an early advocate of Confederation with Canada, as did, famously, his acolyte.

Smallwood was also a great admirer of Sir Richard Squires, and like Squires, he was a strong proponent of change through economic growth, particularly industrial development. His long political career was marked by bold initiatives and costly failures as he struggled to transform the Newfoundland economy.

And so, it was predictable that Smallwood would view the enterprising Walter Seibert with approval, if not admiration, and shortly after Newfoundland became a democracy again, Seibert and Smallwood established a relationship.

It was a time when Smallwood was cultivating a number of relationships with dubious "entrepreneurs." The controversial Alfred Valdmanis, a Latvian economist with a spotty wartime record of collaboration with his country's Nazi occupiers, became

Newfoundland's director general of economic development. Valdmanis was clearly a fan of Walter Seibert and would become influential in persuading Smallwood to provide financial support for Seibert's mining ventures in St. Lawrence.[13]

On November 7, 1949—a brief eight months after Smallwood had taken office—Seibert drafted a long letter to the premier disclosing that he was facing perilous financial times, and that the jobs of 150 Newfoundlanders and a payroll of $30,000 a month could soon go up in smoke. He needed help from Newfoundlanders. Again.[14]

He was under pressure from the Chemical Bank and Trust Co. of New York to liquidate his inventory of finished fluorspar to pay off loans of about $125,000. The bankers were refusing to extend credit to finance winter mining because it would raise his indebtedness by at least another $100,000. The American bank was instructing him to cease production. The Royal Bank of Canada had turned him down two weeks earlier because of his lack of working capital.

He was in this pickle, he explained to Smallwood, because he'd used all his wartime profits for expansion and had never declared a dividend. (He neglected to explain that much of the "expansion" had been at a facility called St. Lawrence Fluorspar located in Wilmington, Delaware.) Briefly stated, he needed a line of credit for up to $250,000.

On December 23, 1949, Seibert dispatched a telegram to the St. Lawrence Workers' Protective Union, now under the leadership of James Cusick, who had replaced the firebrand Aloysius Turpin (temporarily). The telegram was to thank Cusick for agreeing to extend the existing labour–management contract to the end of 1951. Once again, the miners of St. Lawrence were giving Seibert a break.

And on February 2, 1950, Premier Smallwood sent a telegram to Walter Seibert with the happy news that his line of credit had been approved. The last thing Smallwood needed in these precarious times was static from the miners, and even more alarming, a setback in what seemed to be a promising new economic sector.

The $250,000 fix tided the corporation over until 1952, when the US government, now anticipating a third world war—this one with either the Soviet Union or Red China—rescued Walter Seibert once again. This time the Americans wanted 150,000 tons of fluorspar, to be delivered over four years starting in 1953. To ensure delivery, the US Defense Materials Procurement Agency advanced a loan of $1.25 million to expand the corporation's facilities. There was money now for improvements in the workplace, particularly underground, where dust and smoke and water were still major problems.

Most of the money went instead for a new mill in St. Lawrence and improvements at the fluorspar refinery in Wilmington.

The Seibert saga in St. Lawrence had been, for twenty years, a story of audacity and luck. Where else on the planet could he have persuaded a population to work for unsecured promises of future payment and job security? He could not have anticipated, or factored into his ambitious plans, the fortuitous calamities of wars, both hot and cold. Nothing less than luck and the patient tolerance of the ordinary people living in Lawn and St. Lawrence had seen him through.

But luck was running out for Walter Seibert and his St. Lawrence Corporation, and for the men who worked for him. Mr. Isaac Slaney was, in a way, a messenger, bearing news of darker days to come—a canary in a hard-rock mine.

THE unusual autopsy at Isaac Slaney's wake would, even in the absence of forensic detail, become an unofficial benchmark in the evolution of official oversight in workplace health and safety in Newfoundland. Though the province had passed its first workers' compensation regulations in 1950 and silicosis was included as a compensable disease, it was rarely diagnosed and hardly ever recognized as grounds for compensation.

Symptoms were invariably dismissed as evidence of tuberculosis, nothing else. Now there was a case that potentially changed the focus. This was scientific evidence that working in St. Lawrence mines caused silicosis. Isaac Slaney had it. Where else could it have come from? But his case opened up the possibility of a flood of compensation claims from survivors of those miners who had mysteriously died of "miners' TB."

Politicians and bureaucrats now realized that there was a looming problem in St. Lawrence—a health problem, of course, but more significantly, a scandal with potential economic and political consequences.

An October 1953 meeting about silicosis in the office of Newfoundland's chief inspector of mines, Fred Gover, left no doubt about the bias of the government. One of the main conclusions of the meeting: "The welfare of the residents of a mining community must be weighed against the possible financial liability of the mine owners should silicosis become prevalent to the point where heavy compensation is necessary."[15]

As late in the discussion as 1954, the Seibert corporation remained defensive. In a letter to the miners' union, Donald Poynter, with a typical rhetorical flourish, commented that according to his informant, "it would take 197 years" working underground in the corporation mines for a man to breathe in enough dust to cause silicosis. His informant was the chief inspector of mines.[16]

It wasn't surprising, then, that in the beginning, both the corporation and the government had attempted to ignore the diagnosis Dr. Pepper first arrived at in 1949, based on x-rays. Now, after his unorthodox autopsy, he had lab results from tests on actual tissue samples from a post-mortem examination. But still, Mary Slaney's claim for compensation, based on Dr. Pepper's evidence that her husband had died from a recognized industrial disease, was rejected by officials.

It was all too much for Rennie Slaney—until then, a loyal supervisor in the Seibert operation. In 1953, he urged his neighbour's widow to sue his employer. It was audacious and it was unprecedented—a widow going up against the corporation. And because, thanks to Dr. Pepper, it was so obvious that Mr. Isaac's widow had a compelling case, the corporation's lawyers capitulated quickly. They handed Mrs. Slaney a settlement of $10,000. There was now a compelling motivation for the families of dead miners to demand autopsies when their loved ones died after dubious diagnoses of TB.

IN 1953, Rennie Slaney was only forty-six—the age at which his neighbour, Mr. Isaac, had died—but his own declining health dictated that he could no longer work underground. He became the corporation's office manager. In 1957, he left mining entirely and became town manager for St. Lawrence. By 1965, he could no longer climb the stairs to reach his office and was forced into an unpaid retirement.

But after 1952, Rennie Slaney had changed in a deep way that would, inevitably, become political. At about the time of Isaac Slaney's death, Rennie's older brother, Arcule, who was fifty-six, began showing symptoms similar to those that had plagued Mr. Isaac for the five years prior to his death. Arcule had been working underground for seventeen years. At nearly forty, he was relatively old when he started out. By 1953, he was too sick to work anywhere. Rennie brought him and another miner to the sanatorium in St. John's. "At this time," Rennie later wrote, "there were several miners who had worked under me [as mine captain] already in the San and there were a few others around St. Lawrence unable to work.

"My brother . . . was at the San for seventeen months. The men received the best of treatment at the San but could not be cured, while cures were being effected in people from other areas in Newfoundland. Those men became fat and healthy-looking but the treatment could not give them back their breath."[17]

He pointed out this anomaly to the director of the tuberculosis hospital, Dr. Raymond E. Bennett. The hospital considered Arcule cured. Rennie noted that his brother could barely walk. What kind of cure was that?

Dr. Bennett sternly lectured Rennie for his ill-informed impertinence.

Arcule was aware that like Isaac Slaney, he was suffering from silicosis, and that he was probably facing the same fate as Mr. Isaac. Rennie felt frustrated and impotent. It was now commonplace in St. Lawrence—this peculiar strain of tuberculosis that defied the medical conventions of the day.

Men like Arcule had largely given up on the medical profession and made hard decisions to cut the TB treatment short. Arcule understood his fate. He had the official diagnosis. He had TB for sure, but also silicosis. He decided to go home and face the music, the inevitable death.

After he went home, Arcule lasted seventeen more months, during which he faded painfully away, his once massive, powerful body reduced to skin and bones. He died in 1957.

ARCULE had satisfied the compensation board that he had silicosis, and in his final months he had been receiving compensation. But when he died, his widow, Minnie Slaney, was declared ineligible for continuing support. The silicosis had been the cause of his disability—the reason he couldn't work—so he qualified for compensation while he was still alive. But the workers' compensation board declared that the cause of his *death* was tuberculosis, which didn't qualify.

Rennie Slaney couldn't overlook the unfairness, the twisted sophistry. He first persuaded and then helped his brother's widow to fight the system. Once again, the lawyers and the bureaucrats backed off. Minnie got her husband's pension. It was another incremental gain, another precedent. But the future loomed as a long, exhausting struggle, case by case, to prove the legitimacy of claims to compensation for having sacrificed health and quality of life in a potentially lethal work environment.

Rennie knew that his own health was failing, and that he, too, probably had silicosis (which would later be confirmed). Struggling to breathe was crippling his heart. He'd lost a brother, close friends and neighbours. He was a former boss with an acute feeling of responsibility for the men who had worked for him—men who were now dying hard deaths and leaving families in poverty.

Circumstances would, inevitably, force him to go public with his private outrage.

THE suffering of the miners of St. Lawrence was exacerbated by a system weighed down by rules and regulations and rigorous bureaucracies set in place to prevent abuse of public money and resources. Viewed from within the system, each claim was a potential rip-off, someone else looking for a free ride at corporate or government expense.

It was an attitude towards public oversight not unlike the official disapproval of needy people who, years before, had requested six cents a day in dole. The need for public assistance was, per se, evidence of deficient character. In the opinion of one senior British bureaucrat, P. A. Clutterbuck, in 1939, there really was no excuse for hunger in rural Newfoundland. The dole, while skimpy, was adequate considering the availability of fresh fish and wild berries, the abundance of free firewood and the fact that most rural Newfoundlanders owned their homes and so didn't have the added burden of paying rent.[18]

The English poor, he noted, lacked such fortuitous advantages.

THE story of the mining industry in St. Lawrence—as well as the attitudes of politicians and public servants in St. John's and London—leaves little doubt that with few exceptions, bureaucratic principles of "numerical validation" consistently placed the burden of proving the merit of claims for compensation on the shoulders of people who lacked the resources to respond. In many cases, these were people already defeated by the awareness that they were about to die.

Rendell Turpin was one of the first miners to receive compensation for his silicosis. Unlike Isaac Slaney, he didn't have to die to have his lungs examined. While Turpin was at the St. John's sanatorium, doctors removed a part of his lung and discovered silicosis, and on the strength of that biopsy, he got compensation based on his earnings at the time that he became ill. But there was no provision for escalation as living costs increased. He would live out his remaining days in tightening financial straits, and as in Arcule Slaney's case, the authorities would try to cut off the compensation as soon as he was gone.

Turpin died at the age of fifty-two.

LEO Loder, one of the miners first on the scene at the Chamber Cove shipwreck on February 18, 1942, died in 1958 at the age of fifty-four. He had been off work, having been diagnosed with silicosis, when he died suddenly of a brain aneurism, and so his family was ineligible for compensation of any kind.

He left his wife, Lillian, and thirteen children. The family struggled for years and survived with the help of the American James Seamans, who never forgot the kindness and the heroism of the Loders when he was a twenty-three-year-old naval ensign.

BY 1953, Isaac Slaney, were he not in his grave, might have taken certain satisfaction that, in part because of his death and its dramatic aftermath, officials were now diligently gathering and recording dust measurements in the St. Lawrence mines. But dust conditions in the mines were, by then, relatively mild compared to when Isaac toiled in the strangling dust at Black Duck and Iron Springs in the thirties and the forties. It would have been cold comfort to Mr. Isaac to know the monitoring revealed that dust pollution in most working areas was, by 1953, well within existing statutory limits.

BY 1953, doctors in St. John's were dealing with a three-prong question: Did miners who developed silicosis have pre-existing tuberculosis that increased their vulnerability to the disease? Or did the silicosis, even in its early stages, make them more likely to get tuberculosis? And when they died, which of these diseases should be listed as the cause? Silicosis created a corporate and government financial liability. Tuberculosis didn't.

It was a classic and insoluble dilemma, which made many of the decisions regarding outcomes in the miners' cases dependent on the subjective disposition of the person or persons handling the claims.

The other catch was that prior to 1954, there was no hospital in St. Lawrence. Precise medical records were nonexistent in many cases. "Numerical validation" was problematic when there were no numbers to consult.

And there might have been yet another factor in the medical conundrum: Did the men of St. Lawrence, who welcomed Walter Seibert and his promises, have another weakness that would make them especially vulnerable to both tuberculosis *and* silicosis?

Throughout the thirties and the forties, Newfoundlanders—in spite of all the fish and berries—suffered from a range of malnutrition-related illnesses, including beriberi. In 1945, a team of eleven British, American and Canadian doctors confirmed Newfoundland's shockingly high incidence of tuberculosis and other serious diseases, all presumably aggravated by the profound economic depression in the years in which the economy and politics of the dominion were disintegrating.

A 1947 report by another British doctor, D.P. Cuthbertson, noted that infant mortality in Newfoundland was two to three times the rate in the United States and almost double that in Canada. The overall death rate from tuberculosis was, as other studies have reported, a shocking three times that in Canada. Dr. Cuthbertson observed that Newfoundland women "appear to age quickly" due to drudgery and malnutrition because the families had "insufficient income to buy food they couldn't produce for themselves," and that "undernourishment in general lowers resistance to the disease [tuberculosis]."[19]

And on and on it went, the interminable discussion: Were Newfoundlanders unusually vulnerable to serious disease because of structural poverty and malnutrition? Were miners in St. Lawrence even more vulnerable to lung and gastric illnesses because of workplace dust and a lack of sanitation? Did the workplace cause tuberculosis or did tuberculosis, perhaps a consequence of hunger, leave the miners more likely to suffer from silicosis?

As early as 1950, the federal health department had been interested in establishing a profile of industrial health in the new Canadian province. The study was "observational" and involved 350 industrial sites. Members of a survey team spent three weeks

USS *Truxtun*. Of 156 men on board when the ship ran aground February 18, 1942, on the south coast of Newfoundland, only 46 survived. Courtesy of St. Lawrence Miners' Museum.

Above: U.S. Navy supply ship *Pollux*. Of the 233 men on board February 18, 1942, the day the ship foundered, 140 survived with the help of rescuers from the communities of St. Lawrence and Lawn. Courtesy of St. Lawrence Miners' Museum.

Right: The remains of the *Pollux*, photographed shortly after the shipwrecks by a young local woman, Ena Farrell. Her photos are the only known visual record of the tragedy. Photo by Ena Farrell Edwards. Reprinted with permission.

Top left: Edward Bergeron, aged eighteen, from the USS *Truxtun*, scaled a steep embankment and made his way over rough terrain and deep snow to Iron Springs mine, where he alerted miners and their managers to the developing disaster in Chamber Cove. COURTESY OF LISA (SLANEY) LODER.

Top right: *Pollux* survivors William Heldt (*left*) and Warren Greenfield. PHOTO BY ENA FARRELL EDWARDS. REPRINTED WITH PERMISSION.

Left: Lanier Phillips, the African American sailor whose life was transformed by the hospitality of the Newfoundlanders. COURTESY OF THE ARMED FORCES RETIREMENT HOME (AFRH).

Graveside service in St. Lawrence, led by Father Augustine Thorne, parish priest. Ninety of the ship-wreck victims were temporarily buried in the local parish cemetery. PHOTO BY ENA FARRELL EDWARDS. REPRINTED WITH PERMISSION.

Ensign James O. Seamans from Salem, Massachusetts, one of the forty-six survivors from the *Truxtun*. The efforts of his father, Richard Seamans, a prominent businessman and Republican, led to a $400,000 congressional appropriation for the construction of a hospital in St. Lawrence. COURTESY OF ARCHIVES AND SPECIAL COLLECTIONS, QE II LIBRARIES, MUN, 16.06.008, CASSIE BROWN COLLECTION.

Chamber Cove, where 110 sailors from the USS *Truxtun* lost their lives February 18, 1942, when their ship ran aground on rocks and reefs below the cliffs that encircle the cove. Pinnacle Point, in the middle distance, is nearly 300 feet high. PHOTO BY THE AUTHOR.

James O. Seamans with Lillian Loder—the St. Lawrence woman who cared for him while he recovered from his brush with death in Chamber Cove—at a 1988 memorial service commemorating the tragedy. COURTESY OF LISA (SLANEY) LODER.

Dr. Warren Smith (*right*), a geologist, was the first mine manager at Black Duck and worked without pay for two years before becoming manager at a new start-up mine. Donald Poynter (*left*), an engineer, became Black Duck's manager in 1939 and ran the Seibert operations in St. Lawrence for more than twenty years. COURTESY OF ST. LAWRENCE MINERS' MUSEUM.

Cornelius Kelleher, an Irish-born American mining engineer, managed Seibert's operations in St. Lawrence from 1935 to 1938, during which time relations with the workforce deteriorated badly. Lizzie Giovannini, here with her daughter Blanche, ran a renowned St. Lawrence boarding house where Kelleher lived during his stay. COURTESY OF ST. LAWRENCE MINERS' MUSEUM.

Claude Howse (*left*), a Newfoundland-born geologist, would eventually become a senior mining official in the colony and, he later learned, an unwitting participant in the Manhattan Project that produced the world's first atomic bomb. COURTESY OF ST. LAWRENCE MINERS' MUSEUM.

The author, Iron Springs mine site, 1945. In 1942 his father, Dan MacIntyre, newly married, moved to St. Lawrence, where he served as underground captain for three years, returning subsequently on various mining jobs until the mid-1960s.
COURTESY OF THE AUTHOR.

Dan MacIntyre with local midwife Mrs. Mary Beck, at St. Lawrence, *circa* 1945. Mrs. Beck delivered Dan's second child, a daughter. COURTESY OF THE AUTHOR.

The author at the Tilt Cove mine site, Newfoundland, 1962. COURTESY OF THE AUTHOR.

The 1951 St. Lawrence soccer team. Four of the men in the back row would die of cancer: Jack Fitzpatrick (*second from right*), Alonzo Walsh (*third from right*), his brother Jack Walsh (*third from left*) and Bob Kelly (*second from left*). St. Lawrence frequently represented Newfoundland at national soccer tournaments. COURTESY OF ST. LAWRENCE MINERS' MUSEUM.

Miners held occasional competitions to demonstrate basic mining skills, like drilling. Here, manager Donald Poynter, in hat and overcoat, clocks driller Sylvester Slaney. COURTESY OF ST. LAWRENCE MINERS' MUSEUM.

Testing for radiation in 1957, in the Director mine, on the 550-foot level.
COURTESY OF ST. LAWRENCE MINERS' MUSEUM.

The St. Lawrence mines were notoriously wet. Miner Jack Keating wades through water as he carries a case of dynamite from storage on the 250-foot level of the Director mine. The water was subsequently found to be the source of radiation in this and other mines in the area.
COURTESY OF ST. LAWRENCE MINERS' MUSEUM.

Miners ending shift in the Director mine. Bob Edwards (*second from left*) died in a massive rockfall there on September 15, 1967, along with two other miners.
COURTESY OF ST. LAWRENCE MINERS' MUSEUM.

Early miners in St. Lawrence, in an undated photograph. *Left to right*: Michael Slaney, Rennie Slaney, Theo Etchegary, Levi Molloy. Three would, in time, die from work-related illness: Michael Slaney and Levi Molloy of cancer; Rennie Slaney of a heart attack, probably precipitated by silicosis. Theo Etchegary worked at the corporation mine for years, but never underground. Courtesy of St. Lawrence Miners' Museum.

Roche Turpin in Toronto, *circa* 1963, en route to British Columbia, where he was interviewed for a new mining job. He was turned down after a medical examination. He died of lung cancer two years later, aged forty-eight. Courtesy of Ellen Turpin.

Roche and Priscilla Turpin's family, in 1967, two years after Roche's death, photographed by Bob Brooks for the *Toronto Star Weekly*. *Left to right*: Hugh (carrying a fishing pole), Cyril, Adrian, Lucille, Priscilla, Ellen and Arden. Courtesy of Ellen Turpin.

in St. Lawrence, and while there, they met Dr. John Pepper. This was two years before his audacious autopsy of Isaac Slaney, but he was already convinced that the ill health of so many miners was related to the workplace.[20]

The federal representatives listened, but there's no evidence that they paid much attention. And when Dr. Pepper later wrote directly to the government of Canada, asking for a formal investigation, he was told, effectively, to buzz off—that Ottawa would respond only to an official request from the health authorities in the government of Newfoundland.

By 1954, Dr. Pepper was gone. He'd been largely ignored by the federal and provincial health establishments and stonewalled by officials of the mining companies, who complained that he seemed to be pursuing a "vendetta" aimed maliciously at them.[21]

His legacy of activism remained, though, and ultimately became a force that could no longer be ignored. In 1954, officials of the departments of health and mines in St. John's were conferring earnestly about the results of dust monitoring in the St. Lawrence mines, and they were committed to producing a code of mining practice for prevention of silicosis.

But it wasn't until 1959, after six years of dust measurement and dry official meetings—and nine years after Dr. Pepper first relayed his concerns about dust and silicosis to public health officials—that the code of practice became law.

By then, there was a whole new protocol for testing the air that miners had been breathing underground for decades, and a brand-new and more sinister cause for worry among people working in the St. Lawrence mines—a far more urgent situation.

EIGHT

The Daughters
of Radon

38.

A history of hardship and self-reliance toughens people. Toughness is evidence of character and strength. We admire toughness and character, especially when they produce perseverance in the face of hardship, and when they contribute to an admirable and preferably silent personal and cultural forbearance.

For Newfoundlanders, the first half of the twentieth century had been a dizzying succession of catastrophes: natural disaster; horrific wartime casualties; poverty, plagues and riots; the collapse of a democracy and a divisive national debate about the political future of the island.

Now it was becoming obvious to almost everyone that the island had another problem—a sinister and creeping menace that was mysteriously killing men who had been working in the St. Lawrence mines. Tuberculosis and malnutrition had offered easy explanations, excuses for a weary resignation. But evidence of silicosis produced another, generally unwelcome, possibility: a deadly mix of negligence and naiveté, which raised hard questions of responsibility.

The process of accountability and blame inevitably involves a bitter dialectic, a chorus of retrospective accusations—who should have done what and when—and the political antithesis, the contrite apologies and assurances. Lessons had been learned; compensation would be guaranteed, if necessary.

In the end there might be accommodation, but first, there would be tension and unpleasantness, bad publicity and angry fallout, both political and economic—and therefore a reluctance to initiate, never mind accelerate, correction.

And so, even in the face of growing certainty that St. Lawrence had a problem and it was related to the workplace, the human impulse to evade responsibility would persist for years. The instinct to delay the reckoning—to forestall a painful, costly process—would prevail throughout the fifties and into the next decade, fuelled by factors that would become more significant than self-preservation.

ARGUABLY, the Burin Peninsula had, at least since 1929, been the most troubled part of the struggling economy, and patient perseverance seemed to have produced rewards. By the early forties, viewed from afar, the situation there was hopeful. There was a mining business up and running, and it was sending little ripples of optimism through the region, especially around St. Lawrence.

Now, entering the second half of the century, there was something ominous about the situation there. But even with the new evidence of silicosis, there was a reluctance to point accusing fingers at the workplace. There was unquestionably an uncommon lot of sickness, but it was, perhaps, caused by an organic weakness in Newfoundlanders, a result of generations of poverty. It was particularly hard on miners, usually fatal. The most convenient conclusion was that they were just more susceptible to illness than other people. That wasn't anybody's fault. And of course, it was far from certain that everyone was equally vulnerable.

As in every aspect of uncertainty in life, luck, more than anything, would determine outcomes—who would get the sickness, who would survive it. Luck was unmanageable and unpredictable.

You had to look on the bright side, and of course have faith in God, in the mercy of the Ultimate Authority, the Custodian of Luck.

IN the early fifties, even in St. Lawrence, residents, including the corporation manager, Donald Poynter, preoccupied with the daily imperatives of economic survival, might have been forgiven for attributing too much to the plague of tuberculosis, which was the fault of no one in particular. It was probably TB that had carried off Donald Poynter's first wife. TB was a known killer. The place had been raging with TB. This could have been sufficient, for a while at least, to explain the spike in deaths and illnesses in St. Lawrence.

It would also explain why even Poynter was dismissive, in the face of hard evidence, of the reality that, among the miners, TB and silicosis had joined forces to confound the people and the doctors by creating a hybrid illness that could not be cured.

That it could have been prevented really wasn't worth discussing—not yet anyway.

What was the point in complaining? Of course, anyone with any basic knowledge of the mining industry should have known the consequences of insufficient ventilation. The law, as of 1951, was clear: underground workplaces were supposed to be adequately ventilated. Even without the law, the top decision-makers in the corporation—and later, at Newfluor—could and should have built proper ventilation into their designs for underground production.

But that was history. We learn from history. That's worth something, isn't it? Enlightenment?

Progress is a learning curve. And now that people knew more about the perils accompanying the benefits of employment, the problems would be solved. Newfoundland, by 1950, had a real government. Legislators would lay down the law; inspectors would enforce the regulations.

But people working for the mining companies were about to get yet another lesson in the reality of life in a resource-dependent economy. Hard-rock mines are not designed to last indefinitely, and they generally don't. In the absence of stern, objective oversight, the powers that be will spend money on amenities like health and safety grudgingly, if at all.

Almost twenty years into the relationship with the people of St. Lawrence, the St. Lawrence Corporation was inclined to take a hard look at any planning that might involve investment in a future that was starting to look shaky.

Official oversight was, to say the least, tentative, if not myopic.

39.

B Y December 1955, Seibert was again writing to Joey Smallwood, warning about looming difficulties—declining demand in the United States and foreign competition, especially from Mexico.

There had been an unexpected surge in demand for fluorspar because of US strategic requirements during the Korean War. It had been a godsend for St. Lawrence. Without it, the mine would have been out of business. But the boom was almost over. Seibert was giving notice that if St. Lawrence mining jobs were to be protected, he'd need the help of government, again.

"My firm belief is that in another 12 or 14 months the mining operations of the St. Lawrence Corporation at St. Lawrence will be closed down tight," he wrote, "and approximately 250 men will be thrown out of work unless we do get some protection in Canada to keep out the flow of European and Mexican fluorspar."[1]

The obvious solution to the problem was a hefty tariff on

imported fluorspar. The Americans had one. Why not Canada? "[L]et me assure you that I detest tariffs and I prefer to see the world on a free trading basis," Seibert insisted, "but the future of St. Lawrence is extremely bleak unless something is done."[2]

There is no available record of Smallwood's answer, but it's clear that within a little over two years—when Seibert's begging became explicit—he started running out of patience with the American. Surely Smallwood would have been aware that before his time in government, the commissioners who ran the island from 1934 to 1949 had expressed doubts among themselves about the competence of Mr. Seibert.

And by 1957, Smallwood would have reason to entertain similar concerns. It looked like Iron Springs was phasing out. Blue Beach mine had a big role to play in the corporation's future. But then, on an otherwise unexceptional morning in March 1957, Blue Beach collapsed. Miraculously there were no injuries or deaths. But it was an operational disaster, and an omen.

It happened at the beginning of a shift after days of flooding and small cave-ins. Almost from the moment the workday started, at eight in the morning, miners sensed that something serious was happening around them. Strange sounds issued from the rock— snaps and crackles; stone breaking; the walls spitting granite; bits of stone striking bodies, striking faces. It was as if the miners were inside a living thing, a distressed and angry thing.

After an hour of growing turbulence and anxiety, the miners gathered up their gear and retreated towards the shaft, signalled for the cage, piled in and headed for the surface. The assistant manager, Howard Farrell, described what happened next: "At 9.30 a.m. all hell broke loose, there were a succession of blasts accompanied by the rumbling of falling rock . . . [T]he caving continued all day and did not subside until 7.30 that evening."[3]

~~~

KEVIN Pike wasn't especially concerned when he was summoned to the boss's office late on the morning of June 6, 1957. He was the St. Lawrence Corporation warehouse manager, a job held by his father before him.[4]

Kevin had been working for the corporation since he was eleven, doing chores and carrying messages from the office on the St. Lawrence waterfront to the various mine sites, like Iron Springs, which was two and a half miles away. When his dad, the disabled First World War veteran Tom Pike, died suddenly in 1949, Donald Poynter had held the warehouse job open until nineteen-year-old Kevin finished high school.

Young Kevin and Donald Poynter respected each other and got along well, and while the call from Poynter's secretary was unusual, Pike had no reason to anticipate anything out of the ordinary. This changed the moment he saw Poynter slumped behind his desk.

The boss was distant. He was normally assertive and commanded any room he occupied. Now he seemed, as Kevin would remember, "emotional." The first thought that entered Pike's mind was that there was something wrong in Poynter's family. His parents had visited St. Lawrence from New Jersey, and Kevin had met them socially.

He asked the boss directly: "Is there something wrong back home?"

Poynter studied him for a moment. "No, Kev," he said. "I'll be blunt." He looked at his watch. It was ten minutes before eleven. "Go up and tell your people not to come back this afternoon."

Kevin laughed. Not come back?

"I'm serious," he said. "I just had a call from New York, from Seibert. We're closing down."

Donald Poynter would convey similar instructions that day to the people running Seibert's last two mines in St. Lawrence— two relatively small operations at Hay Pook and Hare's Ears.

～～～

IT WAS a tactical move by Seibert, and he clearly hadn't shared the strategy with his local manager, Donald Poynter. Years later, however, Howard Farrell would acknowledge what was probably the real purpose behind the phone call. In a casually oblique reference in a historical account of the St. Lawrence mining saga, Farrell noted, without elaboration, that the shutdown was "an attempt [by Seibert] to get the industry subsidized."[5]

If Farrell was correct, it was blackmail, pressure on the government of Newfoundland and a blunt statement to Seibert's employees in and near St. Lawrence. The prosperity they had helped to achieve by hard work and sacrifice was fragile. What they'd established in the course of twenty-five years could be eliminated by a single phone call from New York.

The message wasn't lost on anybody. It was loud and clear to the miners and the merchants in St. Lawrence, as well as the politicians and bureaucrats in St. John's. And for a crucial four-year period, it would reset priorities in Newfoundland. Worries about livelihood would overwhelm anxieties about life itself.

40.

～～～

EVEN before he'd left town, Dr. Pepper had created a nervous buzz in St. John's, but it didn't last long. Senior people in the provincial health department were reassured by their own dust studies in the St. Lawrence mines, and satisfied that Dr. Pepper had been mistaken. There was, however, the troubling reality of a rising toll of sick and dying miners, and their problems all seemed to be related to their lungs.

It was time, perhaps, to bring in the feds with their expertise and credibility. By 1956, St. John's was ready for that federal dust study that Dr. Pepper had been asking for six years earlier. The feds had the technology and expertise to answer all the questions about dust. As would later be observed in the report of a royal commission, the motivation behind the 1956 request was essentially self-serving: "[M]ining inspectors had . . . found the dust concentrations were within the permissible limits. They wanted this confirmed."[6]

In 1957, the federal government dispatched one of the top occupational health specialists in the Department of National Health and Welfare, Jack P. Windish, to document the dust conditions in the St. Lawrence mines. By then, of course, access to the mines was seriously compromised by the fact that most were idle. The Director mine, run by Alcan's subsidiary, Newfluor, offered the only fully operating workplace for Jack Windish to conduct his studies.

In mid-1958, Windish reported his findings, and the conclusions presented openings for argument—there were areas where the dust exceeded the limits for safe working conditions, but the readings were not excessive; on the other hand, particular circumstances could change long-term outcomes from exposure. There was plenty of material for debate, certainly for more discussion.

Two observations, however, would give reasons for concern: where there was inadequate ventilation (or none at all), the levels of dust were potentially lethal; and Windish found such readings even where the water poured into the workspace nonstop, an explicit contradiction of past expert opinions that the water neutralized the dust and smoke and danger.

These were precisely the conditions in which St. Lawrence miners had worked for years on end, all through the thirties and the forties, at Black Duck, Iron Springs, the Director and other mines. But that was yesterday. Now, in most places where men worked, the dust was tolerable. All good. Dust measurement continued.

But by 1958, there was another problem, a new conundrum to perplex officialdom. Shortly after Dr. Pepper left St. Lawrence, another doctor came to town to run the new US Memorial Hospital. The new doctor, Cyril J. Walsh, wasn't there for long when he began to notice another anomaly in the health profile of the town: lung cancer.

One miner, thirty-nine-year-old Thomas Lake, was known to have died of lung cancer in 1949. Augustus Pike, who was only twenty-seven, may well have died of cancer in 1946. Patrick Rennie, who died in 1951, was believed to have been suffering from stomach cancer. Two more lung cancer cases were confirmed in 1952.[7] In 1953, the number of confirmed lung cancer cases doubled, to four. In 1954, the year Dr. Walsh took charge of the new hospital, there were two more cases.

In July 1955, Michael Quirke, who as a young man gave up his job on a deep-sea diving tender to work at Black Duck mine, was told he had lung cancer. He had been working underground for twenty-two years. He died two months later, in September, at the age of fifty-one. He was one of two lung cancer deaths officially recorded that year. The other was Robert Pike, who had worked underground for seventeen years and was only thirty-six when he died. New cases continued to appear at the rate of two or three a year.

An autopsy on one of the miners who had died in 1953 revealed that he had tuberculosis aggravated by silicosis (or vice versa), and that he had developed lung cancer that proved fatal. The provincial workers' compensation board dismissed a claim on grounds that the cancer couldn't have been caused by conditions in the workplace. Lung cancer at the time was usually attributed to smoking or radiation in mines producing uranium. Fluorspar was definitely not radioactive.

But by 1956, Dr. Walsh realized that no matter where the cancer originated, it was a serious problem. There had been six deaths from the disease in the two years since his arrival. It was a small town. That was a lot. All the victims had worked as miners. They had also all been smokers, and the world was waking up to the link between tobacco and cancer. But six deaths in two years? In a place the size of St. Lawrence?

Everybody smoked in those days, and there was lung cancer everywhere. The incidence of lung cancer in Canada in 1931 was 3 cases per 100,000 people. By 1961, it had risen eightfold—to 24.6 per 100,000. But even in the context of that shocking trend, there was something tragically unusual about St. Lawrence.

Maybe it was time to move on from the discussions about dust and silicosis. Maybe it was time for a broader epidemiological investigation.

By 1958, another federal official was on the scene. His name was Dr. A.J. deVilliers, and he was another expert in the field of workplace health and safety. Official interest was now acute. But it was still too soon for action. The situation in St. Lawrence called for new studies, including an expanded air-quality analysis with more precise measurements, epidemiological and clinical investigations, laboratory studies.

St. Lawrence was a puzzle. It was a perplexing challenge for scientists and doctors. Politicians and public servants were waiting nervously on the sidelines. Nobody wanted this thing to turn out to be what it was beginning to look like. A scandal. No one wanted to be in the spotlight if or when the search for answers moved from causes to responsibility.

Mine managers offered reassurance by minimizing what was happening, attributing illness to causes over which they had no control, blaming agitators for cultivating controversy.

Inside the puzzle, men were withering and dying. Families were growing frantic.

Dr. deVilliers had first visited St. Lawrence as part of an earlier Windish dust survey. He'd met Dr. Walsh, who told him then about the unusual trend of cancer deaths among miners. Now he was back, and one of his main objectives was to find out what was causing all the cancer. Might there be something in the dust? Radiation, perhaps? The worst of the dust came from the granite in which the fluorspar was embedded. Perhaps there should be a closer look at the composition of the surrounding rock.

Like Jack Windish, Dr. deVilliers was facing one practical problem—his investigations would, for the most part, be limited to the Alcan operation, Newfluor's Director mine. As of June 1957, most of Iron Springs was flooded. Blue Beach was a pile of rubble. Black Duck, where many of the sick miners had started out, had been abandoned many years earlier—in late 1941.

One of the first people Dr. deVilliers informed of the worrisome lung cancer problem in St. Lawrence was Dr. Frank Brent, Alcan's chief medical officer. Brent was shocked, and in late October 1957, he visited St. Lawrence to personally evaluate the situation. A few months later, in mid-February 1958, he briefed Alcan's head office in a detailed account of what he saw as a potential crisis. It looked bad, he reported, but all the observational and anecdotal information available had to be corroborated now that Alcan was exposed.[8] There would have to be statistical analyses of mortality figures, more intensive dust measurement, animal tests on carcinogenicity and more precise analyses of air quality for evidence of radioactivity. Alcan's managers weren't about to jump to conclusions that might have incriminated them while Walter Seibert and his corporation sat darkly on the sidelines.

IT WAS genuinely mysterious. There was nothing about fluorspar that might explain a link to lung cancer. And yet miners were dying in unusual numbers from the disease. A comparison with similar communities in Newfoundland revealed that the incidence of death from lung cancer in St. Lawrence was twenty-nine times what was expected in a community that size.[9]

Like federal officials in the early fifties when Dr. Pepper called for a study of dust, Alcan managers at first resisted Dr. Brent's suggestion that there should be measurements to confirm the existence and the nature of radioactivity. Radon was a well-established cause of lung cancer among uranium miners. Radon gas had a short half-life, measured in minutes, and was known to quickly break down into cancer-causing "daughters" that circulated in the air. But Alcan wasn't mining uranium, and Dr. Brent was no expert on radiation. His judgement would require intensive validation—and time.

Time, however, had become an existential problem for miners in St. Lawrence. Men who had worked underground, or even in the mill, now felt exposed. People in town were conscious of the pervasive dust that gusted through the place during dry weather. There were fluorspar stockpiles near the harbour. The dusty roads were made from mine waste.

Maybe the dust was radioactive. The experts checked. It wasn't.

Dr. Brent finally urged health officials in the provincial government to officially ask Ottawa to launch a cancer-focused epidemiological study of the whole mine environment. And soon after that, Jack Windish was sampling the air for radiation.

By 1958, Alcan seemed to be in little doubt about what was coming down the turnpike. Dr. Brent was close enough to the reality that he could almost smell approaching controversy. It was time to factor optics into future planning—dying miners, cancer, careless corporations, bad ventilation, "radon daughters."

He instructed Alcan's man in town, Rupert Wiseman, then the manager of the Newfluor mine, to do what was necessary to counter the appearance that the company had been callous in its response to the evolving situation. It was time for anticipatory damage management. There could no longer be any doubt that radiation was, at the very least, a factor in the rising roll call of death among the men who had worked at mining fluorspar. But the puzzling continued. Radiation was killing miners, but fluorspar wasn't radioactive.

The sense of urgency was growing, but soon there would be a new distraction. Miners were dying, but the St. Lawrence Corporation also seemed to be on its deathbed.

41.

A s of June 6, 1957, it was clear: the corporation was in rough shape, seriously ill. But it wasn't dead. Not yet. Donald Poynter's football-playing instinct kicked in again. The team was trailing badly, but there was still time on the clock. Seibert's call and his order to shut down just amounted to a tactical time out.

Poynter continued to make plans to save the game on the ground, mining and finding markets for fluorspar. Let Walter Seibert deal with the governments of Newfoundland and Canada. He could make the case for public assistance to overcome what he saw as unfair competition from outside—mostly from Mexico, where production costs were lower than in St. Lawrence. Donald would stick to his game, doing what he was good at. Let Seibert do the bullshit part, manipulating other big shots.

In St. John's, however, the Smallwood government seemed to have already given up on the Seibert operation. There were discreet inquiries to potential buyers, and the provincial economist even suggested that the ministry of mines take over.[10]

For Seibert, one answer to his problems was protection in the form of a hefty tariff to squelch the low-cost imports from Mexico. It would take a federal government initiative, but he wanted Smallwood's backing in requesting it. The Canadian tariff on a ton of imported fluorspar should be ten dollars, he proposed.

In January 1958, the Canadian tariff board agreed to conduct an inquiry to determine whether Seibert's company deserved such provocative support. There would be a public hearing in Ottawa in May.

Clearly Ottawa was not enthusiastic, and it would not have helped Walter Seibert's cause that his company's union nemesis, Aloysius Turpin, was again leading the St. Lawrence miners— and expressing his animosity towards the corporation in a letter to the local federal MP. "We the people are fed up with the St. Lawrence Corporation of Newfoundland Ltd.," he wrote, "and at times feeling you are only fighting a battle for Siebert [sic], who's not, after all, worth fighting for."[11]

On February 5, 1958, Premier Smallwood sent a brief, sharp telegram to Walter Seibert, saying he was "considerably disturbed by the prolonged inactivity" at the corporation mines in St. Lawrence. People were being forced to leave town. More than 250 jobs were melting away. "Come and see me," Smallwood wrote.[12]

Seibert showed up, as instructed, to meet the premier and members of the provincial cabinet on February 19, 1958, but he was unapologetic—the shutdown was not his fault. He'd warned Smallwood in December 1955 that he was facing problems. Now he desperately needed help. He could put fifty to seventy-five miners back to work if the government would agree to buy $250,000 worth of fluorspar and stockpile it for future sale back to the corporation.

The provincial economist was convinced that the corporation had a larger problem—St. Lawrence fluorspar was being marketed at twice the cost of product coming out of Mexico, and wages weren't the only cause. The government would likely not have any more success unloading high-cost fluorspar, no matter how long it was kept in reserve. They probably wouldn't recover their money no matter whom they sold it to. The economist had doubts that the corporation would ever again be in a position to fulfill its end of the bargain Seibert was proposing.

American mining operations had higher wages, the economist pointed out, and still had lower overall production costs. One significant problem was Seibert's inability to cultivate goodwill among his workers—"persistent, though generally unwitting, passive resistance among miners" was part of his dilemma.

But with Walter, situations were never quite as simple as they might seem after rational analysis by scientists and economists and public servants. Seibert had deals with the US government, details of which would have been surprising to most people in Newfoundland. There was that refinery, for instance, named after the little town on the Burin but located in Delaware. There was the secret deal to supply fluorspar from St. Lawrence for use in the creation of an atomic bomb. With Walter, there were deals and then deals within deals. Like wheels within wheels—brilliant, as long as they were turning.

In 1955, he had quietly bought controlling interest in a Mexican fluorspar mine—money he could have spent to improve productivity in Newfoundland. Now he was admitting he couldn't even sell cheap Mexican fluorspar in Canada.

The only hope for St. Lawrence was to raise a barrier against all foreign competition—including his own Mexican operation.

Walter had obviously concluded that his move into Mexico, a good idea early on, had since turned into a big miscalculation—that North American steelmakers had formed durable relationships with other Mexican suppliers while he was enjoying his sweetheart status with the US government.

He was ready to bail out of Mexico, perhaps, return to square one—the dream of a "fluorspar empire" in Newfoundland.

Whatever his motivation, the tariff was a non-starter. Almost all the affected parties—especially the steel companies—were opposed. A tariff was a bad idea. And because it would also affect

American producers, it would result in retaliation. Alcan sold a lot of stuff in the United States and Mexico. Alcan was against the tariff.

And in the end, the federal government was against it too. Analysts on the tariff board couldn't find a single point in Seibert's arguments with which they could agree, and in September, they advised the federal minister of finance that the tariff Seibert wanted was unwarranted and would probably cause significant harm to Alcan and the Canadian economy.

It seemed to be game over for the St. Lawrence Corporation. But Donald Poynter still wasn't ready to give up.

Now he was fighting for survival on two fronts. The growing pile of evidence that his mining operations, and Alcan's, were probably the cause of illness and death for many of his neighbours was too much to concede, so he continued to resist it. If there was radiation in the mines, he said dismissively, improved ventilation would surely "blow those nasty little radiation bugs out to sea," and everyone could safely get on with the more important task of mining.

By mid-1959, his determination to sell St. Lawrence fluorspar seemed to bear encouraging results. The corporation had found new openings to sell metallurgical-grade fluorspar to Canadian steel companies. For all Seibert's mismanagement, St. Lawrence fluorspar was still top quality. With Poynter's aggressive mining and salesmanship, Seibert seemed to have recovered some small but steady markets in the United States.

Poynter had restarted production in several small St. Lawrence mines and had high hopes for the future. In 1960, he went to New York and returned with a "pocket full" of orders. The Hay Pook mine was up and running once again.

But Donald Poynter's energetic optimism was being overshadowed by the relentless progress of a killer stalking his community.

42.

~~

THE daughters of radon appear briefly as ionized particles when radon gas, a product of uranium, breaks down. They stick to microscopic specks of dust and moisture. Inhaled, they are capable of destroying human tissue. Radon daughters "rip up any body cells in their path . . . like bolts of lightning striking a house."[13] But where were these deadly radon daughters coming from? The answer wasn't far away.

As long ago as 1948, a geologist's report on mineral deposits in the St. Lawrence area described significant alpha radioactivity and "radiogenic heat" coming from the local rock.[14] It seems that nobody took special note of that observation at the time.

Later studies of the geology would confirm that the local granite, which hosts so much fluorspar, is also unusually rich in uranium.[15] Jack Windish, alerted to the high incidence of lung cancer among St. Lawrence miners, had logically looked for uranium in or around the fluorspar. But he couldn't find it. He'd tested the ore coming from the mine. There was no evidence of radioactivity. There had to be another source. He would discover it was all around him and over him and under his feet, running down his neck, leaking into his boots.

The figurative bolts of lightning were coming from the water.

The Director mine was a veritable Niagara Falls of water—its pumps struggled to discharge up to three thousand gallons per minute from the workings.

Cracks and fissures in the granite carried surface water great distances, and as it passed through uranium along the way, the water picked up radon gas. As the water-borne radon reached the open spaces of the mine, it released its "progeny," the infamous cancer-causing daughters.

The continuous pumping of water, without which there could

be no mining, seemed to have created a deadly loop of radio-activity—a cyclical flow from rainfall and surface water sources, through uranium-bearing granite, into the drifts and stopes where miners worked, to be pumped back out again. And then the cycle would repeat itself—surface water returning through uranium, back again to where the men were working. Pumped out, only to begin the journey back.

Windish and his associate Dr. deVilliers would find in their early studies that radon transported in this way produced radio-activity readings that were between two and a half and ten times above safe working levels. The villains were finally identified, but like the dust, they had already done their damage. And it would take another year to come up with a response.

In late 1959, Windish reported his findings to the companies and to health officials in St. John's. Because the Director mine had been his main focus, Alcan officials scrambled to head off an anticipated backlash. Newfluor miners were dying, but almost all of them had worked for the St. Lawrence Corporation before moving to the Director mine. From Alcan's point of view, it was hardly fair that the fortuitous timing of Seibert's corporate misfortune left Alcan to face the public and political backlash all by itself.

The company immediately began planning better ventilation, but the Alcan medical director, Dr. Frank Brent, also sought political cover—a commitment from the provincial minister of health, James McGrath, that the company would get advance notice of any public statements from the government of Newfoundland.

In the meantime, Alcan seemed to be getting mixed messages from the federal experts, Windish and deVilliers. Windish, who was actually taking measurements where he could in the mines, was candid in his reporting—he had found radiation readings (radon daughters) up to nearly 200 times the maximum allowable levels for a safe workplace, albeit in an unused section of the Director mine. In that same area, he'd recorded a radon gas measurement that was 133 times the suggested safe working level. In that abandoned section, the air was so thin, he said, he was unable to light a match. (At the Ottawa briefing where he made this observation, there was a sceptical reaction.[16] Someone suggested, perhaps facetiously, that maybe there was something wrong with the matches he was trying to light.)

Dr. deVilliers had already offered reassurances, at another meeting weeks earlier, that "reported concentrations of radon are not remarkable."[17] It was acknowledged that in most working areas, radiation readings were sometimes above safe working levels but mostly at or below the standard. When asked about the standard and what he understood to be the practical meaning of the "maximum allowable concentration" for radon in a workplace, deVilliers replied that "it represents a concentration to which a man can be exposed for an eight-hour shift throughout the year, year after year."

Alcan and the bureaucrats seemed to be reassured. But in just a matter of months, political circumstances would raise the temperature of the conversation about the reality of working in the St. Lawrence mines year after year after year.

On March 1, 1960, the radiation menace could no longer be denied. Joey Smallwood, who had been dismissive, now had to act, and he called a meeting for a full discussion of the Windish radiation findings. All the principals were there: politicians, union leaders and Alcan officials. The health minister, James McGrath, later prepared a summary of the findings, and it was a masterful example of transparency and creative obfuscation.[18]

The main points, however, were clear: St. Lawrence miners had a high incidence of lung cancer that couldn't be explained by dust conditions in the mines, and the levels of radiation "were much higher than the permissible limits."

The minister hastily pointed out that the highest readings were in unused sections of the Director mine, but even so, miners were working in areas where radiation was frequently beyond permissible limits. That had to be corrected. "We have been advised . . . that comparatively simple methods of ventilation can bring the concentration down out of the danger zone . . . [and] render the mine safe."

It was, perhaps, an unintended concession that for many years, the St. Lawrence mines had been terribly unsafe, and that hundreds of men had worked for decades in lethal concentrations of dust and radiation that could easily have been remedied.

The minister insisted that "it cannot yet be regarded scientifically proved that the high incidence of cancer and the presence of hazardous radiation are directly effect and cause," but the obvious "coincidence" definitely justified further studies of the problem.

The miners weren't prepared to wait for scientific proof. The St. Lawrence story became—at least for a short while—a public scandal. The St. John's media ran articles about cancer and radiation, and the underlying role of poor ventilation in the mines. The union pulled all its underground members off the job—at the time, Poynter had managed to put twenty-two miners back to work, filling his "pocketful" of orders from the United States. Al Turpin—who knew about the problem from earlier briefings by Windish—now declared that nobody would go back underground until the ventilation issue had been solved.

And it *was* solved—in just a few weeks—but not before an unusual display of defensive denial by the Alcan manager, Rupert Wiseman. The walkout by the miners, he fumed in a press release, wasn't so much a response to the perils in the workplace as a radical reaction to "a distortion of the facts by the press."

Whatever. On April 2, just a month after the decisive meeting with Smallwood, and after a few weeks of proper ventilation, Jack Windish took new readings and found that radiation in both the Director and the smaller corporation mines had miraculously dropped back to safe working levels or better.

On April 5, miners started heading back to work.

IT WAS all so simple—in a matter of months, the companies had achieved, under the threat of scandal, what common sense had instructed decades earlier. Mine safety must include the air that miners breathe. Company and government officials had spent years blaming respiratory problems caused by dust on tuberculosis, which wasn't anybody's fault. But they couldn't duck the radon lightning bolt. Windish had spelled it out clearly, and the fast remediation in the spring of 1960 proved his point: the high radon readings were directly caused by poor or nonexistent mechanical ventilation. And that was the fault of management.

The St. Lawrence mines were, overnight, considerably safer. But for a rising number of St. Lawrence miners, many of whom did not yet know that they were doomed, it was all too late.

BY early April, public interest in the peculiarities of mortality in the St. Lawrence area had faded once again. The priority now, as had always been the case, was employment—and the prospect that the corporation was failing would soon become the primary concern in both St. Lawrence and St. John's.

In 1964, the *British Journal of Industrial Medicine* published a lengthy technical review of the St. Lawrence situation by Windish and deVilliers. There was no pussyfooting here, in a discussion among peers. Their paper was dense with complicated detail, but the conclusions made for a depressing summary of the thirty-year history of the radiation problem.

The death rate among men between twenty and sixty-four in St. Lawrence was well over twice that in nearby Grand Bank, and more than triple the death rate in that age group for all of Newfoundland. Meanwhile, Windish and deVilliers reported, "The death rates for St. Lawrence females in the age group 'all ages' are significantly lower than those for Newfoundland, which, in turn, are lower than those for Grand Bank."[19]

Lung cancer in St. Lawrence afflicted mostly men, all of whom had been miners. The review in the British journal raised the real possibility that there had been an "appreciable under-diagnosis" of lung cancer deaths prior to 1951 because of an absence of post-mortem examinations of people who were believed to have died from tuberculosis.

The obvious conclusion, based on comparisons with the levels of fatal lung cancer among uranium miners in various parts of the world, including the United States and South Africa, was that the fluorspar miners of St. Lawrence had been working in a far more dangerous environment. And the tragic consequences were only starting to appear.

That distant, dire analysis would have excited widespread comment among a readership limited to professionals in the field of occupational health—but it didn't seem to register where it really mattered, in St. Lawrence, Newfoundland. Certainly not right away. But it surely would, and when it did, it would be plain-spoken, from the heart of long experience, from a man who had been a miner with direct and dramatic experience with death. His name was Rennie Slaney.

43.

DONALD Poynter revived the Hay Pook mine in 1960. He also had plans to reopen the Hare's Ears mine. He was confident that the high-quality ore from Hare's Ears would win new customers in the American steel industry. The government of Newfoundland had offered a $200,000 loan guarantee, but it had tight strings attached—evidence that senior government officials finally had serious doubts about the competence, and perhaps even the integrity, of Walter Seibert.

Walter turned the offer down.

There's a telling document among the Smallwood papers in an archive at Memorial University of Newfoundland. It's undated and unsigned. It's stamped "Confidential," and it presents an unflattering portrait of the St. Lawrence Corporation and its owner. "Almost any handyman can build a lean-to," it begins, "add more lean-tos to it, put a couple of more lean-tos on top of it and call it a house. But it is not a house for all it may be called one. At best, it is a crude shelter. In the same way, a bunch of holes dug into the ground all over the place does not constitute a mine, even though it may be called a mine at St. Lawrence. It is at best extensive diggings."[20]

The anonymous author continues: "From observation and from report, I have come to the conclusion that the construction of the fluorspar 'mines' of the St. Lawrence Corporation initially involved only the application of the ingenuity of handymen and the financial outlay of a lean-to . . . Moreover, during the twenty-odd years that these diggings have been expanding there is no visible evidence that anything was done to them by way of engineering design." The policy was "to improvise until there was nothing left to improvise with, and then purchase the cheapest possible make-do to keep things going a little longer."

The document then sets out twelve steps that should have been followed, including the preparation of a master plan and the employment of "a qualified accountant . . . from the start." This observation would have stung Walter Seibert, who was an accountant by profession.

It must be admitted that mines are constructed to make a profit for the owner more than for any other reason. In view of the fact that the St. Lawrence Corporation's operations at St. Lawrence undoubtedly returned a profit for their owner for many years, then the question may well be asked what does it matter whether these diggings were ingenious improvisations or engineered excavations?

The answer is that as soon as an abnormal combination of circumstances, particularly favourable to the owner, disappeared, the operations collapsed flat, the deposits only partly exhausted, and the normal demand for fluorspar greater than ever.

The author noted approvingly "the availability of several superbly ingenious men who were prepared to devote their all to an adventure, and who did just that by going to St. Lawrence in the 1930s." However, "the owner of the deposits was a man with a reputed fanatical devotion to profit," which resulted in many of the problems that were then threatening the existence of the venture.

There is, in the five-page document, no reference to mine ventilation or to health, to silicosis or to cancer. It is, all in all, a lament for lost political and economic opportunities.

The writing has the flair and the journalistic tone, not to mention the wit, to suggest it could have been written by Smallwood himself. The reference to "superbly ingenious men" could reflect the fact that Dr. Warren Smith, the first manager of Black Duck and later boss at Newfluor, and Donald Poynter, who had a warm relationship with the premier, were both well respected among government officials in St. John's and Ottawa.

Whether Joey Smallwood actually penned this vivid document is beside the point—he obviously agreed with it and valued it enough to preserve it among his private papers for posterity.

~~~

On Friday, June 9, 1961, Donald Poynter took another phone call from the United States. On the line this time was Johanna Seibert, Walter's wife. The message was brief: her husband had suffered a massive brain hemorrhage the day before and had died shortly afterwards in St. Mary's Hospital, in Hoboken, New Jersey.

Poynter put the phone down, shaken. He was in his office. He had known Walter Seibert for more than thirty years. Their mothers had introduced them, encouraged them to work together. He and Seibert had become business partners on the strength of promises and a handshake, an arrangement that had never been formalized. He took a deep breath, then walked home to break the news to his wife, Florence Etchegary Poynter.

His son Thomas Poynter recalls that his father "was visibly upset. The wind was clearly taken out of his sails for the moment. I don't think there was any indication that Seibert was ill."

Walter Seibert was, legally, the sole owner of the St. Lawrence Corporation and several other related enterprises in Canada and the United States. The future of the corporation—and now that of its senior employee, Donald Poynter—was suddenly, unexpectedly under a darker cloud than just a day earlier, when the challenge had been simple by comparison: reopen mines, find buyers for fluorspar. Donald Poynter had been confident that both objectives, while difficult, were doable. But what now?

The Seibert family, Johanna and her three sons, visited St. Lawrence to evaluate their mining operations. It quickly became obvious to Poynter that they had no interest in hanging on to them—they would soon be up for sale.

It also became clear that the family had no intention of honouring Walter's informal promises that Donald would one day be a full partner and would own a substantial block of shares in the corporation. Poynter's plans to reopen one of the idle mines were abruptly shelved.

Two of Seibert's sons had actually lived and worked in

St. Lawrence in the early fifties. They would undoubtedly have been aware of the looming tragedy of miners who had worked in corporation mines. To that point, because the corporation had been relatively inactive since 1957, Seibert had avoided the growing controversy about dust and radiation in his mines. He'd been unwavering in his focus on the business of selling fluorspar and making money from it. He had cleared a reported $10 million on his contract with the US government in the early fifties.

Newfluor, so far, had been taking all the heat in the emerging controversy over miners' health. And as of 1961, there would be new regulations that required rigorous radiation monitoring underground and even in surface facilities. There would be intense public scrutiny. Newfluor would be on the firing line for years to come. There was no way around that reality.

There were many reasons, on the other hand, why the Seibert family would want to cut and run, and effectively avoid accountability for the industrial carnage that was directly attributable to Walter's early scheme to make his fortune. The financial compensation owed to the dead and dying miners and their families would inevitably become a liability. The Seibert family had been handed, in Walter's sudden death, a golden opportunity to avoid it.

St. Lawrence Corporation assets were soon up for sale, but the same factors that had made the Seibert family reluctant to continue running the mines were also daunting for prospective buyers. Alcan was already in the middle of the mess. There was little downside to picking up the pieces of what was left of their old competitor. They had their eye, especially, on the Blue Beach property. The Smallwood government, reluctant to allow one company to have total control of the resource, discouraged the deal at first.[21]

The search went on for more than three years, until finally the Seibert family asked Alcan to revive its original offer to buy the corporation assets. And this time, they did. Now they had the town of St. Lawrence, afraid that it could soon become a ghost town, onside, and the political objections quickly slipped away.

Poynter, by now aware that he had been betrayed by the man he had long considered his partner, had to endure the additional indignity of working out the details of the sale to Alcan's subsidiary, Newfluor. And on June 9, 1965, four years to the day from the fateful phone call from Mrs. Seibert, he watched the properties he had helped turn into mines pass over to the competition.

Poynter by then had deep roots in St. Lawrence. His wife was born and raised there, part of the prominent Etchegary clan. His five children, with the exception of his eldest daughter, had all been born in Newfoundland, and all had become ardent Newfoundlanders. He might have returned to New Jersey, but instead he took a job in St. John's as an adviser to the provincial government, which was where he ended his career.

He would live out much of his remaining life in Newfoundland, in failing health, until July 26, 1976, when he suffered a heart attack during a holiday at a family retreat in Long Island, New York. He died four days later, surrounded by his wife and adult children.

His final years were bitter. As his son Thomas, a Boston-based entrepreneur, remembers: "It was a difficult time in our house. My family's notion, on the Poynter and the Etchegary sides, of keeping promises was strong. And the Seiberts broke it, again."[22]

The Seibert family, Thomas Poynter still believes, were "uncaring for the miners or the town. From the father to the wife to the sons, just nasty people who give capitalism a bad name."

IN 1965, the year the corporation died, lung cancer claimed the lives of eight more former miners in St. Lawrence, most of whom had started their careers in corporation mines.

One of them was forty-five-year-old Arcule Slaney Jr., whose father, Rennie Slaney's brother, also named Arcule, had died from "miners' disease" eight years earlier.

NINE

~

Dying by Inches

44.

A ND now they were dying quietly, one by one. The tragedies
were personal, not public, not historical. It was understandable that no one seemed to notice—no one beyond the family or
the edge of town.

Four thousand people died in a single storm off the coast of
Newfoundland, and it's hardly mentioned in the history books.
Twenty-seven people died in the space of a few minutes in a tsunami.
Hardly anyone remembers. Two hundred and three American
sailors perished just outside St. Lawrence on a stormy day in 1942.
Who, outside of Newfoundland, knows about it now?

But Rennie Slaney couldn't get it off his mind, that slow
attrition in his town all through the fifties, maybe earlier, and
now accelerating in the sixties. The number of his neighbours and
family and friends dropping off. Men his age and much younger.
There had been scientific analyses of dust, measurements of radiation, epidemiological surveys. Learned papers written and published far and wide for learned people.

But it didn't seem to register outside St. Lawrence as a human
crisis. It didn't come across as what he was seeing: the endless
funeral procession winding through his town, day after day. Maybe
that's why there was so much dithering in St. John's and Ottawa.
They didn't seem to get it, the personal dimensions of this puzzle.
The puzzle lacked a personality.

So maybe he should do something to wake up the big shots. After all, he felt some personal responsibility. He had been a boss. He remembered how he'd once offered assurances to the mine inspector from Ontario that the corporation would be driving ventilation shafts. For sure.

That's what he'd been told by Poynter. And Poynter had been told by Walter Seibert in New York that the money would be there. So why wouldn't Rennie Slaney, the supervisor, assume that it was going to happen?

But still, people who knew Rennie Slaney would know that he'd felt guilty when it didn't happen when he said it would. And that he'd count this lapse among the causes of the misery that was playing out around him. The misery, in his mind, was personal and painful. The misery had names and faces. It had his brother's face. And he knew he didn't have to look too far into the future to see his own face.

And so, on the morning of February 15, 1965, Rennie Slaney sat at his typewriter and started writing down the names. It's possible to say with some precision when he made his list, because Roche Turpin's name was there, among the dead. And Roche Turpin had just died that very day.

WHEN Roche Turpin got his death sentence, it would have consisted of just four words: "Abnormality. See your doctor."[1]

It would have been a simple notation on an x-ray report. It was a woefully common occurrence those days. For Turpin, it would mark the beginning of an ordeal that was all the more daunting because of its familiarity. He knew what was in store for him.

By 1963, when he got his verdict, Roche Turpin had already seen it many times—the withering of strong men, neighbours, relatives. Men he'd known and worked with. And he would have felt it coming on well before the x-ray, the ebbing energy, the difficulty breathing, the nocturnal terrors. And the private moments of bitterness and grief.

He had become an old man and yet he was just forty-six when they told him. So much life unfinished.

He'd been a miner for more than half his life. He'd started out, as his people had for centuries, as a fisherman. Over the next two years after the dreadful diagnosis, he'd have many moments when he wished he'd never left the sea.

But his fishing days were back before 1938. The fishery, especially on the south coast of Newfoundland, was a dead end. It had been like that since the great tidal wave of November 1929. For years, the catch was a fraction of what it had been before the tsunami. Foreign markets had either disappeared in the Depression or been taken over by Icelanders and aggressive continental Europeans.

St. Lawrence and Lawn were lucky, though, blessed by an accident of geology. They were sitting on great wealth, and as of 1933, bold investors from St. John's and the United States were determined to exploit that wealth. In the long run, everyone would benefit.

In the short run, though, there would be sacrifices. Mining fluorspar was pure drudgery, but it was steady work, and while conditions were still primitive and the pay insulting, even in the midst of hard times everywhere, there was a future and that was priceless.

And then there was a new mining company in town, American Newfoundland Fluorspar. In 1938, Roche Turpin went to work for the newcomers, who were beginning to develop a major property that would become the Director mine, later owned by Alcan.

~~~

FOR weeks, Roche had been fighting a series of heavy, persistent colds and eventually what seemed to be bronchitis. He'd always been a strong and vigorous man, frequently heading off into the bush after a hard day's work to clear his mind, or fish or hunt or gather firewood, or just walk and think. Now he was feeling weak and listless and struggling with no small amount of frustration over his diminished physical abilities. So he went to see his doctor.[2]

He might have had a lurking suspicion that the symptoms were more than the common cold. He'd recently returned from British Columbia. He'd come to a major decision—to leave Newfoundland and find work in another mine, preferably in BC, where the perils were more commonplace and there were higher standards for health and safety in the workplace.

He'd flown out to Vancouver, had an interview; he seemed confident. But then his prospective new employers had sent him for a medical, which included a chest x-ray. And he'd failed it, and because he'd failed it, he didn't get the job.

He should go back home, they told him, get checked out there. Now he was feeling awful, heavy respiratory symptoms. And now he was facing Dr. Hollywood.

DR. Brian Hollywood, chief of medicine at the US Memorial Hospital, had been in St. Lawrence since 1960. He grew up in Ireland. He felt at home in St. Lawrence, understood the culture and the people. He was familiar with complaints like the ailments that brought Roche Turpin to his office. He would have felt a weary sense of despair as Roche sat before him, describing symptoms Dr. Hollywood had heard many, many times before from men who wanted to believe that he could offer some relief.

It's just a cold, right? Sometimes the symptoms hang on longer than they should. Right? The flu, perhaps. I'll take some medicine, a bit of rest. All it's going to take to be as good as new. Right? When can I go back to work?

The doctor would have projected hope, perhaps offered a prescription. Maybe he'd even given Roche a note for his supervisors—the man needs time off to recuperate. Working underground was not conducive to recovery from a respiratory problem. Shortly after that meeting, the company assigned Roche to a surface job.

What the doctor would have known but could not say was that working underground for nearly half his life had already done its damage, and it couldn't be reversed.

HOPE dies slowly, even in the face of certainty. Priscilla Turpin, who would outlive her husband by more than fifty years, said, "Deep down, I don't know if he ever convinced himself that he had cancer. He used to say to me a few times, 'When I get a bit better, you and I are going to go in to St. John's and I'm going to see a specialist.' I'd say, 'Yes.' [But] I knew."[3]

With the normal terror at the prospect of personal extinction, there is the burden of worry about the inevitable hardships the family will face. Roche and Priscilla had six children. The youngest, Ellen, was only four. And yet they were infinitely better off than the family of Thomas Lake, who'd died of lung cancer in 1949 at the age of thirty-nine.[4]

Thomas Lake left eight kids. He had continued working until two weeks before he died, knowing there would be no steady income after he was gone, except perhaps from welfare. His wife died three months after he did. Their oldest boy raised his seven siblings.

Because Thomas Lake had been forced to stop working two years before the Workmen's Compensation Act came into effect in Newfoundland, the family's later claim for compensation was turned down. In any case, lung cancer wasn't then recognized as a compensable disease. The children survived with meagre help from social assistance and money from their grandfather.

Roche Turpin would have been aware that, mercifully, his condition qualified for compensation under regulations that had taken effect in 1960. There was no doubt about that. Lung cancer was now covered, if that was really what he had. He also had the comfort of some insurance coverage from the company and a policy he'd taken out and paid for on his own.

He might also have taken solace from the fact that his wife, Priscilla, was relatively well educated. She had attended high school and had completed a course that qualified her to teach, which she had done for several years before taking a job as a file clerk with Newfluor. She'd be all right in the long run, after he was gone.[5]

Priscilla had worked in the Alcan office until the early fifties, when she married Roche, who was then approaching his mid-thirties and was working for the same company as an underground electrician. And after Roche was gone, she would take a part-time job at the St. Lawrence post office, where she continued to work until she could retire in 1985. Her limited financial security did not, however, reduce the burdens of single parenthood, the loneliness, the coping with the needs of kids who would never fully understand why "poor Daddy" wasn't there anymore.[6] "At first the youngsters, if I couldn't come up until six o'clock . . . they'd be all up in the window; every pane there had a face in it waiting for Mom to come home."[7]

Then Mom laid down the law. They were given jobs. Lucille, who was thirteen, became the cook, and Mom made it clear to all of them that she expected a tidy house and supper on the table when she came home from work. Gradually the anxious faces in the windows disappeared.

~~~

THE Turpin story illustrates the private agonies behind each diagnosis—and by 1965, there had been dozens of them and there would be dozens more.

Priscilla Turpin could not forget the slow drift towards the inevitable. A mysterious and persistent illness late in 1963. September 1964, Roche is in a St. John's hospital. October 1964, Priscilla makes the long and by now prohibitively expensive journey to the city to visit him; she's shocked to see him—he's dropped nearly sixty pounds. He's in a ward with five other seriously sick and injured people; he's in despair. His bedside table is stacked with cards and letters that he hasn't even opened. There has been confirmation of his darkest fears—it is definitely lung cancer. Untreatable. November 1, his brother travels to St. John's to bring him home, but it becomes quickly apparent, especially to Roche, that the family lacks the strength and physical resources to look after him. December 22, Dr. Hollywood offers him a hospital bed. He accepts.

Priscilla went to see him every day, often more than once. Initially she brought the children but soon decided it wasn't helpful. "I brought them in a couple of times to see him, but they always made him very unhappy, and he always cried. And the doctor said I'd better not bring them too often. It made him very lonely."

After less than two months in the hospital, Roche was dead at the age of forty-eight.

WHEN Roche Turpin first went underground, in 1938, it would have been with the sense of achievement of someone who, perhaps for the first time, had steady work and the prospect of a firm financial future. And working underground—for the men who chose what for many would seem an impossibly dangerous, claustrophobic occupation—offered certain psychic rewards that matter greatly to a particular breed of individual: the collegiality that exists among workers who must rely on one another for survival, routinely doing jobs that others couldn't or wouldn't even think of trying.

It probably would not have mattered much to him that he was working in an industry that was, for all practical purposes, unregulated, and that his health and safety were dependent on the enforcement of only one law—as would be acknowledged officially many years later—"the law of self-preservation."[8]

He was twenty-two years old when he started out. He was strong. He was, as far as he could tell, healthy. So what if the mining regulations that applied then had been devised thirty years earlier and were hopelessly irrelevant to the workplace he now inhabited? So what if Newfoundland was run by unelected bureaucrats who refused to risk industrial development by nitpicking about health and safety in the workplace?

It's unlikely that Roche Turpin was aware that in 1936, an Ontario mine inspector, who had visited St. Lawrence to assess working conditions, had urged the commission running the government to introduce new regulations that would require the owners of the St. Lawrence mines to meet the kind of industrial standards that applied in other places. There were rules and they were getting stricter in the provinces of Canada and in the United States. The commissioners didn't listen then, nor would they four years later, in 1940, when he repeated his critique.

The Ontario consultant, A.E. Cave, was ignored until after 1949, when Newfoundland became a part of Canada. By 1951, the new province had put in place protective legislation, including a system for financial compensation for work-related injury or other disability, or death. The new laws stopped short of pre-employment screening for miners, a practice that in other provinces included chest x-rays to identify people with pre-existing problems or obvious vulnerabilities to the perils of working in a damp and dusty environment, like a mine.

In reality, most miners would have quietly approved of such an omission. An x-ray could raise another barrier to a livelihood, as Roche Turpin learned when he looked for work in British Columbia. Most miners smoked cigarettes. Many had survived some contact with tuberculosis. Many miners from the early days of Black Duck and Iron Springs had evidence of silicosis. There were many reasons for a prospective miner to be nervous about having to step in front of an x-ray machine.

Miners, like many industrial workers at the time, faced a commonplace dilemma—weighing the potential risk of illness, disability and death against the very real prospect of unemployment and poverty, a kind of living death with which so many were already only too familiar.

The choice, especially if a man was young and strong and hard up for a job, was easy.

45.

THE day Roche Turpin died—February 15, 1965—was the day that Rennie Slaney was transformed from a silent witness (or in special cases, quiet advocate) for the dead or dying. Because of what he did that day, he would become the public face and voice for a story that could no longer be ignored.

He had nothing left to lose. He was fifty-eight years old, but the years he'd spent working as a miner had so severely compromised his health that he could no longer work, not even in a relatively easy office job.

He was by then town manager for St. Lawrence, but he could barely climb the stairs to his office and would soon have to retire from that position. His lungs were shot. He was suffering from chronic bronchitis, obstructive emphysema, infective asthma and cor pulmonale, a usually terminal heart disease caused by lung failure.[9] He'd had his first serious heart attack in 1952, when he was forty-five. That was when he had to stop working underground. The corporation gave him an office job, but in 1957, when Seibert's company started to shut down, Rennie Slaney, after twenty-three years in mining, was out of work.

For most of the years he spent working for the Seibert outfit, he was a boss—an underground shift boss and eventually a mine captain, which is a kind of general foreman. He'd started out the hard way, at the Black Duck mine, and on many days in that brutal place, he'd have asked himself why he gave up working on the coastal steamers.

But he was married then and the kids were coming quickly. In his peak working years, he had twelve of them still living at home. And now he knew his working days were over. He could not have known he was starting something that, even if it didn't pay much, would energize the last years of his life.

On that day, he typed up five single-spaced pages and set out for an appearance before a special committee appointed by the Smallwood government to review the provincial Workmen's Compensation Act. In his written presentation, he mentioned that Roche Turpin had died that day, and that another miner, Harry Clarke, was in the same St. Lawrence hospital "just awaiting his time." Harry Clarke, in fact, died three days later.

It was a brief and pointed statement, but he started with an apology: "You may ask why I did not take an active interest in the situation long before. Well, I was not a member of the local union, and was not protected by it, and I was raising a family of twelve children, and one did not have to do very much to be expelled from a position."[10]

He explained that he had spent twenty years underground as a supervisor and knew almost all the men who had died or were dying. He gave a brief history of the mining industry in St. Lawrence—how local fishermen and merchants pitched in to get it started, how they endured hardship and poverty through the early years. "The work was pure slavery," he said, "made all the harder because of lack of good equipment and material and because the miners were ill-clad and ill-fed."

And the situation didn't improve much when the corporation started earning profits. The pay was minimal and paydays were irregular. Working conditions improved slowly—it would take years to get amenities like hard hats, proper lighting, workwear that was waterproof. The mines never got proper ventilation until the rising death toll made it unavoidable in 1960.

He spared no graphic detail. "From Sunday night to Saturday night the mine was full of dust and smoke, and myself and the men would have to leave the drift and come to the station, where we would throw up for as long as an hour, and then some. After a while the throw-up would be mostly blood."

And then the fatal sickness started.

In my neighbourhood alone, around twenty young men have died in the worst of agony only a matter of months after they had to quit the mine. Some of the men who died had difficulty to get compensation . . . I did see a fisherman ex-miner who was receiving partial compensation trying to fish. He was brought in from the fishing grounds and hauled up over the wharf with a rope.

This is not human treatment, after a man worked in the mine under the conditions that existed here for ten or twelve years, when everyone knows that he was exposed to dust and the curse of radioactivity.

But the main point that he had to make was about the living, the survivors of all those dead miners. There were hundreds of children and widows struggling to get by on stingy, hard-won compensation benefits or welfare. The system was too adversarial. Government officials were denying compensation arbitrarily.

The most powerful section of his brief was at the end: a list of names, ninety-one men he knew personally—men he had worked with, neighbours and friends—now dead from mining accidents or illnesses they had contracted in the workplace. And the names of twenty others—men so sick they couldn't work.

And then he tabled his list.

He went home, unsure if anybody had been listening to him. He reviewed his own words. Maybe he felt he had said too much, or maybe not enough. But he kept his five typewritten pages handy and, in his own handwriting, continued adding to the list. Sylvester Edwards. David Joseph Clarke. Jack Fitzpatrick . . .

It took two years for the committee to report its findings to the legislature. But when it did, Rennie Slaney's words reverberated across the land.

46.

AFTER 1959, it was no longer speculative that for the previous twenty-five years, St. Lawrence miners had been working in unsafe levels of dust and radioactivity. The scientists who'd gathered proof published what they'd found out about the St. Lawrence mines in a British journal in 1964. Their paper would eventually turn up in Newfoundland, and one of the first Newfoundlanders to read it was Rennie Slaney. He would pass it on to Aloysius Turpin, who was once again at the helm of the St. Lawrence miners' union.

Slaney and Turpin were aware that the investigators, Windish and deVilliers, had established beyond any doubt that there was significant radioactivity in the mines, and that poor ventilation had caused frequent lethal spikes in radiation levels. They went further in the scientific journal and spelled out the consequences. The health profile presented in their paper made grim reading for the former senior supervisor.

Approximately two thousand people had been employed by the mining companies between 1933 and 1961. It was still early in a continuum that would curve up dramatically in the years ahead. But as of 1961, of the total mine-related workforce, 630 of those employees had worked underground. Sixty-nine of the underground workers had already died from work-related illnesses—twenty-five from lung cancer.[11]

The average age of the miners who had died from lung cancer was about forty-seven years. The average underground working life of the men who'd died was about eighteen years—which explained why the incidence of lung cancer would begin to soar in the early sixties and continue rising through the seventies and eighties and well into the nineties.

The death rate for St. Lawrence men between the ages of twenty and sixty-four was, even by the late fifties, three times the provincial average.

The Windish–deVilliers study acknowledged that the picture was possibly worse. Before 1951, there were no reliable statistics. There were few autopsies, few questions asked. Up to that point, almost every fatal lung disease was called tuberculosis.

WHAT is unexplainable is why it took a decade before anybody in authority responded with any sense of urgency—except to commission studies and convene meetings for long discussions of the findings. There was intense discussion among peers reviewing technical inquiries into the phenomena, but in St. Lawrence, the most pertinent concern was with the growing number of fresh graves in the local cemetery.

The bureaucratic, corporate and political sclerosis would inevitably end. The beginning of the end came on February 15, 1965, the day Roche Turpin died and Rennie Slaney laid out the facts of life and death in St. Lawrence in terms that could no longer be deferred, ignored or contradicted.

But Slaney would have to wait two more years before he could understand the impact he'd made in his appearance before the review committee on February 15, 1965. The committee members had listened after all, and they included his entire text in their final report, which Joey Smallwood tabled in the provincial legislature in February 1967. The report described Slaney's submission in bold words: grim, startling, extraordinary.

Responding to the list of specific names of dead and dying miners, a list well beyond the cautious science-based estimates of the Windish–deVilliers analysis, the committee had asked the Workmen's Compensation Board (WCB) to review its files and present its own official numbers. The contrasts were stark but unsurprising, as the board files could reflect only those cases for which compensation had been approved—four deaths from silicosis/tuberculosis.

According to the board's files, nobody died from work-related illnesses in St. Lawrence prior to 1951, which was when the WCB was created. Where Rennie Slaney had named fifty-eight miners he knew personally who had died from lung cancer, the board had records for thirty-four—all after 1960, when the board became obliged to notice.

The committee members decided that Slaney's lists were "clearly much nearer the truly ghastly totals" of death from work-related illnesses among St. Lawrence miners, and they boiled their opinion of the St. Lawrence mining crisis down to one blunt observation: "The only recommendation we feel we can make is that this act be ignored altogether. The tragedy has far exceeded the scope of the act. On the grounds of cost alone, it is impossible to apply."

The committee members recommended a formal inquiry, perhaps even a royal commission, into the history of fluorspar mining in St. Lawrence "in every aspect," including the impact on the miners' health. Premier Smallwood disagreed. The St. Lawrence crisis was old news, "past history," he declared. The basic problems had all been fixed. The mining companies had improved ventilation. And that was good enough.

But Smallwood had underestimated the impact of the blunt words of an ailing former miner from St. Lawrence, now published in the daily St. John's *Telegram*, the graphic tale of exploitation and suffering, the names of more than a hundred people in a small town and the certainty that there would soon be hundreds more—men dead or dying for having worked to earn a living.

Soon, the story of the St. Lawrence miners was making headlines everywhere—"A National Disaster," it was now called in bold type over stories that described what many felt had really been a national disgrace.

SMALLWOOD eventually buckled before a rising storm of public outrage. Newspapers in Newfoundland were on the story, now tenaciously, and the headlines were sensational. Shortly after the compensation committee report was tabled, national reporters were on the ground in St. John's and St. Lawrence.

Soon the dying and dead miners of St. Lawrence were acquiring names and personalities in the homes of strangers across Canada, their stories being told in detail. On April 5, 1967, the government announced the Royal Commission Respecting

Radiation, Compensation and Safety at the Fluorspar Mines of St. Lawrence. In June, the national newsmagazine *Maclean's* published the shocking story of the St. Lawrence tragedy, told by writer Ian Adams in the voices of the victims and their families.

One of those voices belonged to Rennie Slaney. Another to his friend Jack Fitzpatrick, whom Adams had interviewed at length that spring. But Jack Fitzpatrick—who was, like Rennie Slaney, a soccer standout in his youth—never got to see his story in *Maclean's*. He died before the magazine came out.

THERE were some raised eyebrows when Smallwood's choice for chair of the royal commission became known: Fintan J. Aylward, a lawyer and past president of the provincial Liberal Party. But Aylward's personal resume also included the fact that his brother was a merchant and the mayor of St. Lawrence. Their father, while he never worked in any aspect of the mining industry, had been the first head of the St. Lawrence miners' union.

One of the first decisions by the royal commission, and a signal that it planned to take its mission seriously, was to hire Rennie Slaney to write a first-hand history of the mining industry in St. Lawrence, its primitive beginnings and its tragic evolution.

Priscilla Turpin was one of the many Newfoundlanders who felt that the formal investigation was long overdue, and that it never would have come about but for Rennie Slaney's whistle-blowing. She would appear before the royal commission with a brief that described the daily struggles of the widows and their families. Her words, like Rennie Slaney's before the compensation review committee, had a profound impact. In its final report, the commissioners would make special mention of Priscilla Turpin and Margaret Pike, another St. Lawrence widow, for their "very thorough brief."

"Nowhere else in Newfoundland, and indeed, nowhere else in Canada . . . can one find so many widows of so many individuals who worked and died in the same industry," the commissioners reported. "The widows of St. Lawrence find themselves in a community where they can find little or no help from their next-door neighbour, as their next-door neighbour is, in many instances, in a similar position."[12]

THE definitive account of what had happened in St. Lawrence and the communities around it appeared in 1969 with the publication of the final report of the royal commission that Smallwood had grudgingly appointed two years earlier.

The mining companies got off lightly. After all, Seibert and his company were, by then, both dead. Alcan's Newfluor had been scrambling since 1960 to improve ventilation, which was commendable. The company was spared censure for past lapses.

The report was mildly critical of the provincial and federal bureaucrats and politicians who had dithered for so long, looking for the hard evidence that would enable them to apportion blame or obscure responsibility for what was happening before their eyes: miners were dying because of where they worked.

But the report was thorough. There had been consultations with international experts and local people who spoke for the many victims. There were three public sessions in St. Lawrence.

The commissioners eventually presented the government with sixty-nine conclusions and recommendations, and it came as no surprise to anyone who had followed the long saga of the St. Lawrence miners that the government rejected many of them.

While the commissioners had resisted blaming any individuals or companies for the tragedy, they were generous towards the victims and their families. They called for a new compensation policy that would give the benefit of any doubt, in cases where miners who had worked underground before 1960 had become disabled or died, to the worker or his family.

In the absence of an autopsy, or when "diagnosis is in doubt" and there is either silicosis or lung cancer, the commissioners wrote, there should be compensation. Even though evidence might be inconclusive about the causes of lung ailments like bronchitis, silicosis, tuberculosis, tumours, radiation fibrosis or cardiac disability, any symptom of "loss of pulmonary function should definitely be taken into account when considering compensation."

The government specifically rejected the proposal that the families of dead miners receive "the benefit of the doubt" in the absence of hard evidence. And they refused to expand the list of compensable respiratory diseases, adding only silico-tuberculosis.

The commissioners recommended a special fund to supplement the available assistance to disabled miners, as well as widows and children of the deceased. The fund was to be financed jointly by the federal and provincial governments, the Newfluor mining company and the Seibert family.

This proposal was implemented, but only partially. Ottawa refused to chip in. The Seibert family didn't even respond to repeated requests for a commitment to contribute.[13]

THE royal commission agreed with the widows of St. Lawrence that even when a family qualified for compensation, the payments were seriously inadequate. The final report called for the removal of a ceiling on payments to the families of dead and dying miners. The cap had been $312.50 per month, regardless of the number of dependents in a family. Many families, even when approved for compensation, were forced to turn to welfare to avoid total destitution.

Robert Kelly, in younger years an admired St. Lawrence soccer star, found himself in such a situation: he'd been working underground for twenty years, for the corporation at Iron Springs and for Newfluor in the Director mine. He'd started feeling unwell in 1965, and by 1969, he couldn't work at all. He had twenty-one children, and most of them were still at home. He had lung cancer.

The family struggled by on welfare, supplemented by earnings from the older kids. It wasn't until 1972 that the government of Newfoundland finally decided, under pressure, to accept the royal commission recommendation to remove the compensation ceiling.

The Kelly family was in dire straits by then. Robert's cancer was being held in check by frequent bouts of radiation treatment. The family lost count when the treatments numbered in the hundreds. The skin on his chest and back became like leather.[14]

But with the removal of the ceiling, the Kellys qualified for a significant retroactive payment—much of which was clawed back by welfare authorities to cover supplemental compensation while Bob Kelly was still alive.

When he died, in 1980, at the age of fifty-three, there were still thirteen children living at home. According to the family, his widow, Eileen Tobin Kelly, had to buy his coffin from a local merchant on an instalment plan.

47.

"Y OU always had the dread over you there."

It was one of the more startling assessments of working in the St. Lawrence mines by witnesses appearing at the royal commission.[15] It came from Boyd Stone, a timberman at the Director mine. He was referring to a particular situation, but he might have been speaking for many St. Lawrence miners who, for years, had worked in the shadow of a nagging consciousness of what was happening to people they knew—what Boyd called "the dread."

By the time he appeared before the commissioners in 1968, the death toll from work-related illnesses among St. Lawrence miners had surpassed 175. There had been, between 1963 and 1967, twenty-four deaths from lung cancer alone. Boyd Stone's reference to "the dread" was, however, more specific. On September 14, 1967, he'd been working in 508 South Stope, a huge cavern on the 550-foot level of the Director mine.

Besides the perils of dust and radiation, the Director mine had been plagued for years by rockbursts, sudden spontaneous explosions of stone from wall or roof, caused by tectonic pressures in the surrounding granite. Sometimes there were warnings— threatening sounds like gunshots or small stone particles spitting. Sometimes there were danger signs the miners could react to— slabs of solid rock hanging from a ceiling or a wall that they could pre-emptively knock down. And sometimes there was no warning at all. It seemed that the peril grew as the mine penetrated deeper into the earth's crust.

By the mid-sixties, rockbursts had become a persistent problem at the Director mine. In a three-year period, from 1961 to 1963, there were 155 "events" recorded, from flaking to major falls of stone. On January 4, 1963, an underground rockfall shook surface buildings. On November 30, 1966, there was a spasm in 508 South Stope that resulted in a 10,000-ton fall of rock and a concussion that shook buildings in town, two miles away.

Fatalities in St. Lawrence, other than from work-related illnesses, were comparatively rare. In a twenty-five-year period, seven miners died while working in the Director. Three of those deaths happened in a sudden rockburst in the early morning hours of September 15, 1967, in 508 South Stope. The shockwaves from this one would be felt far beyond St. Lawrence.

BOYD Stone had been a miner for thirteen years, all of them at Alcan's Newfluor. His partner on the day shift on September 14,

1967, was Ned Stapleton. When Ned was only two years old, his father, also Edward Stapleton, was killed in Black Duck mine, the first mining fatality in St. Lawrence.

Stone and Stapleton knew the history of rockbursts in the Director mine, and especially in the 508 South Stope. When he appeared before the royal commission a year after the three fatalities on the shift that followed his on that mid-September day, Boyd Stone was prompted by the chairman, Fintan Aylward, to elaborate on how he felt, working in the 508 South Stope.

"Could you be a bit more specific as to what you mean by, you know, trouble and the dread you had there?" Aylward asked.

Stone replied, "Well, small cracking in the wall . . . small bits of ground falling, then you'd move back and wait for it to settle and you'd go back to work again."

"Was this a daily experience?" the chairman asked

Stone replied: "No . . . not every day . . . probably twice a week."

On their daytime shift on September 14, he and Stapleton had been slushing—that is, removing rock from the stope using a kind of scoop that was shuttled back and forth by cables powered by a motor safely located under protective timber.

Shortly after midnight on the next shift, when their replacements were working in the stope, a cable became detached from the scoop. The two operators and their supervisor had to move out from the protection of the timber to reattach the cable. They were on the muck pile struggling with the awkward apparatus when the roof fell in on top of them. One of the dead men was Bob Edwards, the night captain. The other two were Noel Warren and John Slaney.[16]

Several miners quit their jobs in the days following the accident. One of them was Boyd Stone. The Director mine was now being called a death trap in the community.

In the long, dark history of mining in St. Lawrence, the 550-foot level at the Director mine captured the essence of the larger tragedy. In 1959, the federal investigator, Jack Windish, reported that while testing air quality there, he'd found there wasn't enough oxygen to keep a match burning. Among measurements to establish the levels of radioactivity in the St. Lawrence mines, his highest readings were at the 550-foot level of the Director.

Within weeks of the accident on September 15, 1967, the royal commission on radiation expanded its terms of reference to include fatalities from other causes, including rockbursts. But it was unclear what, if anything, the commission could achieve by studying the problem. There was little anyone could do to mitigate the risk inherent in a place where peril is a norm.

More sophisticated ventilation by then had improved the quality of air and dramatically reduced the radiation readings. But there seemed to be nothing anyone could do about the rockbursts. There were standard precautions—heavy mesh screening, rockbolts, timbering to prop up unstable ceilings, scaling "loose" from walls and overhead. But it wasn't possible to timber everything, and screens and rock-bolts sometimes failed.

The commission embraced this added tragedy because it was becoming clear that public patience with the mining operation in St. Lawrence was just about exhausted. The least anyone could do was to provide a place to talk about the fear and the misgivings that were now identified as dread.

48.

~~~

THE thrust of Rennie Slaney's presentation to the compensation review committee in 1965 was that perhaps the most tragic cases in St. Lawrence weren't the workers who had died quickly—like Roche Turpin, who lasted only two years after his diagnosis. Scores had died by then, but many of the men, like Robert Kelly, would linger for years or even decades, disabled and tormented by their idleness and hopelessness, their usually large families suffering with them.

The people who needed compensation most were those who would need it longest—men for whom the end would come slowly, over years, as well as the widows and the children of the dead. But these were the cases that received the greatest scrutiny, and for which the "benefit of the doubt" was invariably denied.

The royal commission report and the tepid political response seemed to mark a turning point in public attitudes. A situation that had been clinically identified in 1952, when Dr. John Pepper performed his extraordinary autopsy on Isaac Slaney, was now, nearly eighteen years later, beyond question.

The most striking proof that Dr. Pepper and Rennie Slaney had been prophets in the early fifties was accumulating in the hospitals and homes and St. Cecilia cemetery in St. Lawrence. By 1969, there were more than two hundred former miners who were either dead or dying.

THE royal commission, while it changed little in the short term, seemed to bring a kind of weary public closure for a while. The tragedy of the St. Lawrence miners had now been thoroughly investigated. It came too late for far too many people, but better late than never. No policy or regulation could reverse the damage that was already done. Improvements in the workplace were already under way, and there would be some material relief for people who were sick and for their families. All in all, the situation had been dealt with, from a political and bureaucratic viewpoint.

The story of the St. Lawrence mines would become another episode in a long history of tragedy in a place where, it would seem, destiny had never smiled and never would. But like most tragedies, it too would gradually fade from the public consciousness, except in those small communities where, for decades, it had been conspicuous: St. Lawrence, Little St. Lawrence, Lawn, Lord's Cove, Lamaline . . .

In those places, families and friends would share a continuing sense of frustration. The frustration, as months and even years went by, would metastasize to anger and gradually outrage.

IN the summer of 1974, Priscilla Turpin had a visitor. The anthropologist Elliott Leyton, a professor at Memorial University in St. John's, had been following the St. Lawrence story for years, ever since it became inflamed by the revelations of radiation, cancer and neglect. That summer, he'd decided that it was time the tragedy and its consequences were explained by the people most directly affected—the dying miners and the widows of those who were already in their graves.

He went to the communities of the south coast of the Burin Peninsula and recorded thirty lengthy interviews. Priscilla Turpin, by then nine years a widow, was among those he talked to. He published ten of the recorded interviews in a book that would quickly become a sensation across the country. The book was *Dying Hard*.

Leyton didn't alter the plain and anguished words of the people he spoke to—didn't torque them for impact. His own words, in a brief introduction, were spare and simple and, because of the restraint, all the more shocking.

"Those who have received their death sentence watch each other with intense interest," he wrote. "They listen for the worsening of a cough, the gasping for breath and the vomiting. They watch for the collapse of the skin on the face, the hollowing of the eye sockets and the dulling of the eyes which presage the end of their suffering."[17]

And he reported the reactions of worried, ailing men to the instruction that they should immediately prepare for death. "One man locked himself in his room for a day and a night; others pace the floor, pounding their fists and weeping. Others are so traumatized they wander in a deep depression, tears coming to their eyes when they realize that this might be their last Christmas, or their last summer on the pier watching the skiffs unload."

It was the third time that people beyond the Burin Peninsula had been told the story in shocking human terms: first in 1960, when news of the toxic levels of radioactivity in the St. Lawrence mines initially hit the headlines; again in 1967, when Rennie Slaney's dramatic submission to the workers' compensation review became public; and now the story would be told once again, but this time in the voices of the miners, many of them dead when the book appeared. And once again, the story would find a sympathetic audience.

In her interview with Elliott Leyton, Priscilla Turpin captured what had become and would remain the reality of existence for many families and their communities on the south coast of Newfoundland. "The first few days he came home," she explained, "he made two trips. One down to the meadow and he looked all around the harbour . . . and that was the last time he was out through the door. He'd get up; he'd try to get up and he'd come out and have something to eat.

"It's hard of course when it comes. And it does something to you. There's no way I can explain it, it's just something that you can't explain. But there were nights that I came home, and I knelt, and I asked God to take him. He was suffering."[18]

Dying Hard excited widespread commentary. But inevitably the public indignation faded. There was nothing left to do. The damage had been done.

RENNIE Slaney would briefly celebrate the final report of the royal commission, which was released in July 1969. The commission had been, largely, a response to his passionate submission to the workers' compensation review more than four years earlier.

The volumes of official reporting were confirmation of what he had, in five typewritten pages, described as a human tragedy brought on, to a significant extent, by human negligence. He was not a vindictive man and would probably have been able to shrug off the failure of the commissioners to criticize the companies he held responsible for the carnage, including the St. Lawrence Corporation, where he'd worked for nearly twenty-five years.

He might not have begrudged the commissioners' faint praise for Newfluor's safety record: "It was generally conceded by all individuals who appeared . . . that the working conditions at Newfluor (Alcan), from its inception, were undoubtedly much better than conditions in the mines operated by the St. Lawrence Corporation of Newfoundland, particularly in the early years."[19]

The commissioners even quoted him—Rennie Slaney, who was now working for them—as witness to what they considered a comparatively okay performance by the Alcan company: "Rennie Slaney says of the Director mine, 'there is no doubt that the mine was operated in accordance with good mining principles . . . from the start.'"

He would have understood the words of the Director mine manager, Rupert Wiseman, when he told the royal commission, "[T]here are means for sure of getting any mineral out of the ground without people being exposed but . . . overriding this is the economic picture, and it's not ore unless you can get it out at a profit."[20]

Rennie Slaney had prefaced his own comments in 1965 with the assurance that his intentions were "not to injure anyone, or any company." And he might have agreed with the commission that the origins of the disaster were set in complex historical and political circumstances, exacerbated by an earthquake and a tsunami.

But he might not have been so receptive to the notion,

implicit in the commission's findings, that inaction by the mining companies and the various government agencies, provincial and federal, was probably excusable, considering the complexity of questions, the elusiveness of answers.

And it's probably a blessing that Rennie Slaney would not live to see how grudgingly the Smallwood government responded to so many of the commission's findings and recommendations.

ON Sunday morning, July 20, 1969, along with 530 million other people around the world, Rennie Slaney was watching television. Three Americans in a rocket ship were circling the moon, and before the day was done, they would become the first humans to set foot upon another heavenly body.

Rennie Slaney was, however, being circled by a more immediate distraction—grandchildren. The family had planned to spend the day at a cabin on Salmonier Pond, between St. Lawrence and Burin. History could wait; the children were insistent. Rennie sighed and turned off the television set. He'd catch up with history later. One way or another, historic moments are preserved, remembered.[21]

Slaney was twenty-two years old in 1929 when a tsunami struck and altered the course of history on the south coast of the Burin Peninsula. He was there in the aftermath of a tidal wave that wiped out the infrastructure of St. Lawrence, but mercifully spared the people. He was there when Walter Seibert arrived, promising deliverance from poverty.

He believed the New Yorker, as it seems did everybody in the place, and he pitched in, working for a pittance at Black Duck mine and eventually as a boss at Iron Springs. He was among the first to understand the price that he and his community were paying for material prosperity, and he would have felt a terrible frustration had he been able to foresee how Seibert and his family would evade accountability.

But there was something about this large event that was now unfolding near the moon that gave a kind of perspective to his life on earth. The spectacle of men walking there would be persuasive evidence that the potential for human progress was unlimited when there was unity of purpose.

The royal commission on radiation seemed to have at least demonstrated unity of purpose in confronting the consequences of a catastrophe enabled to a large extent by carelessness. Being of a positive disposition, Slaney would have presumed that justice and correction would inevitably follow the acknowledgement of blame.

But all that was for the months—and more likely, years—ahead. As for the lunar landing, he would watch it later in the endless replays, hear the details in the breathless commentary in the weeks and years ahead. He turned his thoughts back to the children and the pond.

RENNIE had a boat, a recent Father's Day gift from his sons, Gerard and Ray. He'd subsequently won an outboard motor for the boat by entering a contest advertised on a cornflakes box.

They were at the pond by noon. Like his grandchildren, he headed straight to the shore. He'd always loved the water. He felt uniquely peaceful on a boat, a place where, but for random circumstances, he might have spent a lifetime. It would have reminded him of a distant past, when he and Arcule were fishermen—back before the fish mysteriously vanished, before Rennie and Arcule went to work as hard-rock miners.

His plan had been to cross the pond to a place away from where the kids were raising a commotion, splashing and tumbling, where he could do a bit of quiet fishing and, perhaps, remembering.

Halfway across, the outboard engine stalled.

From the shore, the sudden silence caught the attention of his wife, Bertha. The boat was drifting. Rennie was leaning over the engine, concentrating. Bertha remembered precise details of the moment—that he'd tugged the starter cord five times. He seemed to give up then. He picked up a set of oars, seemed about to sit down, to begin to row. But then he toppled.

His granddaughter Lisa Loder, who was seven, recalls the panic among those who witnessed what had happened. "We were all on the beach watching, and I remember Grandmother yelling out that he fell in the boat. His two sons-in-law went in another boat to check on him, but he was already gone."[22]

He was sixty-two years old. He had died from a massive heart attack. An autopsy revealed deep, debilitating silicosis in his lungs. A kidney had already ceased functioning.

For at least two years, he had been denied compensation because he had two adult children who were employed and still living at home. Now, because of the evidence of silicosis and thanks to the groundbreaking autopsy on his neighbour Isaac Slaney, Rennie's widow would be entitled to the compensation he couldn't get while he was living.

He had died at 1:00 p.m. By eight that evening, as the world celebrated the historic moment that he would never see—two Americans in spacesuits walking on the moon—the people of St. Lawrence were gathering in the church for Rennie Slaney's wake.

This time there would be no mystery, and no denial, about the cause of death. No need for subterfuge. Rennie Slaney, like so many of his friends and neighbours, died because of how he'd earned his living.

TEN

Memory

49.

~~~

CYNTHIA Farrell is remembering the morning Ray Slaney died. September 10, 1991.

She is a nurse and one of seven former caregivers who agreed to talk about their work at the US Memorial Hospital during the last three decades of the century, when the plague of fatal illness crested and removed a significant segment of the town's male population.

The women are no longer young, not yet old. For their generation, it is not unusual to have grown up without a grandfather or a father. For them, the past is full of empty spaces where there should be images of warm and vivid personalities.

The mining industry in St. Lawrence broke the continuity of the community in much the same way the First World War robbed Newfoundland of a generation of potential, of memory. The losses in the war, of course, happened over weeks. The mining losses happened over decades.

Cynthia had left her home long before dawn that day in September 1991. Ray Slaney, like many of the men who had worked in the mines and contracted work-related illnesses, had chosen to spend his final days in his own bed. To die in a familiar place was a little bit less frightening. And it would be easier on his family.

Ray had lung cancer as well as cancer in his bones. He knew what the final moments looked and felt like. He, too, had been part of endless vigils at the hospital, while friends and relatives and former colleagues faded slowly.

The hospital was staffed by people he knew, relatives and friends. The patients were also mostly people he knew, had grown up with. But it was a clinical environment just the same. No matter how the nurses tried, or how personal the efforts of the doctors, dying in the hospital was something many of the doomed men wanted to avoid.

And so, nurses like Cynthia Farrell had informally agreed that they would help by visiting the homes with medications or for basic care, whenever it was needed, regardless of the hour, so the dying men could have that final simple comfort.

Cynthia recalls arriving at the Slaney home at 4:00 a.m. with a vial of morphine and a syringe. The injections were fairly regular at this stage. She worked at being cheerful. The house was brightly lit for the early hour, the family gathered round.

Her colleague Betsy Slaney was scheduled for the next morphine visit, later on that morning. But Betsy had her own ordeal at home. Her husband, Steve Slaney, was also sick with cancer— terminally, it would soon become apparent—and she was spending her spare time looking after him.

Cynthia had decided that she would try to relieve Betsy of the later visit. She would come back herself. But she realized shortly after her arrival that Ray wasn't going to last that long. She decided she would stay for however long she felt needed. And Ray died before the sun was up. He was forty-six years old. He was Bertha and Rennie Slaney's youngest son.

Betsy's husband, Steve Slaney, who was not related to Ray, lingered until March 1993. That year, there were seven deaths from cancer among the former miners in St. Lawrence. Steve was forty-nine.

~~~

THESE nurses are the embodiment of local memory. They experienced the personal intensity of the final days, weeks, months of the men who suffered through the hard and ultimately lonely business of dying while still relatively young. They were the fathers or the brothers of their friends—they were, in some instances, their own fathers. Five of the seven nurses were still young women when they lost their fathers to mining accidents or illness.

Sue Tobin and Connie Hendrigan are sisters. Their father had worked in Iron Springs mine for ten years. When men from the mine began to get sick, he decided to quit while he was still ahead, while he was relatively young. But at the age of sixty-three, he was diagnosed with bone cancer. He lingered for five years. His two daughters nursed him through his final days.

Sue Tobin's husband grew up without a father. Sam Tobin was killed in an underground explosion in 1952, at the age of thirty-two.

Carmelita Rowsell's father died when he fell down a mineshaft. She had six uncles who were also miners, and she nursed most of them as they succumbed to work-related illnesses, including cancer. All died in their fifties.

Joan Turpin's father, John Slaney, was one of the three miners killed in the rockfall in the Director mine on September 15, 1967. Joan was fourteen years old, the eldest of ten kids, when her father passed away.

These nurses have an understanding of the mining tragedy that is deeper and more visceral than the insights of all the doctors and the scientists, the lawyers and the politicians, who have studied data and weighed the facts and tried to understand what happened and pass judgement on who, if anyone, should be held responsible.

Their memories extend back to childhood: the chill that would pass through a classroom in the local school when, in the middle of a lesson, they'd hear someone knocking; watch the teacher put her book down, walk briskly to the door; watch the priest enter quietly, whisper to the teacher, grimly scan the room and all the silent ashen faces. Raise a heavy arm and beckon . . .

From the nurses' viewpoint, there could be no accountability sufficient to undo the damage they have lived through, dealt with up close, intimately.

Now, long after their work at the hospital has ended, they stay in touch. They are like legionnaires, survivors of deep and lasting trauma. And like war veterans, they get together socially whenever there's a reason, whenever there's a plausible excuse, and collectively, they share the burden of memories that might have crushed them individually. They share the stories, a necessary form of therapy. And they share laughter, which was what kept them going in the darker days. They could always laugh. At something.

THERE was an old lady who died one night. There were two patients in the room. Both were toothless. It was policy that patients with false teeth had to store them somewhere while in the hospital. Carmelita Rowsell hunted through the dresser drawers for the old lady's false teeth. Finally located a set of dentures and installed them in the deceased. Prepared the body for the wake and funeral. There were no undertakers in St. Lawrence. Sent the dear dead old lady off for a wake and funeral and burial. The teeth were impressive but for one small detail: the family informed her later that their mom had never owned false teeth.

BETSY Slaney had, in her care, a dying miner who had quit smoking. Dr. Hollywood encouraged him to start again. Why not, when you have nothing left to lose?

A MAN arrived in an ambulance one night. He'd been working in the local fish plant. He'd slipped into a machine that tore off both his legs at the knees. He was still wearing work clothes, and Lisa Loder was attempting to cut through a coat sleeve so she could start an intravenous line. She was nervous and the patient noticed. "Be careful with the scissors, love," he said. "I can't afford to lose an arm now, can I?"

LISA Loder is Rennie Slaney's granddaughter.

"Sometimes there would be three or four [miners] on the men's ward at a time," she recalled. "Some of these men, their hearts just stopped, which was a good thing. But I witnessed a good many poor souls when their lungs totally collapsed and they'd bleed out and basically choke on their own blood. It was the worst thing to witness and not much you could do at that time. God bless them all."

One of the miners she nursed through his final days was Ned Stapleton. Stapleton had been working with Boyd Stone in the 508 South Stope in the Director mine, precisely where John Slaney and two other men were killed on the next shift. Boyd Stone packed it in shortly after. As he later tried to explain to the royal commission, there was "a dread" there every time he went to work. Too much dread. And so he quit.

But Ned carried on. Maybe he felt that, as the old saying goes, lightning doesn't strike twice in the same place. When he was only two years old, an accident at Black Duck mine had claimed his dad. Maybe that was enough to satisfy the demons of bad luck.

Ned Stapleton died of cancer in November 1985, at the age of fifty-one.

AND even after they had seen their patients die, the nurses still had obligations that might surprise colleagues working in a more conventional community. The hospital was understaffed. There was one nurse on duty at night and two in daytime, but there was also an outpatient clinic, and the day nurses were obliged to work there too.

Carmelita Rowsell remembers one night when three sick miners died. When a death was confirmed, it was customary for the family to go straight to a local store to buy a casket. Because there was no undertaker, the nurse on duty at the time of death usually had to prepare the body for the wake and funeral and burial.

In later years, when it became essential to establish a precise cause of death—for purposes of compensation—a nurse would be required to help the doctor with a quick post-mortem. And then the family would return from the sombre shopping trip and the nurse would help arrange the body in the casket.

50.

WE can never know what might have been. It's an irresistible temptation to speculate. But it's hard enough to know what really happened in past time, past life. Knowledge of the past is affected by perception in a future moment, what we call memory. But we wonder anyway. We speculate. What if?

Rennie Slaney was, by the demographic realities of St. Lawrence, an old man when he died. He was only sixty-two, but practically immobilized by heart disease and silicosis. What if he had continued in the coastal shipping service where his adult working life began?

Would Michael Quirke, who died of cancer in 1956 at the age of fifty-two, have had a longer, healthier existence if he'd stuck with deep-sea diving out of St. Pierre? Or Roche Turpin, had he moved away, as so many other fishermen did, to Nova Scotia or the United States, where the fishery still offered viable employment in the hungry thirties?

We can say with certainty that Ed Stapleton would not have died in an accident at Black Duck mine in 1936 if he had opted for another line of work. His son might have lived a longer life if, like his buddy Boyd Stone, he'd packed it in back in 1967, when he probably should have.

But all employment has its perils. Who knows what might have happened to him and to his family in other circumstances?

Roche Turpin's widow, Priscilla, lived in fear of what might happen to her six fatherless children. When she learned that her youngest, Ellen, was determined to become a nurse, she was relieved. At least one of them would make something of her life. It was a comfort.

Today, Ellen is a lawyer in St. John's. The eldest girl, Lucille, and one of the four boys became teachers. Two of the boys are engineers. Another, an electrical technician.

Sometimes things just work out. And sometimes they just don't.

AND how might Donald Poynter's life have unfolded had he continued to develop his engineering career in the relative modernity of New York and New Jersey? Would his final days have been burdened by the discomfort of crippling arthritis and the anxieties of heart disease? Would his first spouse have lived a longer, more contented life had they listened to her parents and stayed away from Newfoundland?

And what of Patrick Rennie? We cannot know how his life might have turned out if there hadn't been an earthquake or a tsunami at a time when he might have assumed that he was fundamentally secure. He knew the sea, its perils and its bounty.

We know that when he left home to play cards at a neighbour's house on the evening of November 18, 1929, he had a livelihood, a wife, six healthy children. By eight o'clock that night, his wife, three of his children, his house and his livelihood were gone. This we know.

And we know that at the age of forty-four, he went to work at Black Duck mine, and that in 1951, at the age of sixty, he died of cancer.

Patrick Rennie died in January. By April that year, his son Martin was actively considering a career change. He wrote to Premier Smallwood to inquire about the availability of government assistance to establish a small business venture. He was a St. Lawrence miner, he told Smallwood, and he wanted out. He believed there was potential for a poultry enterprise in the area. Smallwood's reply was brusque: there was no such fund available for such a project.[1]

Perhaps if Joey Smallwood had had more interest in the individual initiative of ordinary Newfoundlanders, the entire economy might have been transformed by dreamers like Martin Rennie.

But Martin, perhaps instructed by what had happened to his father, took better care of himself and managed to survive into the twenty-first century in spite of Joey. He died in 2002 at the age of eighty-three, which was ancient in the tragic demographic of his community.

His brother Albert, also a miner—but one who spent a lot of time away from mining, fishing with his brother—died in 1989 of cancer, but at the relatively advanced age of seventy-four.

Based on the knowledge acquired after 1951, we know that Patrick Rennie fits a tragic profile—average length of time from first exposure to toxic smoke and dust and radiation to death was eighteen years. Rennie inhaled the abrasive dust, waded in the deadly water, got sick and died in approximately seventeen years. At the age of sixty, he was older than the average for dead miners when the mortality statistics were eventually compiled—most died between the ages of forty-eight and fifty-five—but he'd been older starting out. And yet, before 1951, there could be no precise link between the particulars of Patrick Rennie's situation and the grim scenario that was unfolding all around him when he died and for decades after he was gone.

Cause of early death in most cases before 1951? Bad luck.

IN retrospect, it's fair to conclude that the consequences of an earthquake and a tsunami and the shambles of the early mining operations in St. Lawrence were all compounded by a shocking absence of civil oversight. Newfoundland was, for nearly twenty years, from about 1930 to almost 1950, without a government that was in any way effectively accountable to its citizens. The results were unsurprising. Insensitivity and arrogance; public management on purely bureaucratic principles.

In the dying moments of democracy, the government of Sir Richard Squires had managed to respond effectively to the catastrophe that claimed twenty-eight lives and wiped out the economic infrastructure that supported at least ten thousand people on the south coast. But the commitment didn't last for long. Sir Richard's power was rapidly diminishing, his country practically broke.

The commission government that initially replaced the island's imperfect democratic system was dominated by British administrators who, in many cases, were ignorant about the place and indifferent to, if not contemptuous of, its history.

In 1935, the commissioner for natural resources in the unelected government of Newfoundland, Sir John Hope Simpson, was surprised to learn of the tragedy that had happened only six years earlier. On a tour of communities along the south coast, with Father Thorne of St. Lawrence as his chauffeur and tour guide, he made notes on what he saw. "Yesterday we passed the remains of a settlement that was completely wiped out. The people who escaped never returned . . . ," he wrote. "The atmosphere of depression and hopelessness is terrible. I had never realized how bad things are."[2]

Sir John saw much that might have sparked some altruism on that trip, but beyond recording the impressions of a travel writer, he showed little inclination to follow up.

He visited St. Lawrence, calling it "another depressing settlement." It was, he observed, "mainly Catholic-Irish—a bad combination in a country where sturdy hard work and thrift are essential to comfort."[3]

But St. Lawrence, he noted, had "a struggling fluorspar mine . . . which would be a great thing for the place if it had sufficient capital. We went to see it [Black Duck mine]. It is a cleft dug in the ground four feet wide, eighty-five feet deep, and without hoists, except for the mineral. The men go down a complicated arrangement of ladders. I would not like to work down there."

From a tourist, his observations would be astute and even interesting. From one of the most powerful bureaucrats in a country run by bureaucrats, his first-hand exposure should have signalled the beginning of some corrective action. But it didn't.

He understood the reach and the potential of his authority as a commissioner. In a letter to his daughter Mary, on January 31, 1936, he noted that Newfoundland had a new governor (Sir Humphrey Walwyn) who seemed "very energetic . . . who, I think, hopes to make us sit up."[4]

The new governor was also the chairman of the commission of government, of which Sir John was a part. This didn't give him any special authority, however, and actually seemed to mark him as a figurehead and a rubber stamp for whatever the commissioners were inclined to do. Or not do.

"He [Walwyn] was the admiral in charge of the Indian navy and before that he commanded a battleship, in both of which capacities he said 'Go' and they went, or 'Do this' and it was done.

As governor he has to shed that aspect of authority if he wants to avoid trouble."5

With his fellow commissioner, Thomas Lodge, Hope Simpson occasionally revealed a sense of hopelessness when he reflected on the future of the place. At the root of all the problems, he believed, was education. "The next generation is the hope, but will be no better than the present one unless we get to a better system of education."6

It was a view shared by Thomas Lodge, who openly doubted "whether there is a purely white community in the world on such a low cultural level or where complete ignorance of anything outside the daily toil is so widespread."7

And it might have been predictable that even after the return of democracy, it would take years to impose rules of basic oversight on Walter Seibert's company. In 1930, when the allure of power was already strong in Joey Smallwood's vision for prosperity in Newfoundland, he made a telling observation in a private memoir. He predicted that by 1955, Newfoundland would have become "one of the greatest mining countries in the world."8

And so it should not be surprising that the government of Premier J.R. Smallwood, like the unelected government that came before, had done so little, by way of oversight and regulation, to restrain the initiative and enterprising vision of a mining man like Walter Seibert to help assure a safe and healthy workplace.

51.

A S OF 2007, the unofficial number of miners who had died from work-related accidents and illnesses in the St. Lawrence mines had reached 313, and of that total, 191 had died "hard" from cancer of the lung. The total doesn't include the heart attacks resulting from the inefficiencies of lungs damaged by silicosis and bronchitis.[9]

There was a presumption that miners who went to work in the more enlightened years after 1960 wouldn't face the peril of contracting lung cancer. There were new rules and regulations, and new ventilation shafts and fans to move fresh air to where the men were working. But as of 2007, there were twenty-eight more lung cancer cases among men who had gone to work in the St. Lawrence mines after 1960.

By 1969, the social fabric of St. Lawrence had been altered irrevocably. Rick Edwards, whose uncle was the merchant Aubrey Farrell, recalls that when he graduated from high school that year, twenty-six of the forty-four students in his class were fatherless.[10]

Strangely, in the years after 1969, there was a sharp spike in the rate of accidental injury in the St. Lawrence mines. It might be significant that half the increase involved men with less than a year's experience, and many with less than six months', working underground. These would have been men who eagerly took jobs with only an indifferent awareness of why so many of the veteran miners of St. Lawrence were no longer available for employment. They were dead or sick or had opted to leave home for less dreadful mining jobs in other places.

Among those who survived the workplace perils there is, even now, a reluctance to complain, to point fingers. The survivors are old men now, their lives compromised by chronic respiratory and heart ailments—veterans of the early days, like Mick Slaney, living out his final years with family, struggling to breathe, or Peter Quirke, using a wheelchair to get around the seniors' wing of the local hospital. Old men looking back with a surprising wistfulness on years of sacrifice and mourning.

Peter Quirke recalled that his father, Michael, facing death from lung cancer at the age of fifty-two, "never complained . . . he never seemed to realize." Michael Quirke died quickly, just a few months after the cancer diagnosis. "It hit me hard. I thought a lot of my father. He was strict and he was upright. But I would not have traded him for anybody."[11]

His father never wanted Peter to become a miner, but he became one anyway, at the age of seventeen. Mining is as much a culture as a job, which is part of its allure. Peter entered willingly and left reluctantly when the mining in St. Lawrence ended.

At the age of eighty-six, he insisted that he had no mine-related health problems "that I know of." Then he added: "And if I do, they're probably from smoking cigarettes."

Days after that conversation, Peter Quirke died in his sleep, on May 28, 2017.

52.

I T was a potent blend of rising expectations and outrage in the early seventies that set the stage for a final confrontation in St. Lawrence. And when it came, it was shocking not for its intensity and unexpected outcome but for its source.

For nearly forty years, the women of St. Lawrence and the neighbouring communities had suffered quietly as their fathers and sons, brothers and neighbours died or became disabled, leaving them to cope with the responsibility of raising children and running households without partners or sufficient means for meeting basic needs.

By the early seventies, they'd had enough. On April 6, 1971, as contract negotiations between the miners' union and the one surviving mine were breaking down, about thirty women from St. Lawrence and Lawn set up a picket line at the waterfront, at the entrance to the loading dock. The objective was to block an attempt to load an ore carrier with fluorspar that was destined for the Alcan smelter in Arvida, Quebec.

They stayed there for two days and two nights, until the ship sailed away—empty. By late August, after a miners' strike that lasted more than a month, management and union representatives signed a new two-year contract and the men went back to work. But they had discovered, in the summer of 1971, a new potential source of strength—their wives, their mothers and their daughters.

INEVITABLY, acrimony resurfaced in contract talks in 1975. By May 27, negotiations for a new contract had been stalled for six weeks. The likelihood of a strike was nearing certainty. On that day, an ore carrier once again arrived in St. Lawrence to load cargo for the Alcan smelter in Arvida. The women mobilized again.[12]

At twenty-seven, Monica Kelly was the eldest of Bob Kelly's twenty-one children. "We all got together to see what we could do," she recalled. "The men didn't want to go on strike. We thought that if we stopped the boats from loading, they wouldn't need to."[13]

Her militancy was partly driven by her father's situation. He was languishing at home. Both sides of his chest and back were "burned brown" from radiation therapy for the lung cancer that would eventually kill him.

The miners were demanding a hefty wage increase, to stay abreast of the rampant inflation of the time. Monica could identify with their concerns. Ever since her father had stopped working, her large family had been struggling to survive on welfare and small compensation payments. "Mom scrubbed our clothes on a scrub-board. She washed us in the washtub. We were never hungry—there always seemed to be lots of moosemeat. But life was tough."

The women of St. Lawrence once again descended on the

wharf. There had been thirty of them in 1971. Now there were two hundred. The St. Lawrence fluorspar was going to remain in St. Lawrence for as long as was necessary for their men to negotiate a proper contract.

The story was irresistible to the media. Company officials cringed before a new wave of bad publicity. The media loved the warrior women who were possibly more frightening than the miners. When someone unwisely tried to drive a car through their picket line, they flipped it over.

A St. Lawrence resident who'd moved from Ontario as part of a beefed-up security contingent for the company in 1975 married there and stayed. He cannot forget the trepidation he felt when he had to face the women.

The captain of the ship made one attempt to come ashore, but quickly retreated when he was told in lurid terms what would happen to him if he persisted. Word spread.

THE strike ended quietly in February 1976. But there was barely time for celebration before the beginning of a new cycle of bad news.

It started with rumours, possibly a residue from a dire financial picture presented by the company during the long contract dispute. The rumours eventually crystalized as speculation. Alcan was looking for an opportunity to leave.

It was hard to believe. The company was spending money on a new shaft for a state-of-the-art mine to replace the old Director on Salt Cove Brook. Miners on the project described plans for lining the shaft with concrete instead of timber. It was a $10 million project. The company was already into it for nearly $5 million. Was that something that suggested an imminent departure?

But in the alchemy of corporate decision-making, money—large sums of money—rarely gets in the way of pragmatism, whether it's a breathtaking payout to unload an unsuccessful boss or a write-off of an ill-considered investment.

In June 1976, Alcan was also dealing with another strike, this time at a smelter in Quebec. With idle smelters, there was no need for fluorspar, and it looked as though those smelters would be cold for quite some time. Newfluor promptly laid off half its mining workforce in St. Lawrence.

The Quebec strike dragged on into November that year. The paralysis seemed to give Alcan a lot of time for future planning. It was becoming apparent, at least in Montreal, that Newfoundland no longer figured in the company's future.

In early 1977, Alcan was openly expressing pessimism about the mines in Newfoundland. The company was now getting high-quality fluorspar more cheaply from Mexico. The rumours were revived—that in Montreal, dire decisions had been made. But this time the rumours happened to be true. In July, the company announced that mining in St. Lawrence would cease in February 1978.

The government of Newfoundland tried persuasion and offers of assistance to keep the mines from closing. Alcan insisted it was losing too much money. There could be no recovery. When the government noted that in the first half of 1977, the company had turned an overall profit of $85.2 million, it didn't matter.

Newfoundland then turned to hardball—a threat to expropriate all Alcan's assets in St. Lawrence. But before the government could follow through, Alcan dismantled, sold and shipped out every asset that could possibly be moved.

Before November 18, 1929, the economic mainstay of St. Lawrence had been the fishery. In less than an hour, a natural event that people still refer to as a tidal wave wiped out that economy. It took a little longer to wipe out the industry that replaced it. But as of February 1978, St. Lawrence was a mining town no more.

~~~

IN 1983, a British company, Minworth PLC, lured by promises of handouts from the provincial and federal governments, and anticipating a recovery in world fluorspar markets, announced plans to revive the mines in St. Lawrence. They would develop new open-pit operations and sink two new shafts on the rich Blue Beach property.

Between 1980 and 1983, thirty more former miners had died in St. Lawrence, most in middle age and most from cancer. But when the new company started hiring, four hundred people lined up to apply for one hundred jobs.

The first shipment of fluorspar in nearly ten years left St. Lawrence in 1987, but it was rejected by the customer.[14] Future shipments were sporadic. Almost from day one, the company struggled financially. History was beginning to repeat herself—the financial problems were reflected in the workplace, where health and safety were being sacrificed in the panic to improve productivity. Provincial regulators now had legislative muscle, but when it came to enforcement, there wasn't really much they could do other than, as Dr. John Martin would later write, to "persuade and cajole . . . to no avail."[15]

In 1991, the new company went bankrupt. This time the government, having put up cash and loan guarantees, had a lien against the property, mine and buildings, which they promptly sold to the hopeful Greater Lamaline Development Association for a dollar.

AFTER more than thirty years, physical evidence of the mines at Iron Springs, Black Duck, Blue Beach, Salt Cove Brook and half a dozen other operations would have been difficult to find. Where there had been roads and buildings, headframes and stockpiles, the daily rumble of explosions underground, there was now stunted spruce, thorn bushes, weeds, rutted recreation trails and silence.

And then, in 2011, the mining saga of St. Lawrence resumed afresh. A new company arrived in town—Canada Fluorspar Inc. The newcomers announced a plan for new production on the old Tarefare and Blue Beach veins. They hoped that they'd be up and running in about two years.

The plan was delayed by environmental studies, financing arrangements, political negotiations. But overall, there was optimism that this was serious. In May 2014, a San Francisco–based hedge fund, Golden Gate Capital, bought up Canada Fluorspar shares and renewed the planning for new mining in St. Lawrence.

Then the focus changed—geologists had rediscovered a rich new vein called Grebe's Nest. There would be a large open-pit mine developed there. The government of Canada pitched in a $5 million repayable contribution. Newfoundland put up a loan of $17 million.

As development began in 2017, the company was promising a ten-year operation with an annual payroll of $10 million. There would be 350 to 400 construction jobs for two years, and eventually, 200 full-time jobs. The operation would also generate 525 spin-off jobs.

The town and surrounding communities were enthusiastic. The only evidence of trouble was a brief demonstration at the proposed mine site in March 2017, by St. Lawrence residents protesting rumours that the workforce would include people who didn't live in their town.

Apart from this unwelcome interruption, the news that mining was resuming after a pause of more than twenty-five years was met with general relief and celebration. Mining had brought grief to the area, but it had also brought prosperity. It is, as Rupert Wiseman, the Alcan manager, had bluntly told the royal commission, always a trade-off. In the end, "it's not ore unless you can get it out at a profit."

～～

FUTURE choices and decisions will be informed by memory. The memory of bad luck, bad faith, bad management and bad governance should serve the future well. But the future, like the past, will also be determined by necessity.

Everything changes but necessity.

As was the case in the thirties, the economy of Newfoundland is still fundamentally dependent on one staple. It's no longer fish. Now it's oil. Jobs are hard to come by. Politicians still vie for power by promising industrial expansion. The collective power of working people is weakened fundamentally by anti-union sentiment all over North America. Distant capitalists still exercise extraordinary power over vulnerable lives in remote places most of them have never heard of, don't care about, privately consider to be "shitholes."

Vestiges of 1933 still linger.

Perhaps the future is secured somewhat by the fact that Newfoundland has a long memory and many physical reminders of the ever-lurking presence of catastrophe, the consequences of a sudden spasm in the earth's crust or a foreign war or a whimsical decision by someone with a scheme for personal enrichment.

Not far from Burin, on the road to Port au Bras, there's a monument to the victims of the tsunami—an elegant reminder of the perilous fragility and unpredictability of life. And at Chamber Cove, between St. Lawrence and Lawn, where on a stormy winter morning in 1942, two US warships foundered, there's a granite cross to remind posterity that in spite of all the worst impulses of humankind, there is an enduring instinct that, from time to time, produces gallantry and generosity, the virtues that enable people to survive.

St. Lawrence has a small museum and a historical society dedicated to perpetuating the memory of suffering, and perhaps equally important, the story of a communal determination to survive and grow. But just across the road from the museum, beside what was once a trail to Black Duck mine, there are more than two hundred monuments—reminders that the cost of industry can sometimes run unreasonably high—the tombstones marking graves of miners who died hard and slow and prematurely.

Not far west of St. Cecilia cemetery, there are new roads and buildings now, new equipment, new miners opening the earth, exposing all the pretty rocks again, ancient minerals that generate prosperity and economic optimism.

And in between these two dramatic spectacles, a little town where people pray that, this time, the economic benefits will justify the inevitable human costs.

Conversations with the Dead IV

ix.

He came to visit once, when I was at the university. He caught me by surprise. I was seventeen. Maybe his appearance was unwelcome. Being seventeen, away from home, who wants to see a parent? Even if it was only forty miles away from home, it was another world. I didn't need reminding of where I came from. Or maybe it was something deeper, meaner.

He emerged from a scrim of falling snow—thick, wet, heavy snow that plummets and accumulates quickly. He was wearing shapeless work pants, heavy workboots, a plaid wool woodsman's jacket, a ball cap. He looked painfully out of place. I can now imagine he was shy. He seemed pale, but he was always pale, from being underground so much.

He just happened to be in town. Wandered up to the campus.

—Always hankered to go through college.

—Well, here you are.

Both smiling uncomfortably.

We were near my residence. It was a modest little building, more like a barracks. Sancian House, they called it. In fact, I think it was slapped together near the end of the Second World War for an influx of returning veterans with a hankering for higher education. Like many temporary wartime structures, it became temporarily permanent.

—*Would you like to see where I live?*

—*Since I'm here.*

Later on, when we shared accommodations in a couple of mining establishments, I came to realize that my residence at least was part of the university that would have seemed familiar to him. It was like a bunkhouse.

I had three roommates. One of them was an ascetic little guy who was from Detroit. His name was George. George Keene. I never forgot him after that day.

He was in the room when I arrived, my father trailing behind, taking stock of everything. I'd been hoping that the room would be empty. But George was there.

He was a strange character. Unusually gentle in how he spoke and looked. He wore thick glasses. Seemed to be going prematurely bald. Today he'd be called nerdy. But he was unfailingly decent, unassuming. And he was warm and seemed genuinely impressed meeting my father, who, it seemed to me, was about as foreign to a fellow from Detroit as anyone could be. And definitely out of place in a university.

They chatted for a little while as I waited for it to be over. And then it was. I showed him out and he disappeared back into the silent falling snow.

Afterwards, George wanted to know more. And I didn't know how to explain that I really didn't know my father very well. He always seemed to be away as I was growing up. He always had to go away to find work.

George said that he could understand that. And then he hit me with a question that left me speechless.

—*Are you a little bit ashamed of him?*

And when I didn't answer, he just kept talking. To me, he sounded like a priest. One of the better priests. The university, St. Francis Xavier, was run by priests.

—*Well, you shouldn't be ashamed. But if you are, it's okay. It can take a long time to really know somebody. Even a parent. It isn't easy to see people as they really are. And so, if they seem like simple people, well, that's just how we see them. But people are always more than what we see.*

It was a long time ago, but that's the gist of what he said.

He seemed to be waiting for me to respond—to authorize this, I suppose, impertinence. But I couldn't because I somehow knew that what he'd said was true.

And then George said—and I remember this exactly:

—Someday you'll realize how lucky you are to have a dad like that.

A couple of weeks after that, I had a letter from my father. He was in St. Lawrence, working in a mine. He didn't say which one. I still have the letter. There were two letters, actually.

I'd long ago forgotten that I had them. They just turned up when I was researching the St. Lawrence story. Like he knew and wanted to help. Like he wanted to put his two cents' worth in. That I should know he was working in St. Lawrence then, back in 1961, because it wouldn't have meant much to me at the age of seventeen, a college man. But maybe now.

On the day I found the letters, I was in a fallow research stage. Everything seemed stale and uninspiring. The two letters came like whispers from another world.

He was saying: I was there. I knew what everybody knew, when it was too late, when knowing only added to the fear.

He wrote about the weather. It was fine. The pay was good—$2.19 an hour. He was working what I think they called a split shift. Four hours on, from four in the afternoon till eight in the evening. Then four more, from four in the morning until eight.

I suppose I realized that he was doing it for me, helping out with the costs of higher education. But I didn't want to dwell on that. Not then, anyway.

Some men he knew, miners, had been drowned when a car went off the road. The driver of the car was his roommate. He was at the funerals.

He would visit my godmother, Loretta Walsh, to play cards. She had made a fruitcake for me. Would send it. Refused to let him try it first.

Near the end of the first letter, he commented, I've met a lot of old friends, and there's a lot of them dead and gone.

To me, at seventeen, it would have been an unremarkable observation. He was forty-two then. They were all old. Dead and gone was to be expected of people in their forties.

In his second letter, he said, I feel myself puffing out with radiation from all I hear about it. It doesn't add to peace of mind to hear so much about it.

Radiation?

Of course, the miners were only finding out about the radiation in 1961. It was a long time after that before the world found out, and longer still before anyone beyond the town would care.

X.

I was in St. Lawrence in the mid-eighties. I was a journalist then, there on business. It was really my first visit. Iron Springs mine was my first home, but I had no memory of living there.

I visited my godmother. She told me about her brother Alonzo, who was my father's pal and, because of that, became my godfather. And how Alonzo and his two brothers, Fred and Jack, got sick working in the mine and died young.

She told me where to look for Alonzo's grave. I found his headstone. He died in 1969. The same year as my father. And I looked up Rennie Slaney because they were all friends. And I was amazed to see that Rennie had also died in 1969. Alonzo was a little older than my father when he died. He was fifty-one. Rennie was older than both of them.

I had a ways to go then before I'd hit fifty-one. But maybe because I was at that point in my forties, it suddenly seemed terribly young for someone to be dead and gone.

Then I went to the hospital. The US Memorial Hospital, paid for by the American people. A thank you to St. Lawrence and Lawn for saving so many Americans from a terrible shipwreck in 1942. There was a plaque.

I introduced myself to the hospital director, Dr. Hollywood. I used to think it was a nickname. But it was for real. Dr. Brian Hollywood. An Irishman.

When I told him that my father used to work at Iron Springs mine, he said he wanted me to meet someone.

It was a patient. He was skeletal and weak. He'd been a miner at Iron Springs, and he was dying of lung cancer. Had maybe only days to live. When the doctor introduced me to him, the man just stared off into space for a while, and then he said,

—That's an uncommon name around here.

And he looked at me with a strange intensity.

—I knew only one other fellow with that name. It was quite a while ago. He was a boss. MacIntyre, his name was.

—That would have been my father, I told him.

He seemed pleased.

—He was a good boss.

I could tell that talking made him tired. Dr. Hollywood was hovering. I remembered, This man is dying. I should go. But then he asked,

—And how is he now, Danny MacIntyre?

I hesitated. Searching for a lighter way to say something that is heavy. An easy way of saying something hard. Standing next to death makes the mention of it awkward.

He was smiling, waiting for my answer, remembering someone alive and young and strong and friendly—the way he was himself once, this dying man. And maybe for just a moment, he could feel that way again by reliving it through memory, a brief lifetime when, in the midst of all the drudgery, there were jokes and card games, beer and joy, and celebration of what they were and what they had. When they were all hard young men but looking out for one another. A time when there was a future full of possibilities.

And suddenly I didn't have the words to tell the truth.
—He's good, I said.
Afterwards, I realized I didn't have the man's name. I didn't write it down. But there were so many names by then. So many people he might have been.

Facts need testimony to be remembered and trustworthy witnesses
to be established in order to find a secure dwelling place
in the domain of human affairs.
—HANNAH ARENDT

Acknowledgements

T HIS book wouldn't have been possible without the dedication of many Newfoundlanders in pursuing, recording and preserving the personal stories of their fellow islanders, whether through formal scholarship of large political events or personal attention to the plain-spoken memories of people periodically caught up in moments of unusual significance and drama.

I am especially indebted to Peter Neary, for *Newfoundland in the North Atlantic World, 1929–1949* and *White Tie and Decorations: Sir John and Lady Hope Simpson in Newfoundland, 1934–1936;* Patrick O'Flaherty, for his exhaustive *Lost Country: The Rise and Fall of Newfoundland, 1843–1933;* Cassie Brown, for *Standing into Danger: The True Story of a Wartime Disaster,* her admirable account of the disastrous grounding of US Navy ships on Newfoundland's south coast in February 1942; Dr. John R. Martin, for *The Fluorspar Mines of Newfoundland: Their History and the Epidemic of Radiation Lung Cancer*; Dr. Richard (Rick) Rennie, for *The Dirt: Industrial Disease and Conflict at St. Lawrence, Newfoundland,* his plain-spoken account of the exploitation and denial that yielded so much tragedy and grief in his hometown, and for his 489-page doctoral thesis, "'And There's Nothing Goes Wrong': Industry, Labour, and Health and Safety at the Fluorspar Mines, St. Lawrence, Newfoundland, 1933–1978."

The most compelling stories are often those that come straight from the hearts and the personal experience of ordinary Newfoundlanders, as in Elliott Leyton's powerful collection of personal narratives, *Dying Hard: The Ravages of Industrial Carnage*; Garry Cranford's *Not Too Long Ago*, as well as his other collections of personal reminiscences by survivors of the 1929 earthquake and tsunami; and Rennie Slaney, for *More Incredible Than Fiction: The True Story of the Indomitable Men and Women of St. Lawrence, Newfoundland, from the Time of Settlement to 1965*, a personal memoir of work, life and death in the St. Lawrence mines.

Rennie Slaney's most dramatic contribution to the story was, of course, his brief, blunt presentation in February 1965 to a committee reviewing workers' compensation legislation. When his words became public two years later, they stamped an indelible human character on what was, by then, a tragic narrative that would continue to play out for decades.

Alan Ruffman, of Geomarine Associates Ltd., Halifax, has been tireless in his research and writing about the 1929 tsunami, its human consequences and what we must learn from it to prepare for the possibility of even worse marine disasters in the future. He has been generous in sharing his deep expertise and research. Dr. Allison Bent, of the Geological Survey of Canada, and a leading authority on earthquakes and in particular the Grand Banks quake of 1929, was generous and patient with her responses to questions that were usually naive and ill-informed.

Joan Ritcey, now retired from her position as head of the Centre for Newfoundland Studies at Memorial University Libraries, offered crucial direction towards information sources, and without her guidance and support, the project would have foundered in its infancy. I'm also grateful for help I received from Colleen Quigley and Linda White, of Archives and Special Collections, Memorial University Libraries, and Glenda Dawe, who helped track down elusive information about Sir Percy Thompson.

Larry Dohey, manager of collections and special projects at the provincial archives of Newfoundland and Labrador, and the archive staff, especially Charles Young, have been unfailingly helpful in navigating the vast storehouse of documents available at and through the Rooms in St. John's.

In St. Lawrence, Lisa Loder and the dedicated members of the local historical society accommodated frequent and often unannounced requests for access to their museum and archive. Lisa's deep knowledge of local history and the legacy of her grandfather, Rennie Slaney, became vital to my understanding of the personal and cultural undercurrents that informed the mining tragedy. Lisa's mother, Therese Slaney, offered vivid insights based on her personal connection with the story and her knowledge of the social, cultural and historical links between the south end of the Burin Peninsula and the French Islands of St. Pierre and Miquelon. I'm also grateful to Laurella Stacey and Paula Lambert for their knowledge of St. Lawrence history. Paula created shortcuts to archive documents that were crucial to the storytelling.

Through Ellen Turpin of St. John's, I think I got to know her indomitable mother, Priscilla, and to better understand the terrible reality of a family too soon deprived of a husband and a father and a friend—an experience that defined generations of families in and near St. Lawrence.

Gus Etchegary of St. Lawrence and St. John's has a unique position in the story as, probably, the last living human with a personal memory of all the events in this narrative—from the earthquake and tsunami, to the beginning of mining and its tragic consequences for his hometown, through the shipwrecks of February 1942, where he was a rescuer. He might attribute his robust health and longevity to the fact that he was able to avoid employment in the mines.

I am particularly grateful to his nephew Thomas Poynter of Boston, the son of the former mine manager, Donald Poynter, for sharing memories of his father and his family, and making possible a more developed portrait of a man whose central role in the unfolding story has been too often controversial and sometimes poorly understood.

Jim Gifford of HarperCollins Canada and Shaun Bradley, my agent, remembered long-ago anecdotes about my personal connection to a dramatic series of events in the history of Newfoundland and persuaded me to attempt this book. Noelle Zitzer and Janice Weaver provided crucial guidance in the final stages of the project.

Carol Off provided sound advice and restorative encouragement throughout the process.

Unavoidably, in a story so late in the telling, some of those who made the most meaningful contributions didn't survive to see the final product. I came to regard Peter Quirke and Kevin Pike as friends, and when they died midway through what I viewed as a kind of collaboration, the sense of loss was accentuated by shock. They had survived so much so long, it was easy to forget that they, too, were mortal.

I thank them both, in absentia.

Notes

Epigraphs

Peter Neary, ed., *White Tie and Decorations: Sir John and Lady Hope Simpson in Newfoundland, 1934–1936* (Toronto: University of Toronto Press, 1997), p. 197.

Dan Rory MacIntyre, letter to author, January 27, 1961.

Isak Dinesen, interview, *The New York Times*, November 3, 1957.

Prologue

1. Allison L. Bent, "A Complex Double-Couple Source Mechanism for the Ms 7.2 1929 Grand Banks Earthquake," *Bulletin of the Seismological Society of America* 85, no. 4 (August 1995): 1003–20.
2. Allison L. Bent, email to author, October 18, 2017. She wrote, regarding a strike-slip earthquake, "An analogy to explain the slip would be that if you push on a heavy piece of furniture with the same force over a long period of time, it doesn't move steadily but rather nothing happens for a while and then it moves a bit or a lot, and if you keep pushing it will happen again. The amount it moves and the time between movements [aren't] necessarily constant, even though the forces acting on it are. This analogy applies to earthquakes in general and not just to strike-slip ones."
3. Bruce C. Heezen and William Maurice Ewing, "Turbidity Currents and Submarine Slumps, and the 1929 Grand Banks Earthquake," *American Journal of Science* 250 (December 1952): 849–73.
4. Isaac V. Fine, Alexander B. Rabinovich, Brian D. Bornheld, Richard Thomson and Evgueni A. Kulikov, "The Grand Banks Landslide-Generated Tsunami of November 18, 1929: Preliminary Analysis and Numerical Modeling," *Marine Geology* 215 (February 28, 2005): 45–57.
5. Fine et al., "Landslide-Generated Tsunami."

One: The Quake

1. Therese Slaney, interviews with author, May 15 and December 5, 2017; and September 24, 2018.
2. Augustine (Gus) Etchegary, interviews with author, October 24, 2016; December 6, 2017; and September 23, 2018.
3. Alice Donohue MacIntyre (1916–2017), mother of author, interviewed at various times, 2015, 2016, 2017.
4. Alan Ruffman and Violet Hann, "The Newfoundland Tsunami of November 18, 1929: An Examination of the Twenty-Eight Deaths of the 'South Coast Disaster,'" *Newfoundland and Labrador Studies* 21, no. 1 (2006): 1719–26. The SS *Nerissa* was torpedoed by a German U-boat on the night of April 30, 1941, and sank within four minutes. Only 84 of the 290 passengers and crew, many of them Canadian servicemen on their way to war, survived.
5. Garfield Fizzard, *Master of His Craft: Captain Frank Thornhill* (Grand Bank, NL: Grand Bank Heritage Society, 1988), pp. 33–34.
6. Alan Ruffman, "The 1929 Earthquake and the Search for John MacLeod," *Cape Breton's Magazine*, no. 67 (August 1, 1994): 56.
7. Garry Cranford, "Eloise Morris—Tidal Wave: My Experience," *Not Too Long Ago* (St. John's, NL: Seniors Resource Centre, 1999), p.129.
8. Alan Ruffman, "The Multidisciplinary Rediscovery and Tracking of the Great Newfoundland and St. Pierre et Miquelon Hurricane of September 1775," *The Northern Mariner* 6, no. 3 (July 1996): 11–23.
9. *The Annual Register: Or a View of the History, Politics, and Literature, for the Year 1775* (London: J. Dodsley, 1776), vol. 18, p. 157.

Two: The Wave

1. Vivian Wiseman, interviewed by Lynn Anne Marie Matte, "Oral Narratives of the 1929 Newfoundland Tidal Wave: Narrative Functions, Gender Roles and Commodification" (MA thesis, Memorial University of Newfoundland Folklore Archive, 2006).
2. Ernest Cheeseman, "Letter from Burin, 1929," *Newfoundland Ancestor* 8, no. 4 (Winter 1992): 147–48.
3. Matte, "Oral Narratives," p. 128.
4. Cranford, "Louise (Emberley) Hollett: On Great Burin Island," *Not Too Long Ago*.
5. Gerald Jones, "The South Coast Disaster of 1929," *Newfoundland Quarterly* 71, no. 2 (January 1975): 36.
6. Cassie Brown, "Earthquake and Tidal Wave: The Hillier Story," *St. John's Woman Magazine* (May 1963).
7. Alan Ruffman, *Tsunami Runup Mapping as an Emergency Preparedness Tool: The 1929 Tsunami in St. Lawrence, Newfoundland*, vol. 1 (Ottawa: Emergency Preparedness Canada, 1997).

8. Cranford, "Louise Hollett," *Not Too Long Ago*, p. 77.

9. Cranford, "Marion (Kelly) Moulton: Kelly's Cove," *Not Too Long Ago*, p. 137.

10. Cranford, "Pearl (Brushett) Hatfield: Adrift in a House," *Not Too Long Ago*, p. 70.

11. Cranford, "Mary (Walsh) McKenna: Tidal Wave at Lord's Cove," *Not Too Long Ago*, p. 105

12. Kevin Pike (son of Tom Pike), interviewed at various times, 2016, 2017.

13. Cranford, "Mary (Walsh) McKenna," *Not Too Long Ago*, p 108.

14. There are contradictory accounts of the rescue of Margaret Rennie from the submerged house. Maura Hanrahan, in *Tsunami: The Newfoundland Tidal Wave Disaster* (St. John's, NL: Flanker Press, 2006), named the rescuers as Jim Walsh, Herb Fitzpatrick and John Joe Fitzpatrick; Ruffman and Hann, "Newfoundland Tsunami," said they were David Fitzpatrick, William Lambe and John Joe Fitzpatrick; Mary (Walsh) McKenna, who was twenty years old in November 1929, gave a detailed eyewitness account of the rescue in Garry Cranford, *Our Lives* (St. John's, NL: Flanker Press, 2000), in which she identified her father, Jim Walsh, and a neighbour, Maurice Harnett, as the men who rowed out to the house and found Margaret Rennie in her upstairs crib. A third man, Clement Harnett, remained on shore with Patrick Rennie and his sons Martin and Albert, according to McKenna's account.

15. The 1921 census for Lord's Cove records that Jim Walsh was a widower living with four unmarried daughters, including Mary.

16. Cranford, *Our Lives*, p. 13.

17. Sarah Brake, interview with author, February 17, 2017.

18. The "wall of water" described by witnesses to the tsunami refers to amplitude, the maximum elevation of the "wave" above the normal ocean surface. The run-up height refers to the difference between the normal height of a high tide and the height reached during the strongest tsunami pulse. The maximum wave height/amplitude in 1929 is believed to have been at Taylor's Bay (Alan Ruffman, correspondence with author, March 14, 2018), where there was a moving "wall of water" twenty-five feet high. Tsunami run-up heights, the "climb" up a rising shoreline, reached about forty-five feet in some places. Man-made structures built lower than that height above sea level would have been endangered. In the fishing villages of Newfoundland at the time, it was not unusual to build homes and other structures near the shore and almost at sea level.

19. Alan Ruffman, "Atlantic Tsunamis: 'Like a River Returning'" (illustrated lecture, Maritime Museum of the Atlantic, Halifax, NS, January 18, 2005). Also correspondence with author, March 2018.

20. Ruffman, "Atlantic Tsunamis."

21. It's relevant to quote directly from the last paragraph in Alan Ruffman's study of the 1775 hurricane, which claimed an estimated four thousand lives in or near Newfoundland: "At one time, storm deaths occurred almost entirely at sea when a tempest overtook unsuspecting or ill-equipped vessels. Now such deaths are increasingly on the land, as more urban growth is located in low-lying coastal areas. The threat from catastrophic hurricanes and related storm surges is still real

and indeed increasing as we urbanise our coastlines and build shore properties." Ruffman, "Great Newfoundland and St. Pierre et Miquelon Hurricane."

22. U.S. Geological Survey, reported in *National Geographic*, December 27, 2004, https://news.nationalgeographic.com/news/2004/12/deadliest-tsunami-in-history.

23. Estimate of the population and communities affected is according to the South Coast Disaster Committee, *Report of the South Coast Disaster Committee* (St. John's, NL: Manning & Rabbitts, Printers, 1931).

24. Ella Hillier, "The 1929 Tsunami: Through Dinah's Eyes," *Downhome Magazine*, November 7, 2011.

25. Ruffman and Hann, "Newfoundland Tsunami," p. 123.

26. Brown, "Earthquake and Tidal Wave."

27. Robert C. Parsons, "A Wall of Water," *Newfoundland Lifestyle* 11, no. 1 (Spring 1993): 13–15.

28. Caroline Skinner-Hickman, "The Day My World Fell Apart, Or So I Thought," *Downhome Magazine* 12, no. 7 (December 1999): 31. Caroline is the daughter of Thomas Hillier.

29. Matte, "Oral Narratives."

30. Matte, "Oral Narratives."

31. Parsons, "Wall of Water." This article quotes Robert Hillier, whose mother survived the tsunami because "she was safe at a neighbour's house on higher land, where she tended a woman in childbirth."

32. Michael Staveley, review of *Tsunami: The Newfoundland Tidal Wave Disaster*, by Maura Hanrahan, *Newfoundland and Labrador Studies* 21, no. 2 (2006): 413. Professor Staveley writes: "The property damage of roughly $1 million does not readily register in the inflated fiscal measures of the early 21st century—until we realize that, in 1929, the total GNP of Newfoundland was, at a rough guesstimate, about $30 million, and colonial public revenues were in the region of $10 million." In 1931–32, Newfoundland's total revenues were $7.9 million, against total expenditures of $11.9 million—of which $1.1 million went to "able-bodied relief" and $4.7 million to interest on debt.

33. Ruffman and Hann, "Newfoundland Tsunami."

34. Ruffman and Hann, "Newfoundland Tsunami."

35. Patrick O'Flaherty, *Lost Country: The Rise and Fall of Newfoundland, 1843–1933* (St. John's, NL: Long Beach Press, 2005), pp. 297–98.

36. Jones, "South Coast Disaster."

37. Ruffman and Hann, "Newfoundland Tsunami."

38. "Voyage of the Relief Ship *Meigle* to Scene of Tidal Wave Disaster, Lamaline to Rock Harbour, Districts Burin East and West," unpublished report, November 28, 1929, Centre for Newfoundland Studies (hereafter CNS), Memorial University of Newfoundland, St. John's, NL (hereafter MUN).

39. *Daily News* (St. John's), November 22, 1929.

40. Cranford, "Pearl (Brushett) Hatfield: Adrift in a House," *Not Too Long Ago*, p. 70.

41. Interview with Capt. Chesley Abbott, "Tsunami, 1929: The Silence of the Sea" (Burin, NL: Burin Heritage House, 2005), www.virtualmuseum.ca.

42. Abbott, "Silence of the Sea."

43. Father James Anthony Miller, interviewed in St. John's by a reporter from the *Evening Telegram*, said: "At Port au Bras, a fisherman saw his house being swept away. He tried to save his wife and family but was blocked by another floating house. He was helpless as his imprisoned family whirled into darkness. His home was pulled out to sea faster than a boat could steam." *Evening Telegram* (St. John's), November 24, 1929.

44. Ruffman and Hann, "Newfoundland Tsunami."

45. Jones, "South Coast Disaster."

46. Cheeseman, "Letter from Burin, 1929."

47. *Daily News* (St. John's), November 27, 1929. NONIA was the Newfoundland Outport Nursing and Industrial Association, a charitable venture that was largely financed from sales of crafts and knitted goods made by rural women.

48. Cranford, "Eloise Morris: My Experience," *Not Too Long Ago*, p. 130.

49. Cranford, "Eloise Morris," p. 130.

50. Eloise Morris was one of the many hundreds of Newfoundlanders who departed the island after 1929. She spent most of her adult life teaching in a private school in Rhode Island. After she retired, she returned to Newfoundland and lived in Burin, where she died in 1999. She's remembered in the community as a quiet single woman who loved music and wrote poetry.

51. Matte, "Oral Narratives."

52. Wendy Martin, *Once upon a Mine: Story of Pre-Confederation Mines on the Island of Newfoundland* (Montreal: Canadian Institute of Mining and Metallurgy, 1983), pp. 66–73.

THREE: LEGACY OF CHAOS

1. Dr. W.S. Smith, unpublished notes on the history of fluorspar mining in St. Lawrence, Newfoundland (eventually expanded to "Fluorspar at St. Lawrence"), 1957, GSB #001L/14/0016, Geological Survey Branch, Department of Mineral Resources, St. John's, NL.

2. Smith, "Fluorspar at St. Lawrence."

3. John R. Martin, *The Fluorspar Mines of Newfoundland: Their History and the Epidemic of Radiation Lung Cancer* (Montreal and Kingston: McGill-Queen's University Press, 2012).

4. O'Flaherty, *Lost Country*, p. 379.

5. O'Flaherty, *Lost Country*, p. 379.

6. Jones, "South Coast Disaster," pp. 35–40.

7. Alan Ruffman has argued in various writings that the failure of the fishery in Newfoundland after the tsunami was probably a coincidental phenomenon. There continues, however, to be a strong anecdotal link that attributes the collapse of the cod fishery at least in part to the earthquake and tsunami.

8. O'Flaherty, *Lost Country*, pp. 329–30.

9. O'Flaherty, *Lost Country*, pp. 329–30.

10. Telegraph communication between the Newfoundland government and J.H. Thomas, British Colonial Secretary, *Documents Relating to the Running of the Government of Newfoundland,* December 1931, HJ13 N4 A46 1932, CNS, MUN.

11. O'Flaherty, *Lost Country*, p. 375.

12. O'Flaherty, *Lost Country*, p. 375.

13. James Hiller, ed., *Debates of the Newfoundland Legislature (1932–33)* (St. John's, NL: Queen's Printer, 2010). Reported in the *Daily News,* February 18, 1932, Queen Elizabeth II Library, MUN. (In those years, legislature debates were not transcribed verbatim but later reconstructed from transcripts, journals and press reporting.)

14. Telegraph communication between the Newfoundland government and J.H. Thomas, *Running of the Government of Newfoundland.*

15. O'Flaherty, *Lost Country*, p. 363.

16. Debates of the Newfoundland Assembly, April 19, 1932, J125 N32 1932, CNS Stacks, MUN.

17. O'Flaherty, *Lost Country*, p. 383.

18. Sean Cadigan, *Death on Two Fronts: National Tragedies and the Fate of Democracy in Newfoundland, 1914–34* (Toronto: Allen Lane, 2013), p. 291.

19. Sir Percy Thompson addressed his letter to "My Dear Harding." A contemporary of his was Sir Edward Harding, permanent secretary of the Dominions Office in London. CNS, MUN.

20. O'Flaherty, *Lost Country*, p. 369, quoting Eugene Cholcott (*Evening Telegram*, May 30 and June 2, 1931), who, with others in St. John's, blamed voter illiteracy for many of the country's woes.

21. Cadigan, *Death on Two Fronts*, p. 293. Sir William Coaker had visited Italy in 1932 and, as Cadigan writes, "witnessed the apparent Fascist miracle of new public works, industry and social order."

22. Peter Neary, *Newfoundland in the North Atlantic World 1929–1949* (Montreal and Kingston: McGill-Queen's University Press, 1988), p. 27.

23. Neary, *White Tie and Decorations*, p. 32.

24. Neary, *White Tie and Decorations*, p. 31.

Four: The Cooperation

1. Adele Poynter, *Dancing in a Jar* (St. John's, NL: Breakwater Books, 2016). While this is a somewhat fictionalized account of her father's early years in St. Lawrence, the book is based on correspondence between Donald Poynter and family members back in the United States. Certain details can be considered factual and have been explored in conversations with the late Ms. Poynter's brother, Dr. Thomas Poynter of Boston, and her uncle, Gus Etchegary of St. Phillips, NL.

2. Dr. Thomas Poynter, interviews with author, January 7, January 24 and April 18, 2017.

3. Rennie Slaney, *More Incredible Than Fiction: The True Story of the Indomitable Men and Women of St. Lawrence, Newfoundland, from the Time of Settlement to 1965* (Montreal: Confederation of National Trade Unions/Confederation des syndicats nationaux, 1975), p. 9.

4. Thomas Poynter, interview.

5. Howard Farrell, unpublished manuscript (cited as "H. Farrell, Fluorspar Deposits" in the Fluorspar Deposits and Operations of the St. Lawrence Corporation Ltd., archives of the Aluminum Company of Canada Ltd., Montreal).

6. Donald Poynter, interviewed by members of a trade dispute panel, January 1942. From notes taken by the panel commissioner, Thomas Lefeuvre, and preserved in the archives of the Museum and Historical Society of St. Lawrence.

7. Slaney, *More Incredible Than Fiction*.

8. Slaney, *More Incredible Than Fiction*.

9. Slaney, *More Incredible Than Fiction*, pp. 15–16.

10. Peter Quirke, interviews with author, October 22, 2016, and February 17 and May 15, 2017.

11. Martin, *Once Upon a Mine*.

12. Slaney, *More Incredible Than Fiction*.

13. Slaney, *More Incredible Than Fiction*.

14. Poynter, *Dancing in a Jar*. She writes in her epilogue, "Although I have no confirmation of this, it appears that Urla had tubercular meningitis . . . [A]t the time, the United States did not have a policy of inoculating young people against the disease, so Urla would have come to Newfoundland with no protection."

15. Neary, *White Tie and Decorations*. Both Sir John and Lady Hope Simpson gave detailed descriptions of their 1935 tour of the Burin Peninsula, including their brief stay in St. Lawrence and their visit to the Black Duck mine.

16. Neary, *White Tie and Decorations*.

17. Sir John Hope Simpson, "Memorandum for Consideration of Commission of Government," GN38, S2-1-11, file 1, Public Archives of Newfoundland and Labrador, St. John's (hereafter The Rooms).

18. Sir John Hope Simpson, undated memo to Natural Resources files, The Rooms, probably in February 1936, nearing the second anniversary of his arrival in Newfoundland.

19. Cornelius Kelleher, personal correspondence with Tom Pike, St. Lawrence, August 20, 1939.

FIVE: REVOLT

1. Claude K. Howse, "Our Story: One Man's Story of His Family History, and His Part in It" (self-published autobiography, 1993), CNS, MUN.

2. Sir Robert Ewbank became commissioner of natural resources for Newfoundland in 1936 on the departure of Sir John Hope Simpson. Like Sir John, Ewbank had spent an illustrious career in the British colonial service, much of it in India

3. Rick Rennie, *The Dirt: Industrial Disease and Conflict at St. Lawrence, Newfoundland* (Black Point, NS: Fernwood Publishing, 2008), p. 24.

4. Rennie, *The Dirt,* p. 24.

5. Claude K. Howse, *Report on Investigation of Conditions at St. Lawrence* (memorandum dated June 8, 1937), GN38, S-1-11, file 1, The Rooms.

6. Howse, *Conditions at St. Lawrence.*

7. L.J. Saint, letter to the director of credit in the Royal Stores, St. John's, June 9, 1937, forwarded to Sir Robert Ewbank, commissioner of natural resources, GN38, S1-11, file 1 (NR 47), The Rooms.

8. Department Natural Resources, draft letter to Walter Seibert, GN38, S-1-11, file 1, The Rooms.

9. Poynter, trade dispute panel interview.

10. Slaney, *More Incredible,* p. 38.

11. Poynter, trade dispute panel interview.

12. Kelleher, letter to Tom Pike.

13. Submission by Newfluor to the *Royal Commission Respecting Radiation, Compensation & Safety at the Fluorspar Mines, St. Lawrence, Nfld.* (July 1967), box III, 131, 15–18, The Rooms.

14. Richard Rennie, "'And There's Nothing Goes Wrong': Industry, Labour, and Health and Safety at the Fluorspar Mines, St. Lawrence, Newfoundland, 1933–1978" (PhD thesis, Memorial University of Newfoundland, 2002), p. 88, quoting from a May 1940 report by the Burin district magistrate on relations between the St. Lawrence Corporation and the St. Lawrence Miners and Labourers Protective Union.

15. Poynter, *Dancing in a Jar.*

16. Rennie, "Nothing Goes Wrong," p. 90.

17. Martin, *Fluorspar Mines,* pp. 16–17. Dr. Martin writes: "His [Liddell's] unflattering observations on almost every aspect of Newfoundland society had to be toned down or deleted before the report could be released."

18. Aloysius Turpin, interview, 1967, accession #84-224, tapes C7239, 7240, 7241, MUN Folklore and Language Archive, St. John's.

19. Quirke, interview.

20. Fred Walsh, in testimony before the trade dispute board, January 1942, describing the effect of the dust. From hand-written notes recorded by Commissioner Thomas Lefeuvre. Document on file at the St. Lawrence Miner's Memorial Museum and Archive.

21. Aloysius Turpin, interview.

22. Aloysius Turpin, interview.

23. Aloysius Turpin, interview.

24. H.V. Morton, *Atlantic Meeting* (London: Methuen & Co., Ltd., 1943).

25. Melvin Baker and Peter Neary, "Governor Sir Humphrey Walwyn's Account of His Meetings with Churchill and Roosevelt, Placentia Bay, Newfoundland, August, 1941," *Newfoundland and Labrador Studies* 31, no. 1 (Fall 2016): 165–80.

26. Neary, *North Atlantic World*, p. 233.

27. Baker and Neary, "Walwyn's Account."

28. Howse, "Our Story."

29. James E. Candow, "An American Report on Newfoundland's Health Services in 1940," *Newfoundland and Labrador Studies* 5, no. 2 (1989): 226. The document reproduces, in an abridged version, the *Report of a Survey on Civil Health Services as They Relate to the Health of Armed Forces in Newfoundland . . . Dec. 3, 1940.*

30. "Settlement of Trade Dispute Board Appointed for the Settlement of a Dispute Between the St. Lawrence Corporation of Newfoundland and the St. Lawrence Workers' Protective Union" (1942). Unpublished document held at CNS MUN.

31. Poynter, trade dispute panel interview.

Six: The Rescue

1. Etchegary, interview.

2. Cassie Brown, *Standing into Danger: The True Story of a Wartime Disaster* (St. John's: Flanker Press, 1999). A detailed and authoritative account of the shipping disaster of February 1942 and the legal aftermath.

3. Dr. Warren S. Smith, "The *Truxtun & Pollux* Disaster" (unpublished account of the rescue effort, February 1942). Made available to the author by individuals in St. Lawrence.

4. Lisa Loder, various interviews and electronic communications with author, 2016, 2017, and 2018. Lisa Loder is Rennie Slaney's granddaughter. Her father was Herb Slaney, who helped facilitate Dr. John Pepper's 1952 unofficial autopsy on Isaac Slaney.

5. Kevin Pike, interviews with author, October 23, 2016; and February 19, May 15 and December 4, 2017.

6. Smith, "*Truxtun & Pollux* Disaster."

7. Etchegary, interview.

8. Cassie Brown, letter to Theo Etchegary.

9. Brown, *Standing into Danger*, pp. 195–97.

10. Brown, letter to Etchegary.

11. Sharon Adams, "Cold Comfort," *Legion Magazine*, February 1, 2017, https://legionmagazine.com/features/coldcomfort. This multimedia feature includes archival photographs and audio recordings of some of the survivors, including Lanier Phillips.

12. Adams, "Cold Comfort."

13. Smith, "*Truxtun & Pollux* Disaster."

14. Judy Turpin, interview with author, May 16, 2017. Turpin is the granddaughter of Robert and Theresa Tobin.

15. Pike, interview.

16. Lanier Phillips obituary, *Globe and Mail*, March 17, 2012.

17. Smith, "*Truxtun & Pollux* Disaster."

18. Brown, *Standing into Danger.*

19. Brown, *Standing into Danger.*

20. Brown, *Standing into Danger.*

21. President Franklin Roosevelt, telegram, February 24, 1942, MG 956, The Rooms.

22. Brown, *Standing into Danger,* p. 336.

23. Loder, interview.

24. James Otis Seamans died on October 13, 2001, aged eighty-three, after a long career in electronics and financial planning.

25. Loder, interview.

26. Rennie, "Nothing Goes Wrong," p. 124.

27. *Report by Investigating Ranger to Chief Ranger, St. John's, on the Haskell Fatality at Iron Springs Mine* (August 1942), GN38, 5.5-4-1, file 6, The Rooms.

28. "Augustus Haskell, Fatal Accident, St. Lawrence," GN 4/1D, G98 to G113/1, The Rooms.

29. Edward F. J. Lake, *Capturing an Era: History of the Newfoundland Cottage Hospital System* (St. John's: Argentia Pilgrim Publishing, 2010), pp. 348–54.

30. Civil Aeronautics Board, *Accident Investigation Report: Eastern Air Lines, Inc. and P-38 Air Collision—Near Washington National Airport, Washington, DC, November 1, 1949* (released September 26, 1950), Internet Archive, https://archive.org/stream/CAB-AAR1949-11-01-Eastern-537/Cab-aar1949-11-01-eastern-537_djvu.txt.

31. Lake, *Capturing an Era.*

32. Lake, *Capturing an Era.*

SEVEN: MR. ISAAC'S (EXTRAORDINARY) WAKE

1. Therese Slaney, interview.

2. *Royal Commission Respecting Radiation*, GN6, 1, case files, The Rooms.

3. Rennie, *The Dirt*, p. 30. This same quote appears in his thesis, "Nothing Goes Wrong," p. 72 (albeit under the pseudonym Mike O'Leary).

4. Rennie, "Nothing Goes Wrong," p. 195. In his thesis, Rennie uses pseudonyms for both Herb and Adrian Slaney, as well as for Richard Clarke, who was his uncle—a practice employed by many scholars in their academic writing.

5. Slaney, *More Incredible*, p. 46.

6. *Royal Commission Respecting Radiation*, GN6, 1, casefiles, The Rooms.

7. Richard Rennie, correspondence with author, May 16–17, 2017.

8. *Royal Commission Respecting Radiation* (final report, 1967), pp. 163–64.

9. Martin, *Fluorspar Mines*, pp. 27–29.

10. Rennie, *The Dirt*, pp. 59–60.

11. Therese Slaney, interview.

12. Harold Horwood, *Joey: The Life and Times of Joey Smallwood* (Toronto: Stoddart Publishing, 1989).

13. Gerhard P. Bassler, *Alfred Valdmanis and the Politics of Survival* (Toronto: University of Toronto Press, 2000), p. 313. Bassler reports that William Stephenson, the famous wartime spy, resigned after only seven months as chair of the Newfoundland development agency, NALCO, "when he realized Smallwood, on the advice of Valdmanis, kept making loans behind his back to the American entrepreneur Walter E. Seibert and others."

14. Walter E. Seibert, letter to J.R. Smallwood, November 7, 1949, Smallwood File, Archives and Special Collections, CNS, MUN.

15. Rennie, *The Dirt*, p. 60. Fred Gover would become Newfoundland's deputy minister of mines and a member of the royal commission established in 1967 to investigate the causes and impact of radiation in the St. Lawrence fluorspar mines.

16. Rennie, *The Dirt*, p. 61.

17. Rennie Slaney, written submission to a review committee examining the Workmen's Compensation Board of Newfoundland, February 15, 1965, made available to author by Slaney's family.

18. Peter Neary, "P.A. Clutterbuck on Morley Richards and the Record of the Commission of Government, 1939," *Newfoundland and Labrador Studies* 27, no. 1 (2012): 1719–26. This was Clutterbuck's response to newspaper articles by Richards, a British reporter for the London *Daily Express*. Richards had described living conditions in Newfoundland as a "stark tragedy" and "a disgrace to the empire." Clutterbuck's note to the UK government, a draft response to the articles, argued that the food items supplied by the dole "added to home-grown produce and the resources available from the sea and the countryside, provide the man in receipt of relief with an adequate basis for subsistence."

19. D.P. Cuthbertson, *Report on Nutrition in Newfoundland* (London: His Majesty's Stationery Office, 1947), p. 27. TX 360 N4 C8 1947 c.2, MUN. This is a survey of contemporary literature on poverty in Newfoundland, and the relationship between poor housing, sanitation, malnutrition and the prevalence of tuberculosis.

20. Martin, *Fluorspar Mines*, pp. 33–34.

21. *Royal Commission Respecting Radiation* (final report), p. 164. The report noted, "It has been suggested that he [Dr. Pepper] was carrying on a 'vendetta' against the mining companies on this matter. It is the conclusion of your commission, however, that Dr. Pepper acted only in the interest of the good health of those for whom he was professionally responsible."

EIGHT: THE DAUGHTERS OF RADON

1. Walter E. Seibert, letter to J.R. Smallwood, December 27, 1955, CNS, MUN.

2. Seibert, to Smallwood.

3. Farrell, "Fluorspar Deposits."

4. Pike, interview, February 19, 2017.

5. Farrell, "Fluorspar Deposits."

6. *Royal Commission Respecting Radiation* (final report, 1967), p. 35.

7. A survey of lung cancer deaths among St. Lawrence miners, conducted for the royal commission in 1967, reported that there were no recorded deaths from lung cancer between 1943 and 1947 (p. 178). Between 1948 and 1953, there were three recorded lung cancer deaths. In the period 1963 to 1967, death by cancer of miners and ex-miners had jumped to thirty-two, of which twenty-four were due to lung cancer. *Royal Commission Respecting Radiation* (final report, 1967), p. 178.

8. Martin, *Fluorspar Mines*, pp. 36–37.

9. DeVilliers and Windish, "Lung Cancer in a Fluorspar Mining Community," *British Journal of Industrial Medicine* 21 (1964): 94–109.

10. Gordon K. Goundrey, confidential memo, July 1957, Smallwood File, Archives and Special Collections, CNS, MUN. The provincial economist wrote, "The present owner has done little exploration work, has proved little or no ore reserves, and appears to be using obsolete methods of mining."

11. Aloysius Turpin, letter to C.W. Carter, MP, January 29, 1958, in the collection of the St. Lawrence Museum and Archives.

12. J.R. Smallwood, telegram to Walter Seibert, February 5, 1958, CNS, MUN.

13. *Royal Commission Respecting Radiation*, p. 53.

14. R.E. Van Alstine, *St. Lawrence Geology*, 1948, QE 199, A142, CNS Stacks, MUN.

15. Kevin Ryan, *First-Year Assessment Compilation Report: St. Lawrence, Burin Peninsula, Uranium/Fluorspar Property* (August 2014). "The St. Lawrence Granite," Ryan wrote, "host to most of the mineral occurrences in the region, is a Devonian alaskitic intrusion, similar in nature to the host rocks at the Rossing uranium mine in Namibia, one of the world's largest producers of Uranium."

16. F.G. Barker, memorandum of meeting to discuss radiation in Director mine, December 10, 1959. Submission by Newfluor to the *Royal Commission Respecting Radiation*.

17. F.G. Barker, memorandum of meeting with Dr. deVilliers, November 19, 1959. Submission by Newfluor to the *Royal Commission Respecting Radiation*.

18. *Royal Commission Respecting Radiation*, pp. 39–40.

19. DeVilliers and Windish, "Lung Cancer," p. 104.

20. Unsigned, undated memorandum, Smallwood File, Archives and Special Collections, CNS, MUN.

21. Martin, *Once Upon a Mine*.

22. Thomas Poynter, interview.

NINE: DYING BY INCHES

1. Elliott Leyton, *Dying Hard: The Ravages of Industrial Carnage* (Oxford: Oxford University Press, 1975). Dr. Leyton spent the summer of 1974 based in Lawn; he conducted thirty interviews in various communities from St. Lawrence to Lamaline. He used pseudonyms throughout his book. One of the interviews was with Priscilla Turpin, widow of Roche Turpin, who is given the name Victoria Janes.

2. Leyton, *Dying Hard*, pp. 114–15. From Elliott Leyton's interview with Priscilla Turpin.

3. Leyton, *Dying Hard*, p. 116.

4. Rennie, *The Dirt*.

5. Ellen Turpin, interview with the author, December 8, 2017. Ellen is the daughter of Roche and Priscilla Turpin.

6. Ellen Turpin, correspondence with author, August 3, 2017.

7. Leyton, *Dying Hard*, pp. 115–16.

8. *Royal Commission Respecting Radiation* (final report), p. 33.

9. *Royal Commission Respecting Radiation* (final report), p.214. "The variable degree of bronchial obstruction often leads to the development of emphysema . . . CO2 retention, anoxia, pulmonary hypertension and cor pulmonale and congestive heart failure."

10. Rennie Slaney, written submission to review committee.

11. DeVilliers and Windish, "Lung Cancer," p. 103.

12. *Royal Commission Respecting Radiation* (final report), p. 261.

13. Martin, *Fluorspar Mines*, p. 82.

14. Judy Turpin, interview with author, May 16, 2017. Judy Turpin is Robert Kelly's daughter.

15. *Royal Commission Respecting Radiation*, evidence transcripts, GN139-125, GN139-136, The Rooms. The testimony from Boyd Stone and Edward Stapleton came under expanded terms of reference to include fatalities on September 15, 1967.

16. *Royal Commission Respecting Radiation*, evidence transcripts.

17. Leyton, *Dying Hard*, pp. 17–18.

18. *Dying Hard*, p. 117.

19. *Royal Commission Respecting Radiation* (final report), p. 35.

20. Rupert Wiseman, testimony before the Royal Commission Respecting Radiation, GN 139, file 139.132, box 3, The Rooms.

21. Loder, interview.

22. Loder, interview.

Ten: Memory

1. J.R. Smallwood, letter to Martin Rennie, Coll.-075, J.R. Smallwood, 3.24.019, Newfoundland Department of Provincial Affairs, Archives and Special Collections, MUN.

2. Neary, *White Tie and Decorations*, pp. 196–97.

3. Neary, *White Tie and Decorations*, p. 193.

4. Neary, *White Tie and Decorations*, p. 261.

5. Neary, *White Tie and Decorations*, p. 261.

6. Neary, *White Tie and Decorations*, p. 113.

7. Neary, *North Atlantic World*, pp. 55–56.

8. Joseph R. Smallwood, *Newfoundland Miscellany* (St. John's: Newfoundland Book Publishers, 1978).

9. Martin, *Fluorspar Mines*, pp. 105–6. Dr. Martin cites, with references, studies and updates from 1988 onwards.

10. Rick Edwards, interview with author, September 24, 2018. His mother was Ena Farrell Edwards, a local writer and historian who photographed the aftermath of the US Navy shipwrecks in February 1942.

11. Quirke, interview.

12. Rennie, *The Dirt*, p. 119.

13. Monica Kelly, interview with author, September 2, 2017.

14. Martin, *Fluorspar Mines*, pp. 101–2.

15. Martin, *Fluorspar Mines*, p. 103.

Closing Epigraph

Hannah Arendt, *New York Review of Books,* November 18, 1971.

Index